Deep Learning

by John Paul Mueller
and Luca Massaron

for
dummies®

A Wiley Brand

Deep Learning For Dummies®

Published by: **John Wiley & Sons, Inc.**, 111 River Street, Hoboken, NJ 07030-5774, www.wiley.com

Copyright © 2019 by John Wiley & Sons, Inc., Hoboken, New Jersey

Media and software compilation copyright © 2019 by John Wiley & Sons, Inc. All rights reserved.

Published simultaneously in Canada

For general information on our other products and services, please contact our Customer Care Department within the U.S. at 877-762-2974, outside the U.S. at 317-572-3993, or fax 317-572-4002. For technical support, please visit https://hub.wiley.com/community/support/dummies.

Wiley publishes in a variety of print and electronic formats and by print-on-demand. Some material included with standard print versions of this book may not be included in e-books or in print-on-demand. If this book refers to media such as a CD or DVD that is not included in the version you purchased, you may download this material at http://booksupport.wiley.com. For more information about Wiley products, visit www.wiley.com.

Library of Congress Control Number is available from the publisher: 2019937505

ISBN 978-1-119-54304-6 (pbk); ISBN 978-1-119-54303-9 (ebk); ISBN ePDF 978-1-119-54302-2 (ebk)

Manufactured in the United States of America

V10010263_051319

Contents at a Glance

Introduction 1

Part 1: Discovering Deep Learning 7
CHAPTER 1: Introducing Deep Learning 9
CHAPTER 2: Introducing the Machine Learning Principles 25
CHAPTER 3: Getting and Using Python 45
CHAPTER 4: Leveraging a Deep Learning Framework 73

Part 2: Considering Deep Learning Basics 91
CHAPTER 5: Reviewing Matrix Math and Optimization 93
CHAPTER 6: Laying Linear Regression Foundations 111
CHAPTER 7: Introducing Neural Networks 131
CHAPTER 8: Building a Basic Neural Network 149
CHAPTER 9: Moving to Deep Learning 163
CHAPTER 10: Explaining Convolutional Neural Networks 179
CHAPTER 11: Introducing Recurrent Neural Networks 201

Part 3: Interacting with Deep Learning 215
CHAPTER 12: Performing Image Classification 217
CHAPTER 13: Learning Advanced CNNs 233
CHAPTER 14: Working on Language Processing 251
CHAPTER 15: Generating Music and Visual Art 269
CHAPTER 16: Building Generative Adversarial Networks............ 279
CHAPTER 17: Playing with Deep Reinforcement Learning........... 293

Part 4: The Part of Tens 307
CHAPTER 18: Ten Applications that Require Deep Learning......... 309
CHAPTER 19: Ten Must-Have Deep Learning Tools 317
CHAPTER 20: Ten Types of Occupations that Use Deep Learning 327

Index 335

Table of Contents

INTRODUCTION 1

    About This Book. 1

    Foolish Assumptions. 2

    Icons Used in This Book 3

    Beyond the Book. 4

    Where to Go from Here 5

PART 1: DISCOVERING DEEP LEARNING 7

CHAPTER 1: Introducing Deep Learning 9

    Defining What Deep Learning Means. 10

        Starting from Artificial Intelligence 10

        Considering the role of AI. 12

        Focusing on machine learning. 15

        Moving from machine learning to deep learning 16

    Using Deep Learning in the Real World 18

        Understanding the concept of learning 18

        Performing deep learning tasks 19

        Employing deep learning in applications. 19

    Considering the Deep Learning Programming Environment 19

    Overcoming Deep Learning Hype. 22

        Discovering the start-up ecosystem 22

        Knowing when not to use deep learning 22

CHAPTER 2: Introducing the Machine Learning Principles 25

    Defining Machine Learning 26

        Understanding how machine learning works 26

        Understanding that it's pure math 27

        Learning by different strategies 28

        Training, validating, and testing data 30

        Looking for generalization 31

        Getting to know the limits of bias 32

        Keeping model complexity in mind 33

    Considering the Many Different Roads to Learning. 33

        Understanding there is no free lunch 34

        Discovering the five main approaches. 34

        Delving into some different approaches 36

        Awaiting the next breakthrough 40

    Pondering the True Uses of Machine Learning. 40

        Understanding machine learning benefits 41

        Discovering machine learning limits. 43

CHAPTER 3: **Getting and Using Python**...........................45

Working with Python in this Book...............................46
Obtaining Your Copy of Anaconda 46
    Getting Continuum Analytics Anaconda 47
    Installing Anaconda on Linux...........................47
    Installing Anaconda on MacOS 48
    Installing Anaconda on Windows 49
Downloading the Datasets and Example Code..................54
    Using Jupyter Notebook 54
    Defining the code repository..........................56
    Getting and using datasets 61
Creating the Application.....................................62
    Understanding cells...................................62
    Adding documentation cells 63
    Using other cell types 64
Understanding the Use of Indentation 65
Adding Comments...66
    Understanding comments 67
    Using comments to leave yourself reminders 68
    Using comments to keep code from executing 69
Getting Help with the Python Language 69
Working in the Cloud 70
    Using the Kaggle datasets and kernels 70
    Using the Google Colaboratory.........................70

CHAPTER 4: **Leveraging a Deep Learning Framework**...........73

Presenting Frameworks 74
    Defining the differences...............................74
    Explaining the popularity of frameworks................75
    Defining the deep learning framework 77
    Choosing a particular framework 78
Working with Low-End Frameworks...........................79
    Caffe2 79
    Chainer 80
    PyTorch...80
    MXNet 81
    Microsoft Cognitive Toolkit/CNTK 82
Understanding TensorFlow 82
    Grasping why TensorFlow is so good 82
    Making TensorFlow easier by using TFLearn.............84
    Using Keras as the best simplifier.....................85
    Getting your copy of TensorFlow and Keras 86
    Fixing the C++ build tools error in Windows 88
    Accessing your new environment in Notebook 89

PART 2: CONSIDERING DEEP LEARNING BASICS 91

CHAPTER 5: Reviewing Matrix Math and Optimization 93

Revealing the Math You Really Need 94
    Working with data 94
    Creating and operating with a matrix 95
Understanding Scalar, Vector, and Matrix Operations 96
    Creating a matrix 97
    Performing matrix multiplication 99
    Executing advanced matrix operations 100
    Extending analysis to tensors 102
    Using vectorization effectively 104
Interpreting Learning as Optimization 105
    Exploring cost functions 105
    Descending the error curve 106
    Learning the right direction 107
    Updating 109

CHAPTER 6: Laying Linear Regression Foundations 111

Combining Variables 112
    Working through simple linear regression 112
    Advancing to multiple linear regression 113
    Including gradient descent 115
    Seeing linear regression in action 116
Mixing Variable Types 117
    Modeling the responses 117
    Modeling the features 118
    Dealing with complex relations 119
Switching to Probabilities 121
    Specifying a binary response 121
    Transforming numeric estimates into probabilities 122
Guessing the Right Features 124
    Defining the outcome of incompatible features 124
    Solving overfitting using selection and regularization 125
Learning One Example at a Time 127
    Using gradient descent 127
    Understanding how SGD is different 127

CHAPTER 7: Introducing Neural Networks 131

Discovering the Incredible Perceptron 132
    Understanding perceptron functionality 132
    Touching the nonseparability limit 134
Hitting Complexity with Neural Networks 136
    Considering the neuron 136
    Pushing data with feed-forward 138

Going even deeper into the rabbit hole 140
Using backpropagation to adjust learning. 143
Struggling with Overfitting 146
Understanding the problem 146
Opening the black box 146

CHAPTER 8: **Building a Basic Neural Network** 149
Understanding Neural Networks 150
Defining the basic architecture 151
Documenting the essential modules .153
Solving a simple problem 155
Looking Under the Hood of Neural Networks 158
Choosing the right activation function 158
Relying on a smart optimizer 160
Setting a working learning rate 161

CHAPTER 9: **Moving to Deep Learning** 163
Seeing Data Everywhere. 164
Considering the effects of structure. .164
Understanding Moore's implications .165
Considering what Moore's Law changes 166
Discovering the Benefits of Additional Data 167
Defining the ramifications of data 168
Considering data timeliness and quality 168
Improving Processing Speed 169
Leveraging powerful hardware 170
Making other investments 170
Explaining Deep Learning Differences from Other Forms of AI 171
Adding more layers 172
Changing the activations 174
Adding regularization by dropout 175
Finding Even Smarter Solutions 176
Using online learning 176
Transferring learning 177
Learning end to end 177

CHAPTER 10: **Explaining Convolutional Neural Networks** 179
Beginning the CNN Tour with Character Recognition 180
Understanding image basics 180
Explaining How Convolutions Work 183
Understanding convolutions 183
Simplifying the use of pooling 187
Describing the LeNet architecture 188

Detecting Edges and Shapes from Images 193
    Visualizing convolutions 194
    Unveiling successful architectures 196
    Discussing transfer learning 197

CHAPTER 11: Introducing Recurrent Neural Networks 201

Introducing Recurrent Networks. 202
    Modeling sequences using memory. 202
    Recognizing and translating speech 204
    Placing the correct caption on pictures 206
Explaining Long Short-Term Memory. 207
    Defining memory differences 208
    Walking through the LSTM architecture. 209
    Discovering interesting variants 211
    Getting the necessary attention 212

PART 3: INTERACTING WITH DEEP LEARNING 215

CHAPTER 12: Performing Image Classification. 217

Using Image Classification Challenges 218
    Delving into ImageNet and MS COCO 219
    Learning the magic of data augmentation 221
Distinguishing Traffic Signs 223
    Preparing image data 224
    Running a classification task 228

CHAPTER 13: Learning Advanced CNNs 233

Distinguishing Classification Tasks 234
    Performing localization. 235
    Classifying multiple objects 235
    Annotating multiple objects in images. 237
    Segmenting images. 237
Perceiving Objects in Their Surroundings 239
    Discovering how RetinaNet works 239
    Using the Keras-RetinaNet code 241
Overcoming Adversarial Attacks on Deep Learning Applications . . . 245
    Tricking pixels. 246
    Hacking with stickers and other artifacts. 248

CHAPTER 14: Working on Language Processing 251

Processing Language 252
    Defining understanding as tokenization 253
    Putting all the documents into a bag 254
Memorizing Sequences that Matter 257
    Understanding semantics by word embeddings 257
Using AI for Sentiment Analysis 261

CHAPTER 15: Generating Music and Visual Art 269

Learning to Imitate Art and Life 270
    Transferring an artistic style 271
    Reducing the problem to statistics 272
    Understanding that deep learning doesn't create 274

Mimicking an Artist 274
    Defining a new piece based on a single artist 274
    Combining styles to create new art 276
    Visualizing how neural networks dream 276
    Using a network to compose music 277

CHAPTER 16: Building Generative Adversarial Networks 279

Making Networks Compete 280
    Finding the key in the competition 280
    Achieving more realistic results 282

Considering a Growing Field 289
    Inventing realistic pictures of celebrities 289
    Enhancing details and image translation 290

CHAPTER 17: Playing with Deep Reinforcement Learning 293

Playing a Game with Neural Networks 294
    Introducing reinforcement learning 294
    Simulating game environments 296
    Presenting Q-learning 299

Explaining Alpha-Go 302
    Determining if you're going to win 303
    Applying self-learning at scale 305

PART 4: THE PART OF TENS 307

CHAPTER 18: Ten Applications that Require Deep Learning 309

Restoring Color to Black-and-White Videos and Pictures 310
Approximating Person Poses in Real Time 310
Performing Real-Time Behavior Analysis 311
Translating Languages 312
Estimating Solar Savings Potential 312
Beating People at Computer Games 313
Generating Voices 314
Predicting Demographics 314
Creating Art from Real-World Pictures 315
Forecasting Natural Catastrophes 316

CHAPTER 19: **Ten Must-Have Deep Learning Tools**...............317

    Compiling Math Expressions Using Theano 317

    Augmenting TensorFlow Using Keras............................318

    Dynamically Computing Graphs with Chainer 319

    Creating a MATLAB-Like Environment with Torch 319

    Performing Tasks Dynamically with PyTorch 320

    Accelerating Deep Learning Research Using CUDA 321

    Supporting Business Needs with Deeplearning4j 323

    Mining Data Using Neural Designer 323

    Training Algorithms Using Microsoft Cognitive Toolkit (CNTK)......324

    Exploiting Full GPU Capability Using MXNet 325

CHAPTER 20: **Ten Types of Occupations that Use Deep Learning** 327

    Managing People..327

    Improving Medicine 328

    Developing New Devices 329

    Providing Customer Support...................................329

    Seeing Data in New Ways.......................................330

    Performing Analysis Faster 331

    Creating a Better Work Environment...........................331

    Researching Obscure or Detailed Information 333

    Designing Buildings...333

    Enhancing Safety..334

INDEX 335

Introduction

When you talk to some people about deep learning, they think of some deep dark mystery, but deep learning really isn't a mystery at all — you use it every time you talk to your smartphone, so you have it with you every day. In fact, you find deep learning used everywhere. For example, you see it when using many applications online and even when you shop. You are surrounded by deep learning and don't even realize it, which makes learning about deep learning essential because you can use it to do so much more than you might think possible.

Other people have another view of deep learning that has no basis in reality. They think that somehow deep learning will be responsible for some dire apocalypse, but that really isn't possible with today's technology. More likely is that someone will find a way to use deep learning to create fake people in order to commit crimes or to bilk the government out of thousands of dollars. However, killer robots are most definitely not part of the future.

Whether you're part of the mystified crowd or the killer robot crowd, we hope that you'll read *Deep Learning For Dummies* with the goal of understanding what deep learning can actually do. This technology can probably do a lot more in the way of mundane tasks than you think possible, but it also has limits, and you need to know about both.

About This Book

When you work through *Deep Learning For Dummies*, you gain access to a lot of example code that will run on a standard Mac, Linux, or Windows system. You can also run the code online using something like Google Colab. (We provide pointers on how to get the information you need to do this.) Special equipment, such as a GPU, will make the examples run faster. However, the point of this book is that you can create deep learning code no matter what sort of machine you have as long as you're willing to wait for some of it to complete. (We tell you which examples take a long time to run.)

The first part of this book gives you some starter information so that you don't get completely lost before you start. You discover how to install the various products you need and gain an understanding of some essential math. The beginning examples are more along the lines of standard regression and machine learning, but you need this basis to gain a full appreciation of just what deep learning can do for you.

After you get past these initial bits of information, you start to do some pretty amazing things. For example, you discover how to generate your own art and perform other tasks that you might have assumed to require many of coding and some special hardware to accomplish. By the end of the book, you'll be amazed by what you can do, even if you don't have an advanced machine learning or deep learning degree.

To make absorbing the concepts even easier, this book uses the following conventions:

>> Text that you're meant to type just as it appears in the book is in **bold**. The exception is when you're working through a step list: Because each step is bold, the text to type is not bold.

>> When you see words in *italics* as part of a typing sequence, you need to replace that value with something that works for you. For example, if you see "Type *Your Name* and press Enter," you need to replace *Your Name* with your actual name.

>> Web addresses and programming code appear in monofont. If you're reading a digital version of this book on a device connected to the Internet, you can click or tap the web address to visit that website, like this: http://www.dummies.com.

>> When you need to type command sequences, you see them separated by a special arrow, like this: File ⇨ New File. In this example, you go to the File menu first and then select the New File entry on that menu.

Foolish Assumptions

You might find it difficult to believe that we've assumed anything about you — after all, we haven't even met you yet! Although most assumptions are indeed foolish, we made these assumptions to provide a starting point for the book.

You need to be familiar with the platform you want to use because the book doesn't offer any guidance in this regard. (Chapter 3 does, however, provide Anaconda installation instructions, and Chapter 4 helps you install the TensorFlow and Keras frameworks used for this book.) To give you the maximum information about Python concerning how it applies to deep learning, this book doesn't discuss any platform-specific issues. You really do need to know how to install applications, use applications, and generally work with your chosen platform before you begin working with this book.

You must know how to work with Python. You can find a wealth of tutorials online (see `https://www.w3schools.com/python/` and `https://www.tutorialspoint.com/python/` as examples).

This book isn't a math primer. Yes, you see many examples of complex math, but the emphasis is on helping you use Python to perform deep learning tasks rather than teaching math theory. We include some examples that also discuss the use of machine learning as it applies to deep learning. Chapters 1 and 2 give you a better understanding of precisely what you need to know to use this book successfully.

This book also assumes that you can access items on the Internet. Sprinkled throughout are numerous references to online material that will enhance your learning experience. However, these added sources are useful only if you actually find and use them.

Icons Used in This Book

As you read this book, you see icons in the margins that indicate material of interest (or not, as the case may be).This section briefly describes each icon in this book.

TIP

Tips are nice because they help you save time or perform some task without a lot of extra work. The tips in this book are time-saving techniques or pointers to resources that you should try so that you can get the maximum benefit from Python or from performing deep learning–related tasks.

WARNING

We don't want to sound like angry parents or some kind of maniacs, but you should avoid doing anything that's marked with a Warning icon. Otherwise, you might find that your application fails to work as expected, you get incorrect answers from seemingly bulletproof algorithms, or (in the worst-case scenario) you lose data.

TECHNICAL STUFF

Whenever you see this icon, think advanced tip or technique. You might find these tidbits of useful information just too boring for words, or they could contain the solution you need to get a program running. Skip these bits of information whenever you like.

REMEMBER

If you don't get anything else out of a particular chapter or section, remember the material marked by this icon. This text usually contains an essential process or a bit of information that you must know to work with Python or to perform deep learning–related tasks successfully.

Beyond the Book

This book isn't the end of your Python or deep learning experience — it's really just the beginning. We provide online content to make this book more flexible and better able to meet your needs. That way, as we receive e-mail from you, we can address questions and tell you how updates to either Python or its associated add-ons affect book content. In fact, you gain access to all these cool additions:

>> **Cheat sheet:** You remember using crib notes in school to make a better mark on a test, don't you? You do? Well, a cheat sheet is sort of like that. It provides you with some special notes about tasks that you can do with Python, machine learning, and data science that not every other person knows. You can find the cheat sheet by going to www.dummies.com, searching this book's title, and scrolling down the page that appears. The cheat sheet contains really neat information such as the most common programming mistakes that cause people woe when using Python.

>> **Updates:** Sometimes changes happen. For example, we might not have seen an upcoming change when we looked into our crystal ball during the writing of this book. In the past, this possibility simply meant that the book became outdated and less useful, but you can now find updates to the book by searching this book's title at www.dummies.com.

In addition to these updates, check out the blog posts with answers to reader questions and demonstrations of useful book-related techniques at http://blog.johnmuellerbooks.com/.

>> **Companion files:** Hey! Who really wants to type all the code in the book and reconstruct all those neural networks manually? Most readers would prefer to spend their time actually working with Python, performing machine learning or deep learning tasks, and seeing the interesting things they can do, rather

than typing. Fortunately for you, the examples used in the book are available for download, so all you need to do is read the book to learn Python for deep learning usage techniques. You can find these files at www.dummies.com. Search this book's title, and on the page that appears, scroll down to the image of the book cover and click it. Then click the More about This Book button and on the page that opens, go to the Downloads tab.

Where to Go from Here

It's time to start your Python for deep learning adventure! If you're completely new to Python and its use for deep learning tasks, you should start with Chapter 1 and progress through the book at a pace that allows you to absorb as much of the material as possible.

If you're a novice who's in an absolute rush to get going with Python for deep learning as quickly as possible, you can skip to Chapter 3 with the understanding that you may find some topics a bit confusing later. Skipping to Chapter 4 is okay if you already have Anaconda (the programming product used in the book) installed, but be sure to at least skim Chapter 3 so that you know what assumptions we made when writing this book.

This book relies on a combination of TensorFlow and Keras to perform deep learning tasks. Even if you're an advanced reader, you need to go to Chapter 4 to discover how to configure the environment used for this book. Failure to configure the environment according to instructions will almost certainly cause failures when you try to run the code.

1

Discovering Deep Learning

IN THIS PART . . .

Understand how deep learning impacts the world around us.

Consider the relationship between deep learning and machine learning.

Create a Python setup of your own.

Define the need for a framework in deep learning.

Chapter **1**
Introducing Deep Learning

You have probably heard a lot about deep learning. The term appears all over the place and seems to apply to everything. In reality, deep learning is a subset of machine learning, which in turn is a subset of artificial intelligence (AI). The first goal of this chapter is to help you understand what deep learning is really all about and how it applies to the world today. You may be surprised to learn that deep learning isn't the only game in town; other methods of analyzing data exist. In fact, deep learning meets a specific set of needs when it comes to data analysis, so you might be using other methods and not even know it.

Deep learning is just a subset of AI, but it's an important subset. You see deep learning techniques used for a number of tasks, but not every task. In fact, some people associate deep learning with tasks that it can't perform. The next step in discovering deep learning is to understand what it can and can't do for you.

As part of working with deep learning in this book, you write applications that rely on deep learning to process data and then produce a desired output. Of course, you need to know a little about the programming environment before you can do much. Even though Chapter 3 discusses how to install and configure Python, the language used to demonstrate deep learning in this book, you first need to know a little more about the options available to you.

The chapter closes with a discussion of why deep learning shouldn't be the only data processing technique in your toolkit. Yes, deep learning can perform amazing tasks when used appropriately, but it can also cause serious problems when applied to problems that it doesn't support well. Sometimes you need to look to other technologies to perform a given task, or figure out which technologies to use with deep learning to provide a more efficient and elegant solution to specific problems.

Defining What Deep Learning Means

An understanding of deep learning begins with a precise definition of terms. Otherwise, you have a hard time separating the media hype from the realities of what deep learning can actually provide. Deep learning is part of both AI and machine learning, as shown in Figure 1-1. To understand deep learning, you must begin at the outside — that is, you start with AI, and then work your way through machine learning, and then finally define deep learning. The following sections help you through this process.

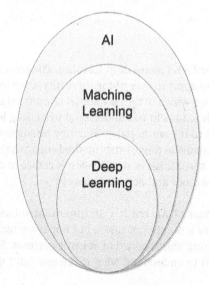

FIGURE 1-1:
Deep learning is a subset of machine learning which is a subset of AI.

AI

Machine Learning

Deep Learning

Starting from Artificial Intelligence

Saying that AI is an artificial intelligence doesn't really tell you anything meaningful, which is why so many discussions and disagreements arise over this term. Yes, you can argue that what occurs is artificial, not having come from a natural source. However, the intelligence part is, at best, ambiguous. People define intelligence in many different ways. However, you can say that intelligence involves certain mental exercises composed of the following activities:

>> **Learning:** Having the ability to obtain and process new information.

>> **Reasoning:** Being able to manipulate information in various ways.

>> **Understanding:** Considering the result of information manipulation.

>> **Grasping truths:** Determining the validity of the manipulated information.

>> **Seeing relationships:** Divining how validated data interacts with other data.

>> **Considering meanings:** Applying truths to particular situations in a manner consistent with their relationship.

>> **Separating fact from belief:** Determining whether the data is adequately supported by provable sources that can be demonstrated to be consistently valid.

The list could easily get quite long, but even this list is relatively prone to interpretation by anyone who accepts it as viable. As you can see from the list, however, intelligence often follows a process that a computer system can mimic as part of a simulation:

1. Set a goal based on needs or wants.

2. Assess the value of any currently known information in support of the goal.

3. Gather additional information that could support the goal.

4. Manipulate the data such that it achieves a form consistent with existing information.

5. Define the relationships and truth values between existing and new information.

6. Determine whether the goal is achieved.

7. Modify the goal in light of the new data and its effect on the probability of success.

8. Repeat Steps 2 through 7 as needed until the goal is achieved (found true) or the possibilities for achieving it are exhausted (found false).

REMEMBER

Even though you can create algorithms and provide access to data in support of this process within a computer, a computer's capability to achieve intelligence is severely limited. For example, a computer is incapable of understanding anything because it relies on machine processes to manipulate data using pure math in a strictly mechanical fashion. Likewise, computers can't easily separate truth from mistruth. In fact, no computer can fully implement any of the mental activities described in the list that describes intelligence.

When thinking about AI, you must consider the goals of the people who develop an AI. The goal is to mimic human intelligence, not replicate it. A computer doesn't truly think, but it gives the appearance of thinking. However, a computer actually provides this appearance only in the logical/mathematical form of intelligence. A computer is moderately successful in mimicking visual-spatial and bodily-kinesthetic intelligence. A computer has a low, passable capability in interpersonal and linguistic intelligence. Unlike humans, however, a computer has no way to mimic intrapersonal or creative intelligence.

Considering the role of AI

As described in the previous section, the first concept that's important to understand is that AI doesn't really have anything to do with human intelligence. Yes, some AI is modeled to simulate human intelligence, but that's what it is: a simulation. When thinking about AI, notice that an interplay exists between goal seeking, data processing used to achieve that goal, and data acquisition used to better understand the goal. AI relies on algorithms to achieve a result that may or may not have anything to do with human goals or methods of achieving those goals. With this in mind, you can categorize AI in four ways:

>> **Acting humanly:** When a computer acts like a human, it best reflects the Turing test, in which the computer succeeds when differentiation between the computer and a human isn't possible (see http://www.turing.org.uk/scrapbook/test.html for details). This category also reflects what the media would have you believe that AI is all about. You see it employed for technologies such as natural language processing, knowledge representation, automated reasoning, and machine learning (all four of which must be present to pass the test).

The original Turing Test didn't include any physical contact. The newer, Total Turing Test does include physical contact in the form of perceptual ability interrogation, which means that the computer must also employ both computer vision and robotics to succeed. Modern techniques include the idea of achieving the goal rather than mimicking humans completely. For example, the Wright brothers didn't succeed in creating an airplane by precisely copying the flight of birds; rather, the birds provided ideas that led to aerodynamics, which in turn eventually led to human flight. The goal is to fly. Both birds and humans achieve this goal, but they use different approaches.

>> **Thinking humanly:** When a computer thinks as a human, it performs tasks that require intelligence (as contrasted with rote procedures) from a human

to succeed, such as driving a car. To determine whether a program thinks like a human, you must have some method of determining how humans think, which the cognitive modeling approach defines. This model relies on three techniques:

- **Introspection:** Detecting and documenting the techniques used to achieve goals by monitoring one's own thought processes.

- **Psychological testing:** Observing a person's behavior and adding it to a database of similar behaviors from other persons given a similar set of circumstances, goals, resources, and environmental conditions (among other things).

- **Brain imaging:** Monitoring brain activity directly through various mechanical means, such as Computerized Axial Tomography (CAT), Positron Emission Tomography (PET), Magnetic Resonance Imaging (MRI), and Magnetoencephalography (MEG).

After creating a model, you can write a program that simulates the model. Given the amount of variability among human thought processes and the difficulty of accurately representing these thought processes as part of a program, the results are experimental at best. This category of thinking humanly is often used in psychology and other fields in which modeling the human thought process to create realistic simulations is essential.

» **Thinking rationally:** Studying how humans think using some standard enables the creation of guidelines that describe typical human behaviors. A person is considered rational when following these behaviors within certain levels of deviation. A computer that thinks rationally relies on the recorded behaviors to create a guide as to how to interact with an environment based on the data at hand. The goal of this approach is to solve problems logically, when possible. In many cases, this approach would enable the creation of a baseline technique for solving a problem, which would then be modified to actually solve the problem. In other words, the solving of a problem in principle is often different from solving it in practice, but you still need a starting point.

» **Acting rationally:** Studying how humans act in given situations under specific constraints enables you to determine which techniques are both efficient and effective. A computer that acts rationally relies on the recorded actions to interact with an environment based on conditions, environmental factors, and existing data. As with rational thought, rational acts depend on a solution in principle, which may not prove useful in practice. However, rational acts do provide a baseline upon which a computer can begin negotiating the successful completion of a goal.

HUMAN VERSUS RATIONAL PROCESSES

Human processes differ from rational processes in their outcome. A process is *rational* if it always does the right thing based on the current information, given an ideal performance measure. In short, rational processes go by the book and assume that "the book" is actually correct. Human processes involve instinct, intuition, and other variables that don't necessarily reflect the book and may not even consider the existing data. As an example, the rational way to drive a car is to always follow the laws. However, traffic isn't rational. If you follow the laws precisely, you end up stuck somewhere because other drivers aren't following the laws precisely. To be successful, a self-driving car must therefore act humanly, rather than rationally.

You find AI used in a great many applications today. The only problem is that the technology works so well that you don't even know it exists. In fact, you might be surprised to find that many devices in your home already make use of this technology. The uses for AI number in the millions — all safely out of sight even when they're quite dramatic in nature. Here are just a few of the ways in which you might see AI used:

>> **Fraud detection:** You get a call from your credit card company asking whether you made a particular purchase. The credit card company isn't being nosy; it's simply alerting you to the fact that someone else could be making a purchase using your card. The AI embedded within the credit card company's code detected an unfamiliar spending pattern and alerted someone to it.

>> **Resource scheduling:** Many organizations need to schedule the use of resources efficiently. For example, a hospital may have to determine where to put a patient based on the patient's needs, availability of skilled experts, and the amount of time the doctor expects the patient to be in the hospital.

>> **Complex analysis:** Humans often need help with complex analysis because there are literally too many factors to consider. For example, the same set of symptoms could indicate more than one problem. A doctor or other expert might need help making a diagnosis in a timely manner to save a patient's life.

>> **Automation:** Any form of automation can benefit from the addition of AI to handle unexpected changes or events. A problem with some types of automation today is that an unexpected event, such as an object in the wrong place, can actually cause the automation to stop. Adding AI to the automation can allow the automation to handle unexpected events and continue as though nothing happened.

- >> **Customer service:** The customer service line you call today may not even have a human behind it. The automation is good enough to follow scripts and use various resources to handle the vast majority of your questions. With good voice inflection (provided by AI as well), you may not even be able to tell that you're talking with a computer.

- >> **Safety systems:** Many of the safety systems found in machines of various sorts today rely on AI to take over the vehicle in a time of crisis. For example, many automatic braking systems rely on AI to stop the car based on all the inputs that a vehicle can provide, such as the direction of a skid.

- >> **Machine efficiency:** AI can help control a machine in such a manner as to obtain maximum efficiency. The AI controls the use of resources so that the system doesn't overshoot speed or other goals. Every ounce of power is used precisely as needed to provide the desired services.

Focusing on machine learning

Machine learning is one of a number of subsets of AI and the only one this book discusses. In machine learning, the goal is to create a simulation of human learning so that an application can adapt to uncertain or unexpected conditions. To perform this task, machine learning relies on algorithms to analyze huge datasets.

REMEMBER

Currently, machine learning can't provide the sort of AI that the movies present (a machine can't intuitively learn as a human can); it can only simulate specific kinds of learning, and only in a narrow range at that. Even the best algorithms can't think, feel, present any form of self-awareness, or exercise free will. Characteristics that are basic to humans are frustratingly difficult for machines to grasp because of these limits in perception. Machines aren't self-aware.

What machine learning can do is perform predictive analytics far faster than any human can. As a result, machine learning can help humans work more efficiently. The current state of AI, then, is one of performing analysis, but humans must still consider the implications of that analysis: making the required moral and ethical decisions. The essence of the matter is that machine learning provides just the learning part of AI, and that part is nowhere near ready to create an AI of the sort you see in films.

REMEMBER

The main point of confusion between learning and intelligence is that people assume that simply because a machine gets better at its job (it can learn), it's also aware (has intelligence). Nothing supports this view of machine learning. The same phenomenon occurs when people assume that a computer is purposely causing problems for them. The computer can't assign emotions and therefore acts only upon the input provided and the instruction contained within an application to process that input. A true AI will eventually occur when computers can finally emulate the clever combination used by nature:

>> **Genetics:** Slow learning from one generation to the next

>> **Teaching:** Fast learning from organized sources

>> **Exploration:** Spontaneous learning through media and interactions with others

To keep machine learning concepts in line with what the machine can actually do, you need to consider specific machine learning uses. It's useful to view uses of machine learning outside the normal realm of what many consider the domain of AI. Here are a few uses for machine learning that you might not associate with an AI:

>> **Access control:** In many cases, access control is a yes-or-no proposition. An employee smartcard grants access to a resource in much the same way as people have used keys for centuries. Some locks do offer the capability to set times and dates that access is allowed, but such coarse-grained control doesn't really answer every need. By using machine learning, you can determine whether an employee should gain access to a resource based on role and need. For example, an employee can gain access to a training room when the training reflects an employee role.

>> **Animal protection:** The ocean might seem large enough to allow animals and ships to cohabitate without problem. Unfortunately, many animals get hit by ships each year. A machine learning algorithm could allow ships to avoid animals by learning the sounds and characteristics of both the animal and the ship. (The ship would rely on underwater listening gear to track the animals through their sounds, which you can actually hear a long distance from the ship.)

>> **Predicting wait times:** Most people don't like waiting when they have no idea of how long the wait will be. Machine learning allows an application to determine waiting times based on staffing levels, staffing load, complexity of the problems the staff is trying to solve, availability of resources, and so on.

Moving from machine learning to deep learning

Deep learning is a subset of machine learning, as previously mentioned. In both cases, algorithms appear to learn by analyzing huge amounts of data (however, learning can occur even with tiny datasets in some cases). However, deep learning varies in the depth of its analysis and the kind of automation it provides. You can summarize the differences between the two like this:

>> **A completely different paradigm:** Machine learning is a set of many different techniques that enable a computer to learn from data and to use what it learns to provide an answer, often in the form of a prediction. Machine learning relies on different paradigms such as using statistical analysis, finding analogies in data, using logic, and working with symbols. Contrast the myriad techniques used by machine learning with the single technique used by deep learning, which mimics human brain functionality. It processes data using computing units, called *neurons,* arranged into ordered sections, called *layers.* The technique at the foundation of deep learning is the *neural network.*

>> **Flexible architectures:** Machine learning solutions offer many knobs (adjustments) called *hyperparameters* that you tune to optimize algorithm learning from data. Deep learning solutions use hyperparameters, too, but they also use multiple user-configured layers (the user specifies number and type). In fact, depending on the resulting neural network, the number of layers can be quite large and form unique neural networks capable of specialized learning: Some can learn to recognize images, while others can detect and parse voice commands. The point is that the term *deep* is appropriate; it refers to the large number of layers potentially used for analysis. The architecture consists of the ensemble of different neurons and their arrangement in layers in a deep learning solution.

>> **Autonomous feature definition:** Machine learning solutions require human intervention to succeed. To process data correctly, analysts and scientist use a lot of their own knowledge to develop working algorithms. For instance, in a machine learning solution that determines the value of a house by relying on data containing the wall measures of different rooms, the machine learning algorithm won't be able to calculate the surface of the house unless the analyst specifies how to calculate it beforehand. Creating the right information for a machine learning algorithm is called feature creation, which is a time-consuming activity. Deep learning doesn't require humans to perform any feature-creation activity because, thanks to its many layers, it defines its own best features. That's also why deep learning outperforms machine learning in otherwise very difficult tasks such as recognizing voice and images, understanding text, or beating a human champion at the Go game (the digital form of the board game in which you capture your opponent's territory).

TECHNICAL STUFF

You need to understand a number of issues with regard to deep learning solutions, the most important of which is that the computer still doesn't understand anything and isn't aware of the solution it has provided. It simply provides a form of feedback loop and automation conjoined to produce desirable outputs in less time than a human could manually produce precisely the same result by manipulating a machine learning solution.

The second issue is that some benighted people have insisted that the deep learning layers are hidden and not accessible to analysis. This isn't the case. Anything a computer can build is ultimately traceable by a human. In fact, the General Data Protection Regulation (GDPR) (https://eugdpr.org/) requires that humans perform such analysis (see the article at https://www.pcmag.com/commentary/361258/how-gdpr-will-impact-the-ai-industry for details). The requirement to perform this analysis is controversial, but current law says that someone must do it.

The third issue is that self-adjustment goes only so far. Deep learning doesn't always ensure a reliable or correct result. In fact, deep learning solutions can go horribly wrong (see the article at https://www.theverge.com/2016/3/24/11297050/tay-microsoft-chatbot-racist for details). Even when the application code doesn't go wrong, the devices used to support the deep learning can (see the article at https://www.pcmag.com/commentary/361918/learning-from-alexas-mistakes?source=SectionArticles for details). Even so, with these problems in mind, you can see deep learning used for a number of extremely popular applications, as described at https://medium.com/@vratulmittal/top-15-deep-learning-applications-that-will-rule-the-world-in-2018-and-beyond-7c6130c43b01.

Using Deep Learning in the Real World

Make no mistake: People do use deep learning in the real world to perform a broad range of tasks. For example, many automobiles today use a voice interface. The voice interface can perform basic tasks, even right from the outset. However, the more you talk to it, the better the voice interface performs. The interface learns as you talk to it — not only the manner in which you say things, but also your personal preferences. The following sections give you a little information on how deep learning works in the real world.

Understanding the concept of learning

When humans learn, they rely on more than just data. Humans have intuition, along with an uncanny grasp of what will and what won't work. Part of this inborn knowledge is instinct, which is passed from generation to generation through DNA. The way humans interact with input is also different from what a computer will do. When dealing with a computer, learning is a matter of building a database consisting of a neural network that has weights and biases built into it to ensure proper data processing. The neural network then processes data, but not in a manner that's even remotely the same as what a human will do.

Performing deep learning tasks

Humans and computers are best at different tasks. Humans are best at reasoning, thinking through ethical solutions, and being emotional. A computer is meant to process data — lots of data — really fast. You commonly use deep learning to solve problems that require looking for patterns in huge amounts of data — problems whose solution is nonintuitive and not immediately noticeable. The article at http://www.yaronhadad.com/deep-learning-most-amazing-applications/ tells you about 30 different ways in which people are currently using deep learning to perform tasks. In just about every case, you can sum up the problem and its solution as processing huge amounts of data quickly, looking for patterns, and then relying on those patterns to discover something new or to create a particular kind of output.

Employing deep learning in applications

Deep learning can be a stand-alone solution, as illustrated in this book, but it's often used as part of a much larger solution and mixed with other technologies. For example, mixing deep learning with expert systems is not uncommon. The article at https://www.sciencedirect.com/science/article/pii/0167923694900213 describes this mixture to some degree. However, real applications are more than just numbers generated from some nebulous source. When working in the real world, you must also consider various kinds of data sources and understand how those data sources work. A camera may require a different sort of deep learning solution to obtain information from it, while a thermometer or proximity detector may output simple numbers (or analog data that requires some sort of processing to use). Real-world solutions are messy, so you need to be prepared with more than one solution to problems in your toolkit.

Considering the Deep Learning Programming Environment

You may automatically assume that you must jump through a horrid set of hoops and learn esoteric programming skills to delve into deep learning. It's true that you gain flexibility by writing applications using one of the programming languages that work well for deep learning needs. However, Deep Learning Studio (see the article at https://towardsdatascience.com/is-deep-learning-without-pro gramming-possible-be1312df9b4a for details) and other products like it are enabling people to create deep learning solutions without programming. Essentially, such solutions involve describing what you want as output by defining a model graphically. These kinds of solutions work well for straightforward problems that others have already had to solve, but they lack the flexibility to do something completely different — a task that requires something more than simple analysis.

Deep learning solutions in the cloud, such as that provided by Amazon Web Services (AWS) (https://aws.amazon.com/deep-learning/), can give you additional flexibility. These environments also tend to make the development environment simpler by providing as much or little support as you want. In fact, AWS provides support for various kinds of serverless computing (https://aws.amazon.com/serverless/) in which you don't worry about any sort of infrastructure. However, these solutions can become quite expensive. Even though they give you greater flexibility than using a premade solution, they still aren't as flexible as using an actual development environment.

You have other nonprogramming solutions to consider as well. For example, if you want power and flexibility, but don't want to program to get it, you could rely on a product such as MATLAB (https://www.mathworks.com/help/deeplearning/ug/deep-learning-in-matlab.html), which provide a deep learning toolkit. MATLAB and certain other environments do focus more on the algorithms you want to use, but to gain full functionality from them, you need to write scripts as a minimum, which means that you're dipping your toe into programming to some extent. A problem with these environments is that they can also be lacking in the power department, so some solutions may take longer than you expect.

REMEMBER

At some point, no matter how many other solutions you try, serious deep learning problems will require programming. When reviewing the choices online, you often see AI, machine learning, and deep learning all lumped together. However, just as the three technologies work at different levels, so do the programming languages that you require. A good deep learning solution will require the use of multiprocessing, preferably using a Graphics Processing Unit (GPU) with lots of cores. Your language of choice must also support the GPU through a compatible library or package. So, just choosing a language usually isn't enough; you need to investigate further to ensure that the language will actually meet your needs. With this caution in mind, here are the top languages (in order of popularity, as of this writing) for deep learning use (as defined at https://www.datasciencecentral.com/profiles/blogs/which-programming-language-is-considered-to-be-best-for-machine):

» Python

» R

» MATLAB (the scripting language, not the product)

» Octave

The only problem with this list is that other developers have other opinions. Python and R normally appear at the top of everyone's lists, but after that you can find all sorts of opinions. The article at https://www.geeksforgeeks.org/top-5-best-programming-languages-for-artificial-intelligence-field/ gives you some alternative ideas. When choosing a language, you usually have to consider these issues:

>> **Learning curve:** Your experiences have a lot to say about what you find easiest to learn. Python is probably the best choice for someone who has programmed for a number of years, but R might be the better choice for someone who has already experienced functional programming. MATLAB or Octave might work best for a math professional.

>> **Speed:** Any sort of deep learning solution will require a lot of processing power. Many people say that because R is a statistical language, it offers more in the way of statistical support and usually provides a faster result. Actually, Python's support for great parallel programming probably offsets this advantage when you have the required hardware.

>> **Community support:** Many forms of community support exist, but the two that are most important for deep learning are help in defining a solution and access to a wealth of premade programming aids. Of the four, Octave probably provides the least in the way of community support; Python provides the most.

>> **Cost:** How much a language costs depends on the kind of solution you choose and where you run it. For example, MATLAB is a proprietary product that requires purchase, so you have something invested immediately when using MATLAB. However, even though the other languages are free at the outset, you can find hidden costs, such as running your code in the cloud to gain access to GPU support.

>> **DNN Frameworks support:** A framework can make working with your language significantly easier. However, you have to have a framework that works well with all other parts of your solution. The two most popular frameworks are TensorFlow and PyTorch. Oddly enough, Python is the only language that supports both, so it offers you the greatest flexibility. You use Caffe with MATLAB and TensorFlow with R.

>> **Production ready:** A language has to support the kind of output needed for your project. In this regard, Python shines because it's a general-purpose language. You can create any sort of application needed with it. However, the more specific environments provided by the other languages can be incredibly helpful with some projects, so you need to consider all of them.

Overcoming Deep Learning Hype

Previous parts of this chapter discuss some issues with the perception of deep learning, such as some people's belief that it appears everywhere and does everything. The problem with deep learning is that it has been a victim of its own media campaign. Deep learning solves specific sorts of problems. The following sections help you avoid the hype associated with deep learning.

Discovering the start-up ecosystem

Using a deep learning solution is a lot different from creating a deep learning solution of your own. The infographic at https://www.analyticsvidhya.com/blog/2018/08/infographic-complete-deep-learning-path/ gives you some ideas on how to get started with Python (a process this book simplifies for you). The educational requirements alone can take a while to fulfill. However, after you have worked through a few projects on your own, you begin to realize that the hype surrounding deep learning extends all the way to the start of setup. Deep learning isn't a mature technology, so trying to use it is akin to building a village on the moon or deep diving the Marianas Trench. You're going to encounter issues, and the technology will constantly change on you.

Some of the methods used to create deep learning solutions need work, too. The concept of a computer actually learning anything is false, as is the idea that computers have any form of sentience at all. The reason that Microsoft, Amazon, and other vendors have problems with deep learning is that even their engineers have unrealistic expectations. Deep learning comes down to math and pattern matching — really fancy math and pattern matching, to be sure, but the idea that it's anything else is simply wrong.

Knowing when not to use deep learning

Deep learning is only one way to perform analysis, and it's not always the best way. For example, even though expert systems are considered old technology, you can't really create a self-driving car without one for the reasons described at https://aitrends.com/ai-insider/expert-systems-ai-self-driving-cars-crucial-innovative-techniques/. A deep learning solution turns out to be way too slow for this particular need. Your car will likely contain a deep learning solution, but you're more likely to use it as part of the voice interface.

AI in general and deep learning in particular can make the headlines when the technology fails to live up to expectations. For example, the article at `https://www.techrepublic.com/article/top-10-ai-failures-of-2016/` provides a list of AI failures, some of which relied on deep learning as well. It's a mistake to think that deep learning can somehow make ethical decisions or that it will choose the right course of action based on feelings (which no machine has). Anthropomorphizing the use of deep learning will always be a mistake. Some tasks simply require a human.

Speed and the capability to think like a human are the top issues for deep learning, but there are many more. For example, you can't use deep learning if you don't have sufficient data to train it. In fact, the article at `https://www.sas.com/en_us/insights/articles/big-data/5-machine-learning-mistakes.html` offers a list of five common mistakes that people make when getting into machine learning and deep learning environments. If you don't have the right resources, deep learning will never work.

Chapter **2**

Introducing the Machine Learning Principles

A s discussed in Chapter 1, the concept of learning for a computer is different from the concept of learning for humans. However, Chapter 1 doesn't really describe machine learning, the kind of learning a computer uses, in any depth. After all, what you're really looking at is an entirely different sort of learning that some people would view as a combination of math, pattern matching, and data storage. This chapter begins by pointing the way to a deeper understanding of how machine learning works.

However, an explanation of machine learning doesn't completely help you understand what's going on when you work with it. How machine learning works is also important, which is the subject of the next section of the chapter. In this section, you discover that no perfect methods exist for performing analysis. You may have to experiment with your analysis to get the expected output. In addition, different approaches to machine learning are available, and each has advantages and disadvantages.

The third part of the chapter takes what you've discovered in the previous two parts and helps you apply it. No matter how you shape your data and perform analysis on it, machine learning is the wrong approach in some cases and will never provide you with useful output. Knowing the right uses for machine learning is essential if you want to receive consistent output that helps you perform interesting tasks. The whole purpose of machine learning is to learn something interesting from the data and then to do something interesting with it.

Defining Machine Learning

Here's a short definition of machine learning: It's an application of AI that can automatically learn and improve from experience without being explicitly programmed to do so. The learning occurs as a result of analyzing ever increasing amounts of data, so the basic algorithms don't change, but the code's internal weights and biases used to select a particular answer do. Of course, nothing is quite this simple. The following sections discuss more about what machine learning is so that you can understand its place within the world of AI and what deep learning acquires from it.

REMEMBER

Data scientists often refer to the technology used to implement machine learning as algorithms. An algorithm is a series of step-by-step operations, usually computations, that can solve a defined problem in a finite number of steps. In machine learning, the algorithms use a series of finite steps to solve the problem by learning from data.

Understanding how machine learning works

Machine learning algorithms learn, but it's often hard to find a precise meaning for the term *learning* because different ways exist to extract information from data, depending on how the machine learning algorithm is built. Generally, the learning process requires huge amounts of data that provides an expected response given particular inputs. Each input/response pair represents an example and more examples make it easier for the algorithm to learn. That's because each input/response pair fits within a line, cluster, or other statistical representation that defines a problem domain. Learning is the act of optimizing a model, which is a mathematical, summarized representation of data itself, such that it can predict or otherwise determine an appropriate response even when it receives input that it hasn't seen before. The more accurately the model can come up with correct responses, the better the model has learned from the data inputs provided. An algorithm fits the model to the data, and this *fitting process* is training.

Figure 2-1 shows an extremely simple graph that simulates what occurs in machine learning. In this case, starting with input values of 1, 4, 5, 8, and 10 and pairing them with their corresponding outputs of 7, 13, 15, 21, and 25, the machine learning algorithm determines that the best way to represent the relationship between the input and output is the formula 2x + 5. This formula defines the model used to process the input data — even new, unseen data —to calculate a corresponding output value. The trend line (the model) shows the pattern formed by this algorithm, such that a new input of 3 will produce a predicted output of 11. Even though most machine learning scenarios are much more complicated than this (and the algorithm can't create rules that accurately map every input to a precise output), the example gives provides you a basic idea of what happens. Rather than have to individually program a response for an input of 3, the model can compute the correct response based on input/response pairs that it has learned.

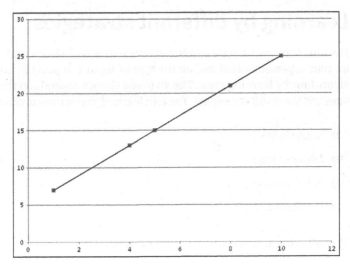

FIGURE 2-1:
Visualizing a basic machine learning scenario.

Understanding that it's pure math

The central idea behind machine learning is that you can represent reality by using a mathematical function that the algorithm doesn't know in advance, but which it can guess after seeing some data (always in the form of paired inputs and outputs). You can express reality and all its challenging complexity in terms of unknown mathematical functions that machine learning algorithms find and make available as a modification of their internal mathematical function. That is, every machine learning algorithm is built around a modifiable math function. The function can be modified because it has internal parameters or weights for such a purpose. As a result, the algorithm can tailor the function to specific information taken from data. This concept is the core idea for all kinds of machine learning algorithms.

Learning in machine learning is purely mathematical, and it ends by associating certain inputs with certain outputs. It has nothing to do with understanding what the algorithm has learned. (When humans analyze data, we build an understanding of the data to a certain extent.) The learning process is often described as training because the algorithm is trained to match the correct answer (the output) to every question offered (the input). (*Machine Learning For Dummies*, by John Paul Mueller and Luca Massaron, [Wiley], describes how this process works in detail.)

In spite of lacking deliberate understanding and of being a mathematical process, machine learning can prove useful in many tasks. It provides many AI applications the power to mimic rational thinking given a certain context when learning occurs by using the right data.

Learning by different strategies

Machine learning offers a number of different ways to learn from data. Depending on your expected output and on the type of input you provide, you can categorize algorithms by learning style. The style you choose depends on the sort of data you have and the result you expect. The four learning styles used to create algorithms are

>> Supervised

>> Unsupervised

>> Self-supervised

>> Reinforcement

The following sections discuss learning styles.

Supervised

When working with supervised algorithms, the input data is labeled and has a specific expected result. You use training to create a model that an algorithm fits to the data. As training progresses, the predictions or classifications become more accurate. Here are some examples of supervised learning algorithms:

>> Linear or Logistic regression

>> Support Vector Machines (SVMs)

>> Naïve Bayes

>> K-Nearest Neighbors (KNN)

You need to distinguish between regression problems, whose target is a numeric value, and classification problems, whose target is a qualitative variable, such as a class or tag. A regression task could determine the average prices of houses in the Boston area, while an example of a classification task is distinguishing between kinds of iris flowers based on their sepal and petal measures. Here are some examples of supervised learning:

Data Input (X)	Data Output (y)	Real-World Application
History of customers' purchases	A list of products that customers have never bought	Recommender system
Images	A list of boxes labeled with an object name	Image detection and recognition
English text in the form of questions	English text in the form of answers	Chatbot, a software application that can converse
English text	German text	Machine language translation
Audio	Text transcript	Speech recognition
Image, sensor data	Steering, braking, or accelerating	Behavioral planning for autonomous driving

Unsupervised

When working with unsupervised algorithms, the input data isn't labeled and the results aren't known. In this case, analysis of structures in the data produces the required model. The structural analysis can have a number of goals, such as to reduce redundancy or to group similar data. Examples of unsupervised learning are

>> Clustering

>> Anomaly detection

>> Neural networks

Self-Supervised

You'll find all sorts of kinds of learning described online, but self-supervised learning is in a category of its own. Some people describe it as autonomous supervised learning, which gives you the benefits of supervised learning but without all the work required to label data.

REMEMBER

Theoretically, self-supervised could solve issues with other kinds of learning that you may currently use. The following list compares self-supervised learning with other sorts of learning that people use.

>> **Supervised learning:** The closest form of learning associated with self-supervised learning is supervised learning because both kinds of learning

rely on pairs of inputs and labeled outputs. In addition, both forms of learning are associated with regression and classification. However, the difference is that self-supervised learning doesn't require a person to label the output. Instead, it relies on correlations, embedded metadata, or domain knowledge embedded within the input data to contextually discover the output label.

>> **Unsupervised learning:** Like unsupervised learning, self-supervised learning requires no data labeling. However, unsupervised learning focuses on data structure — that is, patterns within the data. Therefore, you don't use self-supervised learning for tasks such as clustering, grouping, dimensionality reduction, recommendation engines, or the like.

>> **Semi-supervised learning:** A semi-supervised learning solution works like an unsupervised learning solution in that it looks for data patterns. However, semi-supervised learning relies on a mix of labeled and unlabeled data to perform its tasks faster than is possible using strictly unlabeled data. Self-supervised learning never requires labels and uses context to perform its task, so it would actually ignore the labels when supplied.

Reinforcement

You can view reinforcement learning as an extension of self-supervised learning because both forms use the same approach to learning with unlabeled data to achieve similar goals. However, reinforcement learning adds a feedback loop to the mix. When a reinforcement learning solution performs a task correctly, it receives positive feedback, which strengthens the model in connecting the target inputs and output. Likewise, it can receive negative feedback for incorrect solutions. In some respects, the system works much the same as working with a dog based on a system of rewards.

Training, validating, and testing data

Machine learning is a process, just as everything is a process in the world of computers. To build a successful machine learning solution, you perform these tasks as needed, and as often as needed:

>> **Training:** Machine learning begins when you train a model using a particular algorithm against specific data. The training data is separate from any other data, but it must also be representative. If the training data doesn't truly represent the problem domain, the resulting model can't provide useful results. During the training process, you see how the model responds to the training data and make changes, as needed, to the algorithms you use and the manner in which you massage the data prior to input to the algorithm.

>> **Validating:** Many datasets are large enough to split into a training part and a testing part. You first train the model using the training data, and then you validate it using the testing data. Of course, the testing data must again represent the problem domain accurately. It must also be statistically compatible with the training data. Otherwise, you won't see results that reflect how the model will actually work.

>> **Testing:** After a model is trained and validated, you still need to test it using real-world data. This step is important because you need to verify that the model will actually work on a larger dataset that you haven't used for either training or testing. As with the training and validation steps, any data you use during this step must reflect the problem domain you want to interact with using the machine learning model.

Training provides a machine learning algorithm with all sorts of examples of the desired inputs and outputs expected from those inputs. The machine learning algorithm then uses this input to create a math function. In other words, training is the process whereby the algorithm works out how to tailor a function to the data. The output of such a function is typically the probability of a certain output or simply a numeric value as output.

To give an idea of what happens in the training process, imagine a child learning to distinguish trees from objects, animals, and people. Before the child can do so in an independent fashion, a teacher presents the child with a certain number of tree images, complete with all the facts that make a tree distinguishable from other objects of the world. Such facts could be features, such as the tree's material (wood), its parts (trunk, branches, leaves or needles, roots), and location (planted in the soil). The child builds an understanding of what a tree looks like by contrasting the display of tree features with the images of other, different examples, such as pieces of furniture that are made of wood, but do not share other characteristics with a tree.

A machine learning classifier works the same. A classifier algorithm provides you with a class as output. For instance, it could tell you that the photo you provide as an input matches the tree class (and not an animal or a person). To do so, it builds its cognitive capabilities by creating a mathematical formulation that includes all the given input features in a way that creates a function that can distinguish one class from another.

Looking for generalization

To be useful, a machine learning model must represent a general view of the data provided. If the model doesn't follow the data closely enough, it's *underfitted* — that is, not fitted enough because of a lack of training. On the other hand, if the model follows the data too closely, it's *overfitted*, following the data points like a glove because of *too much* training. Underfitting and overfitting both cause problems because the model isn't generalized enough to produce useful results. Given unknown input data, the resulting predictions or classifications will contain large error values. Only when the model is correctly fitted to the data will it provide results within a reasonable error range.

This whole issue of generalization is also important in deciding when to use machine learning. A machine learning solution always generalizes from specific examples to general examples of the same sort. How it performs this task depends on the orientation of the machine learning solution and the algorithms used to make it work.

REMEMBER

The problem for data scientists and others using machine learning and deep learning techniques is that the computer won't display a sign telling you that the model correctly fits the data. Often, it's a matter of human intuition to decide when a model is trained enough to provide a good generalized result. In addition, the solution creator must choose the right algorithm out of the thousands that exist. Without the right algorithm to fit the model to the data, the results will be disappointing. To make the selection process work, the data scientist must possess

>> A strong knowledge of the available algorithms

>> Experience dealing with the kind of data in question

>> An understanding of the desired output

>> A desire to experiment with various algorithms

The last requirement is the most important because there are no hard-and-fast rules that say a particular algorithm will work with every kind of data in every possible situation. If this were the case, so many algorithms wouldn't be available. To find the best algorithm, the data scientist often resorts to experimenting with a number of algorithms and comparing the results.

Getting to know the limits of bias

Your computer has no bias. It has no goal of world domination or of making your life difficult. In fact, computers don't have goals of any kind. The only thing a computer can provide is output based on inputs and processing technique. However, bias still gets into the computer and taints the results it provides in a number of ways:

>> **Data:** The data itself can contain mistruths or simply misrepresentations. For example, if a particular value appears twice as often in the data as it does in

the real world, the output from a machine learning solution is tainted, even though the data itself is correct.

>> **Algorithm:** Using the wrong algorithm will cause the machine learning solution to fit the model to the data incorrectly.

>> **Training:** Too much or too little training changes how the model fits the data and therefore the result.

REMEMBER

>> **Human interpretation:** Even when a machine learning solution outputs a correct result, the human using that output can misinterpret it. The results are every bit as bad as, and perhaps worse than, when the machine learning solution fails to work as anticipated. (The article at https://thenextweb. com/artificial-intelligence/2018/04/10/human-bias-huge-problem-ai-heres-going-fix/ offers some insights about this issue.)

You need to consider the effects of bias no matter what sort of machine learning solution you create. It's important to know what sorts of limits these biases place on your solution and whether the solution is reliable enough to provide useful output.

Keeping model complexity in mind

Simpler is always better when it comes to machine learning. Many different algorithms may provide you with useful output from your machine learning solution, but the best algorithm to use is the one that's easiest to understand and provides the most straightforward results. Occam's Razor (http://math.ucr. edu/home/baez/physics/General/occam.html) is generally recognized as the best strategy to follow. Basically, Occam's Razor tells you to use the simplest solution that will solve a particular problem. As complexity increases, so does the potential for errors.

Considering the Many Different Roads to Learning

The learning part of machine learning makes it dynamic — that is, able to change itself when it receives additional data. The capability to learn makes machine learning different from other sorts of AI, such as knowledge graphs and expert systems. It doesn't make machine learning better than other AI (as described in Chapter 1), but simply useful for a certain set of problems. Of course, the problem with quantifying what learning entails is that humans and computers view learning differently. In addition, computers use different learning techniques than humans do and some humans may not see the learning part of machine learning as learning at all. The following sections discuss the methods that machine learning algorithms use to learn so that you can better understand that machine learning and human learning are inherently different.

Understanding there is no free lunch

You may have heard the common myth that you can have everything in the way of computer output without putting much effort into deriving the solution. Unfortunately, no absolute solution exists to any problem, and better answers are often quite costly. When working with algorithms, you quickly discover that some algorithms perform better than others in solving certain problems, but that there also isn't a single algorithm that works best on every problem. This is because of the math behind algorithms. Certain math functions are good at representing some problems but may hit a wall on certain other problems. Each algorithm has its specialty.

Discovering the five main approaches

Algorithms come in various forms and perform various tasks. One way to categorize algorithms is by school of thought — the method that a group of likeminded thinkers believed would solve a particular kind of problem. Of course, other ways to categorize algorithms exist, but this approach has the advantage of helping you understand algorithm uses and orientations better. The following sections provide an overview of the five main algorithmic techniques.

Symbolic reasoning

A group called the symbologists relies on algorithms that use symbolic reasoning to find a solution to problems. The term inverse deduction commonly appears as induction. In symbolic reasoning, *deduction* expands the realm of human knowledge, while *induction* raises the level of human knowledge. Induction commonly opens new fields of exploration, and deduction explores those fields. However, the most important consideration is that induction is the science portion of this type of reasoning, while deduction is the engineering. The two strategies work hand in hand to solve problems by first opening a field of potential exploration to solve the problem and then exploring that field to determine whether it does, in fact, solve it.

As an example of this strategy, deduction would say that if a tree is green and that green trees are alive, the tree must be alive. When thinking about induction, you would say that the tree is green and that the tree is also alive; therefore, green trees are alive. Induction provides the answer to what knowledge is missing given a known input and output.

Neural networks

Neural networks are the brainchild of a group called the connectionists. This group of algorithms strives to reproduce the brain's functions using silicon instead of neurons. Essentially, each of the neurons (created as an algorithm that models the real-world counterpart) solves a small piece of the problem, and the use of many neurons in parallel solves the problem as a whole.

TECHNICAL STUFF

A neural network can provide a method of correction for errant data, and the most popular of these methods is *backpropagation*. (The two-part article at http://www.breloff.com/no-backprop/ and http://www.breloff.com/no-backprop-part2/ discusses backpropagation alternatives.) The use of backpropagation, or backward propagation of errors, seeks to determine the conditions under which errors are removed from networks built to resemble the human neurons by changing the *weights* (how much a particular input figures into the result) and *biases* (which features are selected) of the network. The goal is to continue changing the weights and biases until such time as the actual output matches the target output.

At this point, the artificial neuron fires and passes its solution along to the next neuron in line. The solution created by each individual neuron is only part of the whole solution. Each neuron continues to pass information to the next neuron in line until the group of neurons creates a final output.

Evolutionary algorithms

A group called the evolutionaries relies on the principles of evolution to solve problems. This strategy is based on the survival of the fittest, removing any solutions that don't match the desired output. A fitness function determines the viability of each function in solving a problem.

Using a tree structure, the solution method looks for the best solution based on function output. The winner of each level of evolution gets to build the next level of functions. The next level will get closer to solving the problem but may not solve it completely, which means that another level is needed. This particular algorithmic type relies heavily on recursion (see https://www.cs.cmu.edu/~adamchik/15-121/lectures/Recursions/recursions.html for an explanation of recursion) and languages that strongly support recursion to solve problems. An interesting output of this strategy has been algorithms that evolve themselves: One generation of algorithms actually builds the next generation.

Bayesian inference

The Bayesians use various statistical methods to solve problems. Given that statistical methods can create more than one apparently correct solution, the choice of a function becomes one of determining which function has the highest probability of succeeding. For example, when using these techniques, you might accept a set of symptoms as input. An algorithm will compute the probability that a particular disease will result from the symptoms as output. Given that multiple diseases have the same symptoms, the probability is important because a user will see some situations in which a lower probability output is actually the correct output for a given circumstance.

TIP

Ultimately, Bayesian algorithms rely on the idea of never quite trusting any hypothesis (a result that someone has given you) completely without seeing the evidence used to make it (the input the other person used to make the hypothesis). Analyzing the evidence proves or disproves the hypothesis that it supports. Consequently, you can't determine which disease someone has until you test all the symptoms. One of the most recognizable outputs from this group of algorithms is the spam filter.

Systems that learn by analogy

The analogizers use kernel machines to recognize patterns in data. By recognizing the pattern of one set of inputs and comparing it to the pattern of a known output, you create a problem solution. The goal is to use similarity to determine the best solution to a problem. It's the kind of reasoning that determines that using a particular solution worked in a given circumstance at some previous time; therefore, using that solution for a similar set of circumstances should also work. One of the most recognizable outputs from this group of algorithms is recommender systems. For example, when you get on Amazon and buy a product, the recommender system comes up with other, related, products that you might also want to buy.

Delving into some different approaches

It helps to have several views of algorithms so that you understand what they do and why they do it. The previous section looks at algorithms based on the groups that created them. However, you have other approaches you can use to categorize algorithms. The following list categorizes some popular algorithms by similarity:

>> **Artificial neural network:** Models the structure or function of biological neural networks (or sometimes it does both). The goal is to perform pattern matching for regression and classification problems. However, the technique mimics the approach used by biological organisms rather than strictly relying on a true math-based approach. Here are examples of artificial neural network algorithms:

- Perceptron

- Feed-forward Neural Network

- Hopfield Network
- Radial Basis Function Network (RBFN)
- Self-Organizing Map (SOM)

» **Association rule:** Extracts rules that help explain the relationships between variables in data. You can use these rules to discover useful associations within huge datasets that are ordinarily easy to miss. Here are the more popular association-rule algorithms:

- Apriori algorithm
- Eclat algorithm

» **Bayesian:** Applies Bayes' Theorem to probability problems. This form of algorithm sees use for classification and regression problems. Here are examples of Bayesian algorithms:

- Naïve Bayes
- Gaussian Naïve Bayes
- Multinomial Naïve Bayes
- Bayesian Belief Network (BBN)
- Bayesian Network (BN)

» **Clustering:** Describes a model for organizing data by class or other criteria. The results are often centroid or hierarchical in nature. What you see are data relationships in a way that helps make sense of the data — that is, how the values affect each other. The following list contains examples of clustering algorithms:

- K-means
- K-medians
- Expectation Maximisation (EM)
- Hierarchical Clustering

» **Decision tree:** Constructs a model of decisions based on the actual values found in data. The resulting tree structure enables you to perform comparisons between new data and existing data very quickly. This form of algorithm often sees use for classification and regression problems. The following list shows some of the common decision-tree algorithms:

- Classification and Regression Tree (CART)
- Iterative Dichotomiser 3 (ID3)

- C4.5 and C5.0 (different versions of a powerful approach)

- Chi-squared Automatic Interaction Detection (CHAID)

» **Deep learning:** Provides an update to artificial neural networks that rely on multiple layers to exploit even larger datasets and build complex neural networks. This particular group of algorithms works well with semisupervised learning problems in which the amount of labeled data is minimal. Here are some examples of deep learning algorithms:

- Deep Boltzmann Machine (DBM)

- Deep Belief Networks (DBN)

- Convolutional Neural Network (CNN)

- Recurrent Neural Network (RNN)

- Stacked Auto-Encoders

» **Dimensionality reduction:** Seeks and exploits similarities in the structure of data in a manner similar to clustering algorithms, but using unsupervised methods. The purpose is to summarize or describe data using less information so that the dataset becomes smaller and easier to manage. In some cases, people use these algorithms for classification or regression problems. Here is a list of common dimensionality reduction algorithms:

- Principal Component Analysis (PCA)

- Factor Analysis (FA)

- Multidimensional Scaling (MDS)

- t-Distributed Stochastic Neighbor Embedding (t-SNE)

» **Ensemble:** Composes a group of multiple weaker models into a cohesive whole whose individual predictions are combined in some manner to define an overall prediction. Using an ensemble can solve certain problems faster, more efficiently, or with reduced errors. Here are some common ensemble algorithms:

- Boosting

- Bootstrapped Aggregation (Bagging)

- AdaBoost

- Random Forest

- Gradient Boosting Machines (GBM)

>> **Instance-based:** Defines a model for decision problems in which the training data consists of examples that are later used for comparison purposes. A similarity measure helps determine when new examples compare favorably to existing examples within the database. Some people call these algorithms winner-take-all or memory-based learning because of the manner in which they work. The following list provides some common algorithms associated with this category:

- K-Nearest Neighbors (KNN)

- Learning Vector Quantization (LVQ)

>> **Regression:** Models the relationship among variables. This relationship is iteratively refined using an error measure. This category sees heavy use in statistical machine learning. The following list shows the algorithms normally associated with this kind of algorithm:

- Ordinary Least Squares Regression (OLSR)

- Logistic Regression

>> **Regularization:** Regulates other algorithms by penalizing complex solutions and favoring simpler ones. This kind of algorithm often sees use with regression methods. The goal is to ensure that the solution doesn't become lost in its own complexity and delivers solutions within a given time frame using the least number of resources. Here are examples of regularization algorithms:

- Ridge Regression

- Least Absolute Shrinkage and Selection Operator (LASSO)

- Elastic Net

- Least-Angle Regression (LARS)

>> **Support Vector Machines (SVM):** Supervised learning algorithms that solve classification and regression problems by separating only a few data examples (called *supports*, hence the name of the algorithm) from the rest of the data using a function. After separating these supports, the prediction becomes easier. The form of analysis depends on the function type (called a *kernel*): linear, polynomial, or radial basis. Here are examples of SVM algorithms.

- Linear Support Vector Machines

- Radial Basis Function Support Vector Machines

- One-Class Support Vector Machines (for unsupervised learning)

>> **Other:** You have many other algorithms from which to choose. This list contains major algorithm categories. Some of the categories not found in this list belong to those used for feature selection, algorithm accuracy, performance measures, and specialty subfields of machine learning. For example, whole categories of algorithms are devoted to the topic of Computer Vision (CV) and Natural Language Processing (NLP). As you read through this book, you find many other categories of algorithms and may begin to wonder how a data scientist can make any choice, much less the right one.

Awaiting the next breakthrough

Breakthroughs require patience because computers are inherently based on math. You may not see them as such when working with a higher-level language like Python, but everything that goes on beneath the hood requires an extreme understanding of math and the data it manipulates. Consequently, you can expect to see new uses for machine learning and deep learning in the future as scientists continue to find new ways to process data, create algorithms, and use those algorithms to define data models.

REMEMBER

Unfortunately, working with what is available today isn't enough to create the applications of tomorrow (despite what the movies might have you believe). In the future, you can expect advances in hardware to make applications that aren't feasible today quite doable. It's not just a matter of additional computing power or larger memories. Tomorrow's computer will have access to sensors that aren't available today; processors that do things that today's processors can't; and methods of viewing how computers think that haven't been envisioned yet. What the world needs most now is experience, and experience always takes time to accumulate.

Pondering the True Uses of Machine Learning

The fact that you have a number of options to choose from when it comes to AI means that machine learning isn't the only technology you should consider to solve any given problem. Machine learning does excel at helping you solve specific categories of problems. To determine where machine learning works best, you must begin by considering how an algorithm learns and then applying that knowledge to problem classes that you need to solve. Remember that machine learning is about generalization, so it doesn't work particularly well in these scenarios:

>> The result must provide a precise answer, such as calculating a trip to Mars.

>> You can solve the problem using generalization but other techniques are simpler, such as developing software to compute a factorial of a number.

>> You don't have a good generalization of the problem because the problem is misunderstood, no specific relationship exists between inputs and results, or the problem domain is too complex.

The following sections discuss the true uses of machine learning from the perspective of how it learns and then defines the benefits of machine learning given specific problem domains.

Understanding machine learning benefits

How you can benefit from machine learning depends partly on your environment and partly on what you expect from it. For example, if you spend time on Amazon buying products, you might expect machine learning to make useful recommendations based on past purchases at some point. These recommendations are for products that you might not have otherwise known about. Recommending products that you already use or don't need isn't particularly useful, which is where the machine learning part comes into play. As Amazon builds more data about your purchasing habits, the recommendations should become more useful, although not even the best machine learning algorithm will ever guess your needs correctly every time.

REMEMBER

Of course, machine learning benefits you in many other ways. A developer can use machine learning to add an NLP capability to an application. A researcher could use it to help find the next cure for cancer. You may already use it for spam filtering for your e-mail or rely on it when you get into your car as part of a voice interface. With this in mind, the following benefits likely fit more of a business perspective for using machine learning effectively, but keep in mind that many other ways exist as well:

>> **Simplify product marketing:** One of the issues that any organization faces is determining what to sell and when, based on customer preferences. Sales campaigns are expensive, so having one fail usually isn't an option. In addition, an organization might find odd bits of information: Customers may like products in red but not in green. Knowing what the customer wants is incredibly difficult unless you can analyze huge amounts of buying data, which is something that machine learning does well.

>> **Predict future sales accurately:** Being in business can seem a little like gambling because you can't be quite sure that your bets will pay off. A machine learning solution can follow sales minute by minute and track trends before they become obvious. The capability to perform this kind of tracking means that you can more accurately tune sales channels to deliver optimal results and ensure that stores have enough of the right products to sell. It isn't precisely like gazing into a crystal ball, but it's close.

>> **Forecast medical and other employee downtime:** Oddly enough, some organizations end up having problems because employees choose the worst possible times to be absent from work. In some cases, these absences seem unpredictable, such as medical needs, while in others you could possibly predict them, such as a sudden need for personal time. By tracking various trends from easily available data sources, you can track both medical-type and personal-type absences for your industry as a whole, location as a whole, and your organization in particular to ensure that you have enough people to get the job done at any given time.

>> **Reduce data entry errors:** Some kinds of data entry errors are relatively easy to avoid by using form features correctly or incorporating a spell checker into your application. In addition, adding certain kinds of pattern matching can help reduce capitalization errors or incorrect phone numbers. Machine learning can take error reduction to another level by correctly identifying complex patterns that other techniques will miss. For example, a customer order may need one of part A and two of part B to create a whole unit. The pattern matching for these kinds of sales can be elusive, but machine learning can make it possible, reducing errors that are particularly different to find and eradicate.

>> **Improve financial rule and modeling precision:** Keeping the finances straight can prove difficult in an organization of any size. Machine learning enables you to perform tasks such as portfolio management, algorithmic trading, loan underwriting, and fraud detection with greater precision. You can't eliminate human participating in such cases, but the human and machine working together can become an incredibly efficient combination that won't allow many errors to pass unnoticed.

>> **Foresee maintenance needs:** Any system that consists of something physical likely requires maintenance of various sorts. For example, machine learning can help predict when a system will need cleaning based on past performance and environmental monitoring. You can also do things like plan for replacement or repair of certain equipment based on past repairs and equipment statistics. A machine learning solution can even enable you to determine whether replacement or repair is the better option.

>> **Augment customer interaction and improve satisfaction:** Customers like to feel special; in fact, everyone does. However, trying to create a custom plan for each customer manually would prove impossible. You can find a wealth of information about customers through online sources, including everything from recent purchases to consistent buying habits. By combining all this data with a good machine learning solution and customer support personnel who have discerning eyes, you can appear to have personally created a special solution for each customer, even though the time required to do so is minimal.

Discovering machine learning limits

The limits of a technology are often hard to quantify completely because these limits are often the result of a lack of imagination on the part of the creator or consumer of that technology. However, machine learning does have some distinct limits that you need to consider before using this technology to perform any given task. The following list isn't complete. In fact, you may not even completely agree with it, but it does provide a good starting point.

>> **Massive amounts of training data are needed:** Unlike programmed solutions of the past, a machine learning solution relies on massive amounts of data to train it. As problem complexity increases, the number of data points required to model a particular problem increases, making even more data necessary. Although humans generate increasingly larger amounts of data in specific problem domains and the computing power needed to process this data also increases daily, some problem domains simply lack enough data or enough processing power to make machine learning effective.

>> **Labeling data is tedious and error prone:** When using the supervised learning technique (see the "Learning by different strategies" section, earlier in this chapter, for details), someone must label the data to provide the output value. The labeling process for huge amounts of data is both tedious and time consuming, making machine learning difficult at times. The problem is that a human can look at any number of examples of something like a stop sign and know that they're all stop signs, but a computer must have every stop sign individually labelled.

REMEMBER

>> **Machines can't explain themselves:** As machine learning solutions become more flexible and capable; the amount of hidden functionality becomes greater as well. In fact, when dealing with deep learning solutions, you find that the solution contains one or usually more hidden layers that the solution creates but that humans haven't taken the time to explore. Consequently, both machine learning (to some extent) and deep learning (to a greater extent) encounter issues for which transparency is valued and counter to some laws, such as the

General Data Protection Regulation, or GDPR (https://eugdpr.org/). Because the process becomes opaque, a human must now analyze a process that is supposed to be automatic. A potential solution for this problem may come in the form of new strategies, such as Local Interpretable Model-Agnostic Explanations (LIME) (see https://homes.cs.washington.edu/~marcotcr/blog/lime/ for details).

>> **Bias makes the results less usable:** An algorithm can't tell when data contains various mistruths in it (*Artificial Intelligence For Dummies,* by John Paul Mueller and Luca Massaron [Wiley], explains this issue in detail). Consequently, it regards all data as being unbiased and completely truthful. As a result, any analysis performed by an algorithm trained using this data is suspect. The problem becomes even greater when the algorithm itself is biased. You can find countless examples online of algorithms misidentifying common objects like stop signs because of the combination of data containing mistruths and biased algorithms.

>> **Machine learning solutions can't cooperate:** One of the most important advantages of being human is the ability to collaborate with others. Knowledge potential increases exponentially as each party to a potential solution submits its piece of knowledge to create a whole that is much greater than the sum of its parts. A single machine learning solution remains a single machine learning solution because of it can't generalize knowledge and thereby contribute to a comprehensive solution with multiple cooperative parties.

Chapter **3**

Getting and Using Python

Deep learning requires the use of code, and you have numerous language choices available to you. However, this book relies on Python because it works on many different platforms and enjoys significant support in the developer community. In fact, according to the Tiobe Index (https://www.tiobe.com/tiobe-index/) available at the time of writing, Python is the fourth-ranked language in the world and the one that will work best for deep learning, according to multiple sources (see https://www.analyticsindiamag.com/top-10-programming-languages-data-scientists-learn-2018/ for details).

Before you can do too much with Python or use it to solve deep problems, you need a workable installation. You also need access to the datasets and code used for this book. Downloading the sample code and installing it on your system is the best way to get a good learning experience from the book. This chapter helps you get your system set up so that you can easily follow the examples in the remainder of the book. It also explores potential alternatives, such as Google Colaboratory (https://colab.research.google.com/notebooks/welcome.ipynb), also called simply Colab, in case you want to work on an alternative device, such as a tablet.

REMEMBER

Using the downloadable source doesn't prevent you from typing the examples on your own, following them using a debugger, expanding them, or working with the code in all sorts of ways. The downloadable source is there to help you get a good start with your deep learning and Python learning experience. After you see how the code works when it's correctly typed and configured, you can try to create the examples on your own. If you make a mistake, you can compare what you've typed with the downloadable source and discover precisely where the error exists. You can find the downloadable source for this chapter in the `DL4D_03_Sample.ipynb`, `DL4D_03_Dataset_Load.ipynb`, `DL4D_03_Indentation.ipynb`, and `DL4D_03_Comments.ipynb` files. (The Introduction tells you where to download the source code for this book.)

Working with Python in this Book

The Python environment changes constantly. As the Python community continues to improve Python, the language experiences *breaking changes* —those that create new behaviors while reducing backward compatibility. These changes might not be major, but they're a distraction that will reduce your ability to discover deep learning programming techniques. Obviously, you want to discover deep learning with as few distractions as possible, so having the correct environment is essential. Here is what you need to use Python with this book:

>> Jupyter Notebook version 5.5.0

>> Anaconda 3 environment version 5.2.0

>> Python version 3.6.7

TIP

If you don't have this setup, you may find that the examples don't work as intended. The screenshots will most likely differ and the procedures may not work as planned.

WARNING

As you go through the book, you need to install various Python packages to make the code work. Like the Python environment you configure in this chapter, these packages have specific version numbers. If you use a different version of a package, the examples may not execute at all. In addition, you may become frustrated trying to work through error messages that have nothing to do with the book's code but instead result from using the wrong version number. Make sure to exercise care when installing Anaconda, Jupyter Notebook, Python, and all the packages needed to make your deep learning experience as smooth as possible.

Obtaining Your Copy of Anaconda

Before you can move forward, you need to obtain and install a copy of Anaconda. Yes, you can obtain and install Jupyter Notebook separately, but then you lack various other applications that come with Anaconda, such as the Anaconda

Prompt, which appears in various parts of the book. The best idea is to install Anaconda using the instructions that appear in the following sections for your particular platform (Linux, MacOS, or Windows).

Getting Continuum Analytics Anaconda

The basic Anaconda package is a free download from `https://repo.anaconda.com/archive/` to obtain the 5.2.0 version used in this book. Simply click one of the Python 3.6 Version links to obtain access to the free product. The filename you want begins with `Anaconda3-5.2.0-` followed by the platform and 32-bit or 64-bit version, such as `Anaconda3-5.2.0-Windows-x86_64.exe` for the Windows 64-bit version. Anaconda supports the following platforms:

» Windows 32-bit and 64-bit (The installer may offer you only the 64-bit or 32-bit version, depending on which version of Windows it detects.)

» Linux 32-bit and 64-bit

» Mac OS X 64-bit

The free product is all you need for this book. However, when you look on the site, you see that many other add-on products are available. These products can help you create robust applications. For example, when you add Accelerate to the mix, you obtain the capability to perform multicore and GPU-enabled operations. The use of these add-on products is outside the scope of this book, but the Anaconda site provides details on using them.

Installing Anaconda on Linux

You use the command line to install Anaconda on Linux; no graphical installation option exists. Before you can perform the install, you must download a copy of the Linux software from the Continuum Analytics site. You can find the required download information in the "Getting Continuum Analytics Anaconda" section of this chapter. The following procedure should work fine on any Linux system, whether you use the 32-bit or the 64-bit version of Anaconda:

1. **Open a copy of Terminal.**

   The Terminal window appears.

2. **Change directories to the downloaded copy of Anaconda on your system.**

   The name of this file varies, but normally it appears as `Anaconda3-5.2.0-Linux-x86.sh` for 32-bit systems and `Anaconda3-5.2.0-Linux-x86_64.sh` for 64-bit systems. The version number is embedded as part of the filename.

In this case, the filename refers to version 5.2.0, which is the version used for this book. If you use some other version, you may experience problems with the source code and need to make adjustments when working with it.

3. **Type** bash Anaconda3-5.2.0-Linux-x86 **(for the 32-bit version) or** Anaconda 3-5.2.0-Linux-x86_64.sh **(for the 64-bit version) and press Enter.**

   An installation wizard starts that asks you to accept the licensing terms for using Anaconda.

4. **Read the licensing agreement and accept the terms using the method required for your version of Linux.**

   The wizard asks you to provide an installation location for Anaconda. The book assumes that you use the default location of ~/anaconda. If you choose some other location, you may have to modify some procedures later in the book to work with your setup.

5. **Provide an installation location (if necessary) and press Enter (or click Next).**

   You see the application extraction process begin. After the extraction is complete, you see a completion message.

6. **Add the installation path to your** PATH **statement using the method required for your version of Linux.**

   You're ready to begin using Anaconda.

Installing Anaconda on MacOS

The Mac OS X installation comes in only one form: 64-bit. Before you can perform the install, you must download a copy of the Mac software from the Continuum Analytics site. You can find the required download information in the "Getting Continuum Analytics Anaconda" section, earlier in this chapter. The following steps help you install Anaconda 64-bit on a Mac system:

1. **Locate the downloaded copy of Anaconda on your system.**

   The name of this file varies, but normally it appears as Anaconda3-5.2. 0-MacOSX-x86_64.pkg. The version number is embedded as part of the filename. In this case, the filename refers to version 5.2.0, which is the version used for this book. If you use some other version, you may experience problems with the source code and need to make adjustments when working with it.

2. **Double-click the installation file.**

   You see an introduction dialog box.

3. **Click Continue.**

The wizard asks whether you want to review the Read Me materials. You can read these materials later. For now, you can safely skip the information.

4. **Click Continue.**

The wizard displays a licensing agreement. Be sure to read through the licensing agreement so that you know the terms of usage.

5. **Click I Agree if you agree to the licensing agreement.**

The wizard asks you to provide a destination for the installation. The destination controls whether the installation is for an individual user or a group.

WARNING

You may see an error message stating that you can't install Anaconda on the system. The error message occurs because of a bug in the installer and has nothing to do with your system. To get rid of the error message, choose the Install Only for Me option. You can't install Anaconda for a group of users on a Mac system.

6. **Click Continue.**

The installer displays a dialog box containing options for changing the installation type. Click Change Install Location if you want to modify where Anaconda is installed on your system. (The book assumes that you use the default path of ~/anaconda.) Click Customize if you want to modify how the installer works. For example, you can choose not to add Anaconda to your PATH statement. However, the book assumes that you have chosen the default install options, and you don't have a good reason to change them unless you have another copy of Python installed somewhere else.

7. **Click Install.**

You see the installation begin. A progress bar tells you how the installation process is progressing. When the installation is complete, you see a completion dialog box.

8. **Click Continue.**

You're ready to begin using Anaconda.

Installing Anaconda on Windows

Anaconda comes with a graphical installation application for Windows, so getting a good install means using a wizard, much as you would for any other installation. Of course, you need a copy of the installation file before you begin, and you can find the required download information in the "Getting Continuum Analytics Anaconda" section, earlier in this chapter. The following procedure should work fine on any Windows system, whether you use the 32-bit or the 64-bit version of Anaconda:

1. **Locate the downloaded copy of Anaconda on your system.**

   The name of this file varies, but normally it appears as Anaconda3-5.2.0–Windows-x86.exe for 32-bit systems and Anaconda3-5.2.0-Windows-x86_64.exe for 64-bit systems. The version number is embedded as part of the filename. In this case, the filename refers to version 5.2.0, which is the version used for this book. If you use some other version, you may experience problems with the source code and need to make adjustments when working with it.

2. **Double-click the installation file.**

   (You may see an Open File – Security Warning dialog box that asks whether you want to run this file. Click Run if you see this dialog box pop up.) You see an Anaconda 5.2.0 Setup dialog box similar to the one shown in Figure 3-1. The exact dialog box you see depends on which version of the Anaconda installation program you download. If you have a 64-bit operating system, it's always best to use the 64-bit version of Anaconda so that you obtain the best possible performance. This first dialog box tells you when you have the 64-bit version of the product.

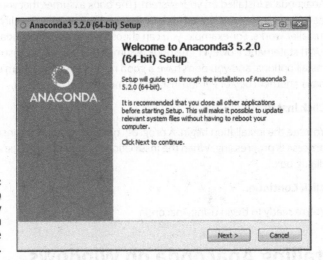

FIGURE 3-1:
The setup process begins by telling you whether you have the 64-bit version.

3. **Click Next.**

   The wizard displays a licensing agreement. Be sure to read through the licensing agreement so that you know the terms of usage.

4. **Click I Agree if you agree to the licensing agreement.**

You're asked what sort of installation type to perform, as shown in Figure 3-2. In most cases, you want to install the product just for yourself. The exception is if you have multiple people using your system and they all need access to Anaconda. The selection of Just Me or All Users will affect the installation destination folder in the next step.

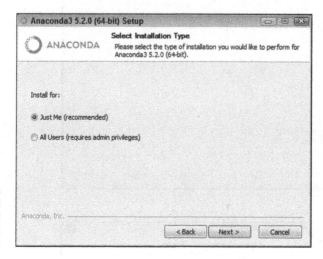

FIGURE 3-2:
Tell the wizard
how to install
Anaconda on
your system.

5. **Choose one of the installation types and then click Next.**

The wizard asks where to install Anaconda on disk, as shown in Figure 3-3. The book assumes that you use the default location, which will generally install the product in your C:\Users\<User Name>\Anaconda3 folder. If you choose some other location, you may have to modify some procedures later in the book to work with your setup. You may be asked whether you want to create the destination folder. If so, simply allow the folder creation.

6. **Choose an installation location (if necessary) and then click Next.**

You see the Advanced Installation Options, shown in Figure 3-4. These options are selected by default and you have no good reason to change them in most cases. You might need to change them if Anaconda won't provide your default Python 3.6 setup. However, the book assumes that you've set up Anaconda using the default options.

TIP

The Add Anaconda to My PATH Environment Variable option is deselected by default, and you should leave it deselected. Adding it to the PATH environment variable does offer the ability to locate the Anaconda files when using a standard command prompt, but if you have multiple versions of Anaconda installed, only the first version that you installed is accessible. Opening an Anaconda Prompt instead is far better so that you gain access to the version you expect.

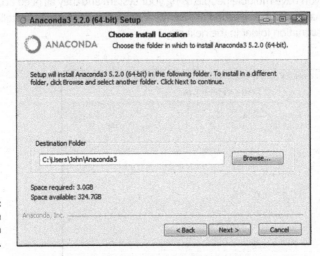

FIGURE 3-3:
Specify an installation location.

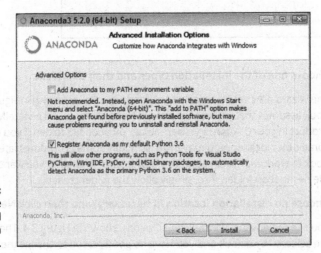

FIGURE 3-4:
Configure the advanced installation options.

7. **Change the advanced installation options (if necessary) and then click Install.**

   You see an Installing dialog box with a progress bar. The installation process can take a few minutes, so get yourself a cup of coffee and read the comics for a while. When the installation process is over, you see a Next button enabled.

8. **Click Next.**

   The wizard tells you that the installation is complete.

9. **Click Next.**

   Anaconda offers you the chance to integrate Visual Studio code support. You don't need this support for this book and adding it might change the way that the Anaconda tools work. Unless you absolutely need Visual Studio support, you want to keep the Anaconda environment pure.

10. **Click Skip.**

    You see a completion screen. This screen contains options to discover more about Anaconda Cloud and to obtain information about starting your first Anaconda project. Selecting these options (or deselecting them) depends on what you want to do next, and the options don't affect your Anaconda setup.

11. **Select any required options. Click Finish.**

    You're ready to begin using Anaconda.

A WORD ABOUT THE SCREENSHOTS

As you work your way through the book, you'll use an IDE of your choice to open the Python and Jupyter Notebook files containing the book's source code. Every screenshot that contains IDE-specific information relies on Anaconda because Anaconda runs on all three platforms supported by the book. The use of Anaconda doesn't imply that it's the best IDE or that the authors are making any sort of recommendation for it — Anaconda simply works well as a demonstration product.

When you work with Anaconda, the name of the graphical (GUI) environment, Jupyter Notebook, is precisely the same across all three platforms, and you won't even see any significant difference in the presentation. The differences you do see are minor, and you should ignore them as you work through the book. With this in mind, the book does rely heavily on Windows 7 screenshots. When working on a Linux, Mac OS X, or other Windows-version platform, you should expect to see some differences in presentation, but these differences shouldn't reduce your ability to work with the examples. This book doesn't use Windows 10 because of the serious issues it can present in making Python installations work as described at http://blog.johnmuellerbooks.com/2015/10/30/python-and-windows-10/. Some readers do successfully use Windows 10, but for the best result, continue to rely on Windows 7.

If you're using Google Colab or another cloud-based product, the screenshots you see will match a combination of your browser and the cloud environment. The screenshots you see in the book won't match what you see on your screen at all. However, the content should be the same, so look for content rather than a precise GUI presentation. In addition, because Colab can't perform some tasks that Notebook does, you may find that some content is missing or that you see an error message in place of the content.

Downloading the Datasets and Example Code

This book is about using Python to perform deep learning tasks. Of course, you can spend all your time creating the example code from scratch, debugging it, and only then discovering how it relates to deep learning, or you can take the easy way and download the prewritten code so that you can get right to work. Likewise, creating datasets large enough for deep learning purposes would take quite a while. Fortunately, you can access standardized, precreated datasets quite easily using features provided in some of the data science libraries. The following sections help you download and use the example code and datasets so that you can save time and get right to work with data science–specific tasks.

Using Jupyter Notebook

To make working with the relatively complex code in this book easier, you use Jupyter Notebook. This interface lets you easily create Python notebook files that can contain any number of examples, each of which can run individually. The program runs in your browser, so which platform you use for development doesn't matter; as long as it has a browser, you should be okay.

Starting Jupyter Notebook

Most platforms provide an icon to access Jupyter Notebook. You simply need to open this icon to access Jupyter Notebook. For example, on a Windows system, you choose Start⇨All Programs⇨Anaconda3⇨Jupyter Notebook. Figure 3-5 shows how the interface looks when viewed in a Firefox browser. The precise appearance on your system depends on the browser you use and the kind of platform you have installed.

If you use a platform that doesn't offer easy access through an icon, you can use these steps to access Jupyter Notebook:

1. **Open an Anaconda Prompt, Command Prompt, or Terminal Window on your system.**

   The window opens so that you can type commands.

2. **Change directories to the \Anaconda3\Scripts directory on your machine.**

   Most systems let you use the CD command for this task.

3. **Type ..\python Jupyter-script.py notebook and press Enter.**

   The Jupyter Notebook page opens in your browser.

THE DIFFERENCE BETWEEN A NOTEBOOK AND AN IDE

A *notebook* differs from a text editor in that it focuses on a technique advanced by Stanford computer scientist Donald Knuth called *literate programming,* which you use to create a kind of presentation of code, notes, math equations, and graphics. In short, you wind up with a scientist's notebook full of everything needed to understand the code completely. You commonly see literate programming techniques used in high-priced packages such as Mathematica and MATLAB. Notebook development excels at

- Demonstration
- Collaboration
- Research
- Teaching objectives
- Presentation

This book uses the Anaconda tool collection because it not only provides you with a great Python coding experience but also helps you discover the enormous potential of literate programming techniques. If you spend a lot of time performing scientific tasks, Anaconda and products like it are essential. In addition, Anaconda is free, so you get the benefits of the literate programming style without the cost of other packages.

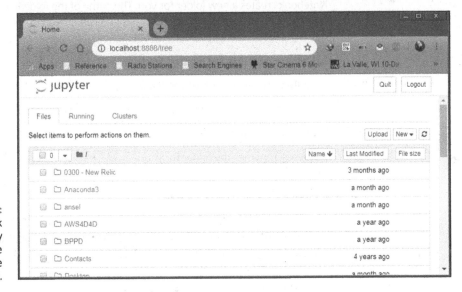

FIGURE 3-5:
Jupyter Notebook provides an easy method to create data science examples.

Stopping the Jupyter Notebook server

No matter how you start Jupyter Notebook (or just Notebook, as it appears in the remainder of the book), the system generally opens a command prompt or terminal window to host Notebook. This window contains a server that makes the application work. After you close the browser window when a session is complete, select the server window and press Ctrl+C or Ctrl+Break to stop the server.

Defining the code repository

The code you create and use in this book will reside in a repository on your hard drive. Think of a *repository* as a kind of filing cabinet where you put your code. Notebook opens a drawer, takes out the folder, and shows the code to you. You can modify it, run individual examples within the folder, add new examples, and simply interact with your code in a natural manner. The following sections get you started with Notebook so that you can see how this whole repository concept works.

Defining the book's folder

You use folders to hold your code files for a particular project. The project for this book is DL4D (which standa for *Deep Learning For Dummies*). The following steps help you create a new folder for this book:

1. **Choose New ⇨ Folder.**

   Notebook creates a new folder for you. The name of the folder can vary, but for Windows users it's simply listed as Untitled Folder. You may have to scroll down the list of available folders to find the folder in question.

2. **Select the box next to Untitled Folder.**

3. **Click Rename at the top of the page.**

   You see the Rename Directory dialog box, shown in Figure 3-6.

4. **Type DL4D and press Enter.**

   Notebook renames the folder for you.

Creating a new notebook

Every new notebook is like a file folder. You can place individual examples within the file folder, just as you would sheets of paper into a physical file folder. Each example appears in a cell. You can put other sorts of things in the file folder, too, but you see how these things work as the book progresses. Use these steps to create a new notebook:

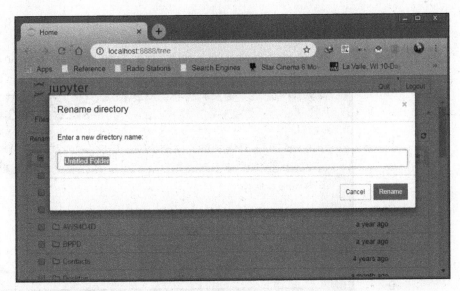

FIGURE 3-6:
Create a folder to
use to hold the
book's code.

1. **Click the DL4D entry on the Home page.**

   You see the contents of the project folder for this book, which will be blank if you're performing this exercise from scratch.

2. **Choose New ⇨ Python 3.**

   A new tab opens in the browser with the new notebook, as shown in Figure 3-7. Notice that the notebook contains a cell and that Notebook has highlighted the cell so that you can begin typing code in it. The title of the notebook is Untitled right now. That's not a particularly helpful title, so you need to change it.

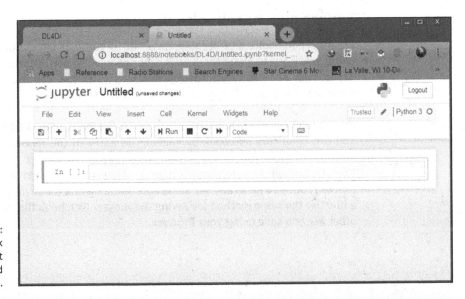

FIGURE 3-7:
A notebook
contains cells that
you use to hold
code.

3. **Click Untitled on the page.**

   Notebook asks what you want to use as a new name, as shown in Figure 3-8.

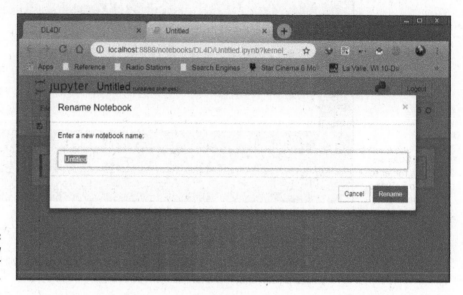

FIGURE 3-8:
Provide a new
name for your
notebook.

4. **Type** DL4D_03_Sample **and press Enter.**

   The new name tells you that this is a file for *Deep Learning For Dummies*, Chapter 3, Sample.ipynb. Using this naming convention will make it easy for you to differentiate these files from other files in your repository.

Exporting a notebook

Creating notebooks and keeping them all to yourself isn't much fun. At some point, you want to share them with other people. To perform this task, you must export your notebook from the repository to a file. You can then send the file to someone else, who will import it into his or her repository.

The previous section shows how to create a notebook named DL4D_03_Sample. You can open this notebook by clicking its entry in the repository list. The file reopens so that you can see your code again. To export this code, choose File⇨Download As⇨Notebook (.ipynb). What you see next depends on your browser, but you generally see some sort of dialog box for saving the notebook as a file. Use the same method for saving the Jupyter Notebook file as you use for any other file you save using your browser.

Saving a notebook

You eventually want to save your notebook so that you can review the code later and impress your friends by running it after you ensure that it doesn't contain any errors. Notebook periodically saves your notebook for you automatically. However, to save it manually, you choose File ⇨ Save and Checkpoint.

Closing a notebook

You definitely shouldn't just close the browser window when you finish working with your notebook. Doing so will likely cause data loss. You must perform an orderly closing of your file, which includes stopping the kernel used to run the code in the background. After you save your notebook, you can close it by choosing File ⇨ Close and Halt. You see your notebook entered in the list of notebooks for your project folder, as shown in Figure 3-9.

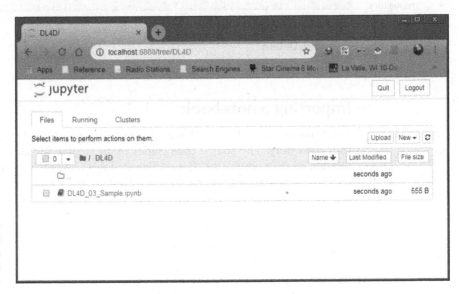

FIGURE 3-9:
Your saved notebooks appear in a list in the project folder.

Removing a notebook

Sometimes notebooks get outdated or you simply don't need to work with them any longer. Rather than allow your repository to get clogged with files you don't need, you can remove these unwanted notebooks from the list. Use these steps to remove the file:

1. **Select the check box next to the DL4D_03_Sample.ipynb entry.**

2. **Click the Delete (trash can) icon.**

   A Delete notebook warning message appears, like the one shown in Figure 3-10.

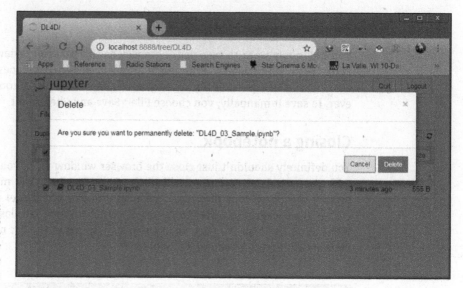

FIGURE 3-10:
Notebook warns
you before
removing any
files from the
repository.

3. **Click Delete.**

   Notebook removes the notebook file from the list.

Importing a notebook

To use the source code from this book, you must import the downloaded files into your repository. The source code comes in an archive file that you extract to a location on your hard drive. The archive contains a list of .ipynb (IPython Notebook) files containing the source code for this book (see the Introduction for details on downloading the source code). The following steps tell how to import these files into your repository:

1. **Click the Upload on the Notebook DL4D page.**

   What you see depends on your browser. In most cases, you see some type of File Upload dialog box that provides access to the files on your hard drive.

2. **Navigate to the directory containing the files that you want to import into Notebook.**

3. **Highlight one or more files to import and then click the Open (or other, similar) button to begin the upload process.**

   You see the file added to an upload list, as shown in Figure 3-11. The file isn't part of the repository yet — you've simply selected it for upload.

4. **Click Upload.**

   Notebook places the file in the repository so that you can begin using it.

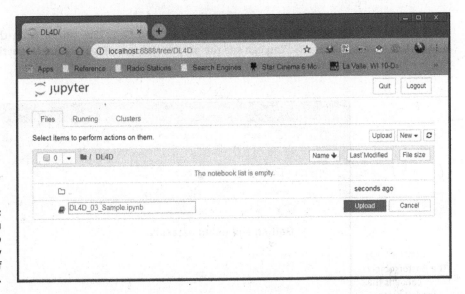

Getting and using datasets

This book uses a number of datasets, some of which you download directly from the web while others appear in Python packages such as the Scikit-learn library. These datasets demonstrate various ways in which you can interact with data, and you use them in the examples to perform a variety of tasks. The following list provides a quick overview of the functions used to import the datasets from Scikit-learn into your Python code:

» `load_boston()`: Regression analysis with the Boston house prices dataset

» `load_iris()`: Classification with the Iris dataset

» `load_digits([n_class])`: Classification with the digits dataset

» `fetch_20newsgroups(subset='train')`: Data from 20 newsgroups

The technique for loading each of these datasets is the same across examples. The following example shows how to load the Boston house prices dataset. You can find the code in the `DL4D_03_Dataset_Load.ipynb` notebook.

```
from sklearn.datasets import load_boston

Boston = load_boston()

print(Boston.data.shape)
```

To see how the code works, click Run Cell. The output from the `print` call is (506, 13). You can see the output shown in Figure 3-12. (Be patient; the dataset load can require a few seconds to complete.)

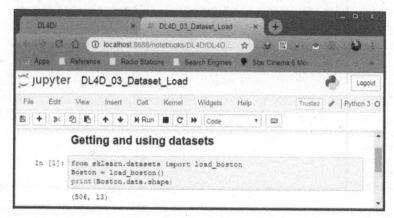

Creating the Application

The "Creating a new notebook" section shows how to create an empty notebook, which is nice but not helpful. You want to use the notebook to hold an application that you can use to discover the inner workings of deep learning. The following sections show how to work with notebook in a manner that lets you create a simple application for any purpose you need. However, before you begin, make sure that you have the DL4D_03_Sample.ipynb file open for use because you need it to explore Notebook.

Understanding cells

If Notebook were a standard IDE, you wouldn't have cells. What you'd have is a document containing a single, contiguous series of statements. To separate various coding elements, you need separate files. Cells are different because each cell is separate. Yes, the results of things you do in previous cells matter, but if a cell is meant to work alone, you can simply go to that cell and run it. To see how this works for yourself, type the following code into the first cell of the DL4D_03_Sample file:

```
myVar = 3 + 4
print(myVar)
```

Now click Run (the right-pointing arrow). The code executes, and you see the output, as shown in Figure 3-13. The output is 7, as expected. However, notice the In [1]: entry. This entry tells you that this is the first cell executed.

FIGURE 3-13:
Cells execute individually in Notebook.

Now place the cursor in the second cell — the one that is currently blank — and type **print("This is myVar: ", myVar)**. Click Run. The output in Figure 3-14 shows that the cells have executed individually (because the In [2]: entry shows the separate execution), but that myVar is global to the notebook. What you do in other cells with data affects every other cell, no matter what order the execution takes place.

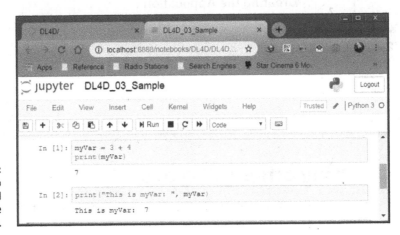

FIGURE 3-14:
Data changes do affect every cell that uses the modified variable.

Adding documentation cells

Cells come in a number of different forms. This book doesn't use them all. However, knowing how to use the documentation cells can come in handy. Select the first cell (the one currently marked with a 1). Choose Insert⇨ Insert Cell Above.

You see a new cell added to the notebook. Note the drop-down list that currently has Code in it. This list allows you to choose the kind of cell to create. Select Markdown from the list and type **# Creating the Application** (to create a level 1 heading). Click Run (which may seem like an extremely odd thing to do, but give it a try). You see the heading turn into an actual heading with darker, larger text.

About now, you may be thinking that these special cells act just like HTML pages, and you'd be right. Choose Insert⇨Insert Cell Below, select Markdown in the drop-down list, and then type **## Understanding cells** (to create a level 2 heading). Click Run. As you can see in Figure 3-15, the number of hash signs (#) you add to the text affects the heading level, but the hash signs don't show up in the actual heading. (You can find complete Markdown documentation for Notebook at https://www.ibm.com/support/knowledgecenter/en/SSGNPV_1.1.3/dsx/markd-jupyter.html, among other places online.)

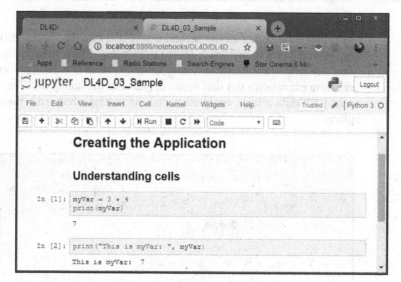

FIGURE 3-15:
Using heading levels provides emphasis for cell content.

Using other cell types

This chapter (and book) doesn't demonstrate all the kinds of cell content that you can see by using Notebook. However, you can add other items, such as graphics, to your notebooks as well. When the time comes, you can output (print) your notebook as a report and use it in presentations of all sorts. The literate programming technique is different from what you may have used in the past, but it has definite advantages, as you see in upcoming chapters.

Understanding the Use of Indentation

As you work through the examples in this book, you see that certain lines are indented. In fact, the examples also provide a fair amount of white space (such as extra lines between lines of code). Python ignores any indentation in your application. The main reason to add indentation is to provide visual cues about your code. In the same way that indentation is used for book outlines, indentation in code shows the relationships between various code elements.

The various uses of indentation will become more familiar as you work your way through the examples in the book. However, you should know at the outset why indentation is used and how it gets put in place. To that end, it's time for another example. The following steps help you create a new example that uses indentation to make the relationship among application elements a lot more apparent and easier to figure out later.

1. **Choose New ⇨ Python3.**

   Jupyter Notebook creates a new notebook for you. The downloadable source uses the filename DL4D_03_Indentation.ipynb, but you can use any name desired.

2. **Type** print("This is a really long line of text that will " +.

   You see the text displayed normally onscreen, just as you expect. The plus sign (+) tells Python that there is additional text to display. Adding text from multiple lines together into a single long piece of text is called *concatenation*. You learn more about using this feature later in the book, so you don't need to worry about it now.

3. **Press Enter.**

   The insertion point doesn't go back to the beginning of the line, as you might expect. Instead, it ends up directly under the first double quote. This feature, called automatic indention, is one of the features that differentiates a regular text editor from one designed to write code.

4. **Type** "appear on multiple lines in the source code file.") **and press Enter.**

   Notice that the insertion point goes back to the beginning of the line. When Notebook senses that you have reached the end of the code, it automatically outdents the text to its original position.

5. **Click Run.**

   You see the output shown in Figure 3-16. Even though the text appears on multiple lines in the source code file, it appears on just one line in the output. The line does break because of the size of the window, but it's actually just one line.

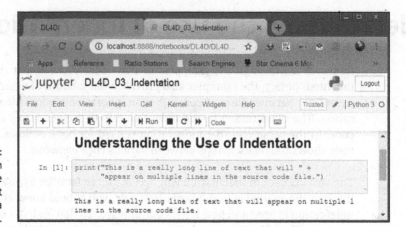

FIGURE 3-16:
Concatenation makes multiple lines of code text appear on a single output line.

Adding Comments

People create notes for themselves all the time. When you need to buy groceries, you look through your cabinets, determine what you need, and write it down on a list or speak it into an app on your phone. When you get to the store, you review your list to remember what you need. Using notes comes in handy for all sorts of needs, such as tracking the course of a conversation between business partners or remembering the essential points of a lecture. Humans need notes to jog their memories. Comments in source code are just another form of note. You add them to the code so that you can remember what task the code performs later. The following sections describe comments in more detail. You can find these examples in the DL4D_03_Comments.ipynb file in the downloadable source.

HEADINGS VERSUS COMMENTS

You may find headings and comments a bit confusing at first. Headings appear in separate cells; comments appear with the source code. They serve different purposes. Headings serve to tell you about an entire code grouping, and individual comments tell you about individual code steps or even lines of code. Even though you use both of them for documentation, each serves a unique purpose. Comments are generally more detailed than headings.

Understanding comments

Computers need some special way to determine that the text you're writing is a comment, not code to execute. Python provides two methods of defining text as a comment and not as code. The first method is the single-line comment. It uses the number sign (#), like this:

```
# This is a comment.
print("Hello from Python!") #This is also a comment.
```

REMEMBER

A single-line comment can appear on a line by itself or after executable code. It appears on only one line. You typically use a single-line comment for short descriptive text, such as an explanation of a particular bit of code. Notebook shows comments in a distinctive color (usually blue) and in italics.

Python doesn't actually support a multiline comment directly, but you can create one using a triple-quoted string. A multiline comment both starts and ends with three double quotes (""") or three single quotes (''') like this:

```
"""
    Application: Comments.py
    Written by: John
    Purpose: Shows how to use comments.
"""
```

REMEMBER

These lines aren't executed. Python won't display an error message when they appear in your code. However, Notebook treats them differently, as shown in Figure 3-17. Note that the actual Python comments, those preceded by a hash sign (#) in cell 1, don't generate any output. The triple-quote strings, however, do generate output. In addition, unlike standard comments, triple-quoted text appears in red (depending on the editor), rather than in blue, and the text isn't in italics. If you plan to output your notebook as a report, you need to avoid using triple-quoted strings. (Some IDEs, such as IDLE, ignore the triple-quoted strings completely.)

You typically use multiline comments for longer explanations of who created an application, why it was created, and what tasks it performs. Of course, no hard rules exist regarding precisely how you use comments. The main goal is to tell the computer precisely what is and isn't a comment so that it doesn't try to interact with the comment as it would code.

FIGURE 3-17: Multiline comments do work, but they also provide output.

Using comments to leave yourself reminders

A lot of people don't really understand comments and don't quite know what to do with notes in code. Keep in mind that you might write a piece of code today and then not look at it for years. You need notes to jog your memory so that you remember what task the code performs and why you wrote it. In fact, here are some common reasons to use comments in your code:

>> Remind yourself about what the code does and why you wrote it

>> Tell others how to maintain your code

>> Make your code accessible to other developers

>> List ideas for future updates

>> Provide a list of documentation sources you used to write the code

>> Maintain a list of improvements you've made

You can use comments in a lot of other ways, too, but these are the most common ways. Look at how comments are used in the examples in the book, especially as you get to later chapters where the code becomes more complex. As your code becomes more complex, you need to add more comments and make the comments pertinent to what you need to remember about it.

Using comments to keep code from executing

Developers also sometimes use the commenting feature to keep lines of code from executing (referred to as *commenting out*). You might need to do this to determine whether a line of code is causing your application to fail. As with any other comment, you can use either single-line commenting or multiline commenting. However, when using multiline commenting, you do see the code that isn't executing as part of the output (and it can actually be helpful to see where the code affects the output).

Getting Help with the Python Language

This book doesn't teach you the Python language, which would require a whole book in itself. Of course, you could always use *Beginning Programming with Python For Dummies*, by John Paul Mueller (Wiley), to obtain what you need. You have many other options for getting help with the Python language as well. In fact, so many options are available that covering them all in this chapter isn't possible. Here are the best methods for obtaining help:

» Choose one of the options on the Help menu of Notebook.

» Open an Anaconda prompt, start a copy of Python, and use text commands to search for help.

» Download the Python documentation from https://docs.python. org/3.6/download.html.

» View the online documentation at https://docs.python.org/3.6/.

» Use any of the following tutorials:

   • **The official tutorial:** https://docs.python.org/3.6/

   • **TutorialsPoint:** https://www.tutorialspoint.com/python/

   • **W3Schools:** https://www.w3schools.com/python/

   • **learnpython.org:** https://www.learnpython.org/

   • **Codecademy:** https://www.codecademy.com/learn/learn-python

REMEMBER

The point is that this book assumes that you already know how to program in Python. This chapter provides you with some tool-related aids to ease your transition from whatever tools you have used in the past to the tools used in this book.

Working in the Cloud

Even though this chapter has presented a local processing approach, you may find a need to interact with cloud resources to perform certain tasks. The following sections discuss two cloud-related activities that you may perform while using this book. The first is to access cloud resources for various needs. The second is to use Google Colaboratory to work with the examples on your tablet instead of a desktop system.

Using the Kaggle datasets and kernels

Kaggle (https://www.kaggle.com/) is a huge community of data scientists and others who need to work with large datasets to obtain the information needed to meet various goals. You can create new projects on Kaggle, view the work done by others on completed projects, or participate in one of its ongoing competitions. However, Kaggle is more than simply a community of really smart people who like to play with data; it's also a place where you can obtain resources needed to learn all about deep learning and to create projects of your own.

TIP

The best place to find out how Kaggle can help you discover more about deep learning is at https://www.kaggle.com/m2skills/datasets-and-tutorial-kernels-for-beginners. This site lists the various datasets and tutorial kernels that Kaggle provides. A *dataset* is simply a kind of database of information used to perform standardized tests on application code. A *tutorial kernel* is a kind of project you use to learn how to analyze data in various ways. For example, you can find a tutorial kernel about mushroom classification at https://www.kaggle.com/uciml/mushroom-classification.

Using the Google Colaboratory

Colaboratory (https://colab.research.google.com/notebooks/welcome.ipynb), or Colab for short, is a Google cloud-based service that replicates Jupyter Notebook in the cloud. This is a custom implementation, so you may find times when Colab and Notebook are out of sync — features in one may not always work in the other. You don't have to install anything on your system to use it. In most respects, you use Colab as you would a desktop installation of Jupyter Notebook. The main reason to learn more about Colab is if you want to use a device other than a standard desktop setup to work through the examples in this book. If you want a fuller tutorial of Colab, you can find one in Chapter 4 of *Python For Data Science For Dummies*, 2nd Edition, by John Paul Mueller and Luca Massaron (Wiley). For now, this section gives you the basics of using existing files. Figure 3-18 shows the opening Colab display.

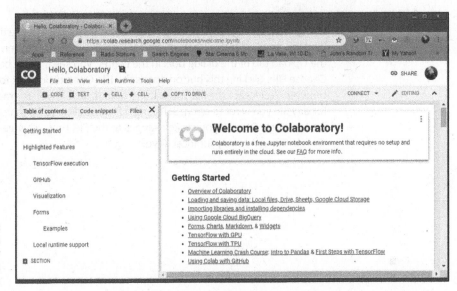

FIGURE 3-18:
Colab makes using your Python projects on a tablet easy.

You can open existing notebooks found in local storage, on Google Drive, or on GitHub. You can also open any of the Colab examples or upload files from sources that you can access, such as a network drive on your system. In all cases, you begin by choosing File⇨Open Notebook. The default view shows all the files you opened recently, regardless of location. The files appear in alphabetical order. You can filter the number of items displayed by typing a string into Filter Notebooks. Across the top are other options for opening notebooks.

TIP

Even if you're not logged in, you can still access the Colab example projects. These projects help you understand Colab but don't allow you to do anything with your own projects. Even so, you can still experiment with Colab without logging into Google first. Here is a quick list of the ways to use files with Colab:

>> **Using Drive for existing notebooks:** Google Drive is the default location for many operations in Colab, and you can always choose it as a destination. When working with Drive, you see a listing of files. To open a particular file, you click its link in the dialog box. The file opens in the current tab of your browser.

>> **Using GitHub for existing notebooks:** When working with GitHub, you initially need to provide the location of the source code online. The location must point to a public project; you can't use Colab to access your private projects. After you make the connection to GitHub, you see a list of repositories (which are containers for code related to a particular project) and branches (which represent particular implementations of the code). Selecting a repository and branch displays a list of notebook files that you can load into Colab. Simply click the required link and it loads as if you were using Google Drive.

» **Using local storage for existing notebooks:** If you want to use the down-loadable source for this book, or any local source, for that matter, you select the Upload tab of the dialog box. In the center, you see a single button called Choose File. Clicking this button opens the File Open dialog box for your browser. You locate the file you want to upload, just as you normally would for any file you want to open. Selecting a file and clicking Open uploads the file to Google Drive. If you make changes to the file, those changes appear on Google Drive, not on your local drive.

Chapter **4**

Leveraging a Deep Learning Framework

This chapter looks at deep learning frameworks because using a deep learning framework can greatly reduce the time, cost, and complexity of developing a deep learning solution. Of course, you must begin by defining the term *framework*, which is an abstraction that provides generic functionality that your application code modifies. Unlike a library that runs within your application, when you're using a framework, your application runs within it. You can't modify basic framework functionality, which means that you have a stable environment in which to work, but most frameworks offer some level of extensibility. Frameworks are generally specific to a particular need, such as the web frameworks used to create online applications. Consequently, even though deep learning frameworks have many characteristics of frameworks in general, they also provide specific functionality that this chapter explores.

Not everyone uses the same ideas and concepts for running deep learning applications. In addition, not every organization wants to invest in a complex deep learning framework when a less expensive and simpler framework will do. Consequently, you find a lot of deep learning frameworks that can provide you with basic functionality that you can use for experimentation and for simpler applications. This chapter explores some of these basic frameworks and compares them so that you have a better idea of what is available.

To provide the best possible learning environment, this book relies on the Tensor-Flow framework for the examples. TensorFlow works better for the situations presented in this book than the other solutions covered earlier, and this chapter explains why. It also tells you precisely why TensorFlow is a good general solution to many deep learning scenarios.

REMEMBER

You don't have to type the source code for this chapter manually. In fact, it's a lot easier if you use the downloadable source. The source code for this chapter appears in the `DL4D_03_Comments.ipynb`, `DL4D_03_Dataset_Load.ipynb`, `DL4D_03_Indentation.ipynb`, and `DL4D_03_Sample.ipynb` source code files (see the Introduction for details on how to find that source file).

Presenting Frameworks

As mentioned in the introduction, your code runs within a framework. In a framework environment, your code makes requests of the framework, which then fulfills the request for you. Consequently, frameworks provide a kind of structure for application development. Because of this structure, frameworks are domain specific, answering specific kinds of application development needs. The following sections discuss frameworks both from an overview perspective and in more detail as a deep learning solution. It's important to remember that these sections don't provide you with complete information on frameworks, but they do help you understand deep learning frameworks well enough to make good decisions about them.

Defining the differences

The problem domain–specific nature of frameworks makes it necessary to locate the right sort of framework for your needs. (A *problem domain* is a description of the expertise and resources required to solve a problem. For example, you don't go to a doctor to solve your plumbing problems —you go to a plumber instead.) Simply asking for a general framework won't do you much good. Here are some examples of framework types, all of which have specific characteristics to meet the needs of their problem domain:

>> Application framework (of the sort used to create end-user applications)

>> Artistic (drawing, music, and other creative forms)

>> Cactus framework (high-performance scientific computing)

- » Decision support system
- » Earth system modeling
- » Financial modeling
- » Web framework (including language-specific frameworks for languages like such as AJAX and JavaScript)

REMEMBER

The diversity of software frameworks is amazing, and you're unlikely to ever need them all. They do have two important things in common. In each case, the framework defines a series of *frozen spots* that define the characteristics of the application and that the developer can't change. In addition, the framework defines *hot spots* that a developer does use to define the specifics to the target software. For example, a frozen spot in a web application might define the interface on which a user relies to make requests, while a hot spot might define how to fulfill that request. Someone designing a book search application would focus on the specifics of book searches while disregarding the requirements of state management and request handling.

Explaining the popularity of frameworks

In thinking about software, you can easily see the progression of tools used to create it. At one time, developers had to input their code using keypunch cards, which was extremely time consuming and error prone. Editors make the job easier because now you can type what you want done. The Integrated Development Environment (IDE) comes next. Using an IDE allows modeling, compilation, and testing of the code in a single environment, along with other things. The use of libraries enables you to create large, complex applications quickly. So, a framework — which is an environment in which a developer needs to consider only the specifies of a particular application — is simply the next step in making developers more productive while also making applications more robust and less error prone. Hence the popularity of frameworks with developers.

REMEMBER

However, a framework is much more than simply a means of creating code faster, with less effort and fewer errors. A framework lets you create a standardized environment in which everyone uses the same libraries, tools, Application Programming Interfaces (APIs), and other programs. The use of a standardized environment enables you to transfer code between systems without fear of introducing odd application issues because of environmental inconsistencies. In addition, team development issues are fewer because the collaboration environment is simplified.

Because a framework handles all the low-level details, you must also consider the makeup of an application team. In the past, the team might need people who were adept at interacting with the hardware or creating user interface basics. The use of a framework means that all these tasks are already completed, so a team is made up of subject-matter experts who can communicate effectively with each other, making a coherent approach to application development possible.

The most important reason that frameworks are so popular now relates to how coding is done today. At one time, developers needed to know how to interact with the hardware and software at an extremely low level. Today, frameworks make coding easy in an environment in which:

>> Most applications consist mainly of API calls strung together to achieve a specific purpose.

>> People need to understand how APIs perform, rather than what they do or how they do it. A developer needs to consider what data structures the API accepts and how well it processes data under pressure.

>> The immense installed base of existing software means keeping that code in place and finding fast, efficient methods to interact with it.

>> The focus is on architecture rather than details. Because most new applications rely heavily on existing code accessed through libraries or APIs, developers don't spend as much time learning the idiosyncrasies of a language; it's better to discover which pile of code can do the work without having to write any of the code yourself.

>> Getting the algorithm correct is what matters most.

>> Tools have become so smart that they often correct minor coding errors and interpret ambiguities in developer code correctly, so the emphasis is on getting ideas down rather than writing perfect code.

>> Visual languages, in which you drag and drop objects in a graphical environment, are becoming more common. At some point, code could actually disappear (at least, for most application developers).

>> Knowing a single platform isn't enough. Most applications today must execute flawlessly on Windows, Linux, OS X, Android, most smartphones, and myriad other platforms because users want software in a form they understand.

Defining the deep learning framework

When thinking about a deep learning framework, what you're really considering is how the framework manages the frozen spots and the hot spots. In most cases, a deep learning framework provides frozen spots and hot spots in these areas:

>> Hardware access (such as using a GPU with ease)

>> Standard neural network layer access

>> Deep learning primitive access

>> Computational graph management

>> Model training

>> Model deployment

>> Model testing

- >> Graph building and presentation
- >> Inference (forward propagation)
- >> Automatic differentiation (backpropagation)

Frameworks address other issues, and the focus on specific issues determines the viability of a particular framework for a particular purpose. As with many forms of software development aid, you need to choose the framework you use carefully.

Choosing a particular framework

The previous sections in this chapter discuss the appeal of frameworks in general and trace how frameworks can create a significantly better work environment for developers. Also covered are features that make a deep learning framework special. Of course, the amount of automation that a framework supplies and the number of typical features it supports are the starting point for finding a framework that meets your needs. You also need to consider issues such as learning curve with regard to the ease of using the framework.

TIP

One of the more important considerations when choosing a framework is to remember that frameworks are domain specific, which means that if you need to create an application that spans domains, such as a deep learning application that includes a web interface, you need multiple frameworks. Getting frameworks that work well with each other can be critical. If you also host your application in the cloud, you need consider which frameworks work with the cloud vendor's offering, too. For example, if you choose to use TensorFlow as your framework, you can also rely on Amazon Web Services (AWS) to host your application (see https://aws.amazon.com/tensorflow/ for details).

REMEMBER

As another option when using TensorFlow, you can go directly to Google Cloud (see https://cloud.google.com/tpu/ for details), where you can train your deep learning solution using GPUs or Tensor Processing Units (TPUs). The TPUs were developed by Google specifically for neural network machine learning use TensorFlow. TPUs are Application-Specific Integrated Circuits (ASICs) optimized for a particular use. In this case, they're for neural network processing using TensorFlow.

Application size and complexity also play a role in deep learning framework choice because you often need a higher-end framework to interact properly with large applications. The need to deal with applications of various sorts is offset by the usual cost and availability concerns. Many of the low-end deep learning frameworks in this chapter will cost you nothing to try and could provide everything needed to get started.

Working with Low-End Frameworks

Low-end deep learning frameworks often come with a built-in trade-off. You must choose between cost and usage complexity, as well as the need to support large applications in challenging environments. The trade-offs you're willing to endure will generally reflect what you can use to complete your project. With this in mind, the following sections discuss a number of low-end frameworks that are incredibly useful and work well with small to medium-size projects, but that come with trade-offs for you to consider as well.

Caffe2

Caffe2 (https://caffe2.ai/) is loosely based on Caffe, which was originally developed at the University of California, Berkeley. It's written in C++ with a Python interface. One of the reasons people really like Caffe2 is that you can train and deploy a model without actually writing any code. Instead, you choose one of the prewritten models and add it to a configuration file (which looks amazingly like JSON code). In fact, a large selection of pretrained models appears as part of Model Zoo (https://github.com/BVLC/caffe/wiki/Model-Zoo) that you can rely on for many needs.

The original Caffe had a number of problems that make it less appealing than Caffe2 to data scientists. The current version of Caffe is still popular, but you really can't use it for anything complex. Caffe2 improves on Caffe in the following ways:

» Better support for large-scale distributed training

» Mobile development

» Added CPU support and support for GPUs through CUDA

MIGRATING CAFFE TO CAFFE2

Even though Caffe (http://caffe.berkeleyvision.org/ and https://github.com/BVLC/caffe) is still around and many people use it, you might find that Caffe2 is the product you really need. If you have some Caffe applications now, you can move them to Caffe2 using the techniques found at https://caffe2.ai/docs/caffe-migration.html, so any investment you made in Caffe is still useful in Caffe2.

You can find other additions in the new version of Caffe. Another reason for Caffe2's popularity is that it can process images quite quickly and without significant scaling issues. It's designed to be lightweight and speedy. Note that Caffe2 and PyTorch are set to unite as a single product at some point in the future (see https://caffe2.ai/blog/2018/05/02/Caffe2_PyTorch_1_0.html for details).

Chainer

Chainer (https://chainer.org/) is a library written purely in Python that relies on the NumPy (http://www.numpy.org/) and CuPy (https://cupy.chainer.org/) libraries. Preferred Networks (https://www.preferred-networks.jp/en/) leads the development of this library, but IBM, Intel, Microsoft, and NVIDIA also play a role. The main point with this library is that helps you use the CUDA capabilities of your GPU by adding only a few lines of code. In other words, this library gives you a simple way to greatly enhance the speed of your code when working with huge datasets.

Many deep learning libraries today, such as Theano (discussed in the "Compiling Math Expressions Using Theano" section of Chapter 19) and TensorFlow (discussed later in this chapter), use a static deep learning approach called define and run, in which you define the math operations and then perform training based on those operations. Unlike Theano and TensorFlow, Chainer uses a define-by-run approach, which relies on a dynamic deep learning approach in which the code defines math operations as the training occurs. Here are the two main advantages to this approach:

>> **Intuitive and flexible approach:** A define-by-run approach can rely on a language's native capabilities rather than require you to create special operations to perform analysis.

>> **Debugging:** Because the define-by-run approach defines the operations during training, you can rely on the internal debugging features to locate the source of errors in a dataset or the application code.

TIP

TensorFlow 2.0 can also use define-by-run by relying on Chainer to provide eager execution.

PyTorch

PyTorch (https://pytorch.org/) is the successor to Torch (http://torch.ch/) written in the Lua (https://www.lua.org/) language. One of the core Torch libraries (the PyTorch autograd library) started as a fork of Chainer, which is described in the previous section. Facebook initially developed PyTorch, but many other organizations use it today, including Twitter, Salesforce, and the University of Oxford. Here are the features that make PyTorch special:

>> Extremely user friendly

>> Efficient memory usage

>> Relatively fast

>> Commonly used for research

Some people like PyTorch because it's easy to read like Keras, but the scientist doesn't lose the ability to use complicated neural networks. In addition, PyTorch supports dynamic computational model graphing directly (see the "Grasping why TensorFlow is so good" section, later in the chapter, for more details on this issue), which makes it more flexible than TensorFlow without the addition of TensorFlow Fold.

MXNet

The biggest reason to use MXNet is speed. It might be hard to figure out whether MXNet (https://mxnet.apache.org/) or CNTK (https://www.microsoft.com/en-us/cognitive-toolkit/) is faster, but both products are quite fast and are often used as a contrast to the slowness that some people experience when working with TensorFlow. (The whitepaper at https://arxiv.org/pdf/1608.07249v7.pdf provides some details on benchmarking of deep learning code.)

MXNet is an Apache product that supports a host of languages including Python, Julia, C++, R, and JavaScript. Numerous large organizations use it, including Microsoft, Intel, and Amazon Web Services. Here are the aspects that make MXNet special:

>> Features advanced GPU support

>> Can be run on any device

>> Provides a high-performance imperative API

>> Offers easy model serving

>> Provides high scalability

It may sound like the perfect product for your needs, but MXNet does come with at least one serious failing — it lacks the level of community support that TensorFlow provides. In addition, most researchers don't look at MXNet favorably because it can become complex, and a researcher isn't dealing with a stable model in most cases.

Microsoft Cognitive Toolkit/CNTK

As mentioned in the previous section, its speed is one of the reasons to use the Microsoft Cognitive Toolkit (CNTK). Microsoft uses CNTK for big datasets — really big ones. As a product, it supports the Python, C++, C#, and Java programming languages. Consequently, if you're a researcher who relies on R, this isn't the product for you. Microsoft has used this product in Skype, Xbox and Cortana. This product's special features are

>> Great performance

>> High scalability

>> Highly optimized components

>> Apache Spark support

>> Azure Cloud support

As with MXNet, CNTK has a distinct problem in its lack of adequate community support. In addition, it tends not to provide much in the way of third-party support, either, so if the package doesn't contain the features you need, you might not get them at all.

Understanding TensorFlow

At the moment, TensorFlow is at the top of the heap with regard to deep learning frameworks (see the chart at https://towardsdatascience.com/deep-learning-framework-power-scores-2018-23607ddf297a for details). TensorFlow's success stems from many reasons, but mainly it comes from providing a robust environment in a relatively easy-to-use package. The following sections help you understand why this book uses TensorFlow. You discover what makes TensorFlow so exciting and how add-ons make it even easier to use.

Grasping why TensorFlow is so good

A product has to offer quite a bit in terms of functionality, ease-of-use, and reliability to make much of a dent in the market when people have many choices. Part of the reason for TensorFlow's success is that it supports a number of the most popular languages: Python, Java, Go, and JavaScript. In addition, it's quite extensible. Each extension is an *op* (as in operation), which you can read about at https://www.tensorflow.org/guide/extend/op. The point is that when a product has great support for multiple languages and allows for significant extensibility, the product becomes popular because people can perform tasks in a manner that best suits them, rather than what the vendor thinks the user needs.

TENSORFLOW SUPPORT ON COLAB

Many developers today rely on online environments, such as Colab, to perform tasks because installing and configuring TensorFlow on a desktop machine can prove difficult, and you must have a GPU that TensorFlow supports (https://developer.nvidia.com/cuda-gpus) if you want accelerated processing. In addition, you have all sorts of other issues to consider (https://www.tensorflow.org/install/gpu).

Colab appears to make things easy. To get CPU support, all you do is select a configuration box. To ensure that you have the proper support, you simply run a little extra Colab-specific code (https://colab.research.google.com/notebooks/gpu.ipynb). However, reality seldom works the same as theory. For one thing, you have to reinstall everything every time you start a new Colab session because the library support isn't persistent (https://www.kdnuggets.com/2018/02/essential-google-colaboratory-tips-tricks.html). Of course, you may not have access to a GPU at all (it's at Google's discretion) or the GPU support may have limits (https://stackoverflow.com/questions/48750199/google-colaboratory-misleading-information-about-its-gpu-only-5-ram-available).

To ensure that you have the best possible learning experience, this book uses an extremely simplified TensorFlow setup that avoids many of the pitfalls that other environments experience. This environment will work for the book, any learning experience you're likely to have in school, small experimental projects, and even projects for small to medium-sized businesses that use small to medium-sized datasets. You could never use this setup to run a Facebook-type project.

The manner in which TensorFlow evaluates and executes code is important as well. Natively, TensorFlow supports only static computational graphs. However, the TensorFlow Fold extension (https://github.com/tensorflow/fold) supports dynamic graphs as well. A *dynamic graph* is one in which the structure of the computational graph varies as a function of the input data structure and changes dynamically as the application runs. Using dynamic batching, TensorFlow Fold can create a static graph from the dynamic graphs, which it can then feed into TensorFlow. This static graph represents the transformation of one or more dynamic graphs modeling uncertain data. Of course, you might not even need to build a computational graph because TensorFlow also supports *eager execution* (evaluating operations immediately without building a computational graph) so that it can evaluate Python code immediately (called *dynamic execution*). The inclusion of this dynamic functionality makes TensorFlow extremely flexible in the data it can accommodate.

REMEMBER

In addition to various kinds of dynamic support, TensorFlow also enables you to use a GPU to speed calculations. You can actually use multiple GPUs and spread the computational model over several machines in a cluster. The capability to bring so much computing power to solving a problem makes TensorFlow faster than much of the competition. Speed is important because answers to questions often have a short life expectancy; getting an answer tomorrow for a question you have today won't work in many scenarios. For example, a doctor who relies on the services of an AI to provide alternatives during a surgery needs answers immediately or the patient could die.

Computational features only help you obtain a solution to a problem. TensorFlow also helps you visualize the solution in various ways using the TensorBoard extension (https://www.tensorflow.org/guide/summaries_and_tensorboard). This extension helps you to

>> Visualize the computational graph

>> Plot graph execution metrics

>> Show additional data as needed

As with many products that include a lot of functionality, TensorFlow comes with a steep learning curve. However, it also enjoys considerable community support, provides access to a wealth of hands-on tutorials, has great third-party support for online courses, and offers many other aids to reduce the learning curve. You'll want to start with the tutorial at https://www.tensorflow.org/tutorials/ and peruse the guide of offerings at https://www.tensorflow.org/guide/.

Making TensorFlow easier by using TFLearn

One of the major complaints people have about using TensorFlow directly is that the coding is both low level and difficult at times. The trade-off that you make with TensorFlow is that you gain additional flexibility and control by writing more code. However, not everyone needs the depth that TensorFlow can provide, which is why packages such as TFLearn (http://tflearn.org/), which stands for TensorFlow Learn, are so important. (You can find a number of packages on the market that attempt to reduce the complexity; TFLearn is just one of them.)

REMEMBER

TFLearn does make working with TensorFlow easier, but in specific ways:

>> A high-level Application Programming Interface (API) helps you to produce results with less code.

>> The high-level API reduces the amount of standardized (boilerplate) code you write.

>> Prototyping is faster, akin to the functionality found in Caffe2 (described earlier in this chapter).

>> Transparency with TensorFlow means that you can see how the functions work and use them directly without relying on TFLearn.

>> The use of helper functions automates many tasks that you normally need to perform manually.

>> The use of great visualization helps you see the various aspects of your application, including the computational model, with greater ease.

You get all this functionality, and more, without giving up the aspects that make TensorFlow such a great product. For example, you still have full access to TensorFlow's capability to use CPUs, GPUs, and even multiple systems to bring more computing power to task on any problem.

Using Keras as the best simplifier

Keras is less of a framework and more of an API (a set of interface specifications that you can use with multiple frameworks as backends). It's generally lumped in as a deep-learning framework, though, because that's how people use it. To use Keras, you must also have a deep learning framework, such as TensorFlow, Theano, MXNet, or CNTK. Keras is actually bundled with TensorFlow, which also makes it the easy solution for reducing TensorFlow complexity.

TIP

This book assumes that you use Keras with TensorFlow, but knowing that you can use Keras with other deep learning frameworks is an advantage. That's why this book doesn't use the Keras version incorporated into TensorFlow, but installs it separately (see `https://medium.com/tensorflow/standardizing-on-keras-guidance-on-high-level-apis-in-tensorflow-2-0-bad2b04c819a` for details). You can use the same interface with multiple frameworks, enabling you to use the framework that you need without having to deal with yet another learning curve. The biggest selling point of Keras is that it puts the process of creating applications using a deep learning framework into a paradigm that most people can understand well.

You can't develop an application of any kind that is both easy to use and able to handle truly complex situations — all while being flexible as well. So Keras doesn't necessarily handle all situations well. For example, it's a good product to use when your needs are simple, but not a good choice if you plan to develop a new kind of neural network.

The strength of Keras is that it lets you perform fast prototyping with little hassle. The API doesn't get in your way while it tries to provide flexibility that you might not need in the current project. In addition, because Keras simplifies how you perform tasks, you can't extend it as you can with other products, which limits your ability to add functionality to an existing environment.

WARNING

More than a few people have complained about the sometimes ambiguous error reporting provided by Keras. However, Keras partially offsets this issue by providing strong community support. In addition, many of the people complaining about the error messages are also apparently trying to do something complex. Keeping the fast prototyping nature of Keras in mind could keep you from trying projects that might be too much for the product to handle.

Getting your copy of TensorFlow and Keras

Your copy of Python that comes with Anaconda doesn't include a copy of Tensor-Flow or Keras; you must install these products separately. To avoid problems with integrating TensorFlow with the Anaconda tools, don't follow the instructions found at `https://www.tensorflow.org/install/pip` for installing the product using pip. Likewise, avoid using the Keras installation instructions at `https://keras.io/#installation`. To ensure that your copy of TensorFlow and Keras are available with Notebook, you must open an Anaconda prompt, not a standard command prompt or a terminal window. Otherwise, you can't ensure that you have the appropriate paths set up. The following steps will get you started with your installation.

1. **At the Anaconda prompt, type** python — version **and press Enter.**

You see the currently installed Python version, which should be version 3.6.5 for this book, as shown in Figure 4-1. The path you see in the window is a function of your operating system, which is Windows in this case, but you may see a different path when using the Anaconda prompt.

TECHNICAL STUFF

The next step is to create an environment in which to execute code that relies on TensorFlow and Keras. The advantage of using an environment is that you maintain a pristine environment for later use with other libraries. You use conda, rather than another environment product such as virtualenv, to ensure that the software integrates with the Anaconda tools. If you use a product such as virtualenv, the resulting installation will work, but you'll have to perform a lot of other steps to access it, and these steps don't appear in the book. The name of the environment for this book is DL4Denv.

2. **Type** conda create -n DL4Denv python=3 anaconda=5.3.0 tensorflow=1.11.0 keras=2.2.4 nb_conda **and press Enter.**

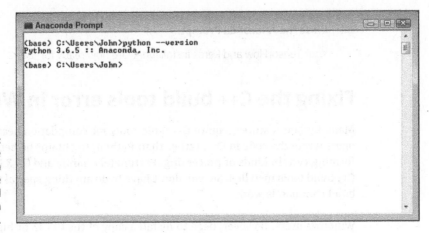

FIGURE 4-1:
Be sure to use
the Anaconda
prompt for the
installation and
check the Python
version.

TIP

You may see a warning message about the availability of a newer version of conda. It's safe to ignore this message (or you can choose to update conda using the command shown by the warning later, if desired). If necessary, type **Y** and press Enter to clear the message so that the creation process will proceed.

This step can require some time to execute because your system will have to download TensorFlow 1.11.0 and Keras 2.2.4 from an online source. After the download is complete, the setup needs to create a complete installation for you. You see the Anaconda prompt return after all of the required steps are complete. In the meantime, reading a good technical article or getting coffee will help pass the time.

3. **Type** conda activate DL4Denv **and press Enter.**

   The prompt changes to show the DL4Denv environment rather than the base or root environment. Any tasks you perform now will affect the DL4D environment rather than the original base environment.

4. **Type** python -m pip install — upgrade pip **and press Enter.**

   This step will require a little time, but not nearly as long as creating the environment. The purpose of this step is to ensure that you have the most current version of pip installed so that later commands (some of which appear in the book's code) don't fail.

5. **Type** conda deactivate **and press Enter.**

   Deactivating an environment returns you to the base environment. You perform this step to ensure that you always end a session in the base environment.

6. **Close the Anaconda Prompt.**

Your TensorFlow and Keras installations are now ready for use.

Fixing the C++ build tools error in Windows

Many Python features require C++ build tools for compilation because the developers wrote the code in C++, rather than Python, to obtain the best speed in performing certain kinds of processing. Fortunately, Linux and OS X both come with C++ build tools installed. So, you don't have to do anything special to make Python build commands work.

Windows users, however, need to install a copy of the C++ 14 or higher build tools if they don't already have them installed. In fact, the Notebook environment is actually quite picky — you need Visual C++ 14 or higher, rather than just any version of C++ (such as GCC, https://www.gnu.org/software/gcc/). If you recently installed Visual Studio or another Microsoft development product, you may have the build tools installed and won't need to install a second copy.

This book uses the most current tools available as of writing, which is C++ 17. Getting just the build tools won't cost you anything. The following steps show a short and easy method for getting your required build tools if you don't already have C++ 14 or above installed:

1. **Download the offline build tools installer from** https://aka.ms/vs/15/
release/vs_buildtools.exe.

Your download application downloads a copy of vs_buildtools.exe. Trying to use the online build tools often comes with too many options, and Microsoft, naturally, wants you to buy its product.

2. **Locate the downloaded file on your hard drive and double-click** vs_
buildtools.exe.

You see a Visual Studio Installer dialog box. Before you can install the build tools, you need to tell the installer what you want to install.

3. **Click Continue.**

The Visual Studio Installer downloads and installs some additional support files. After this installation is complete, it asks which Workload to install, as shown in Figure 4-2.

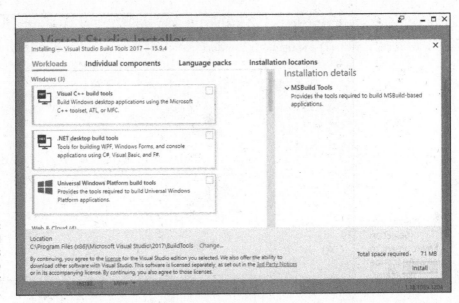

4. **Check the Visual C++ Build Tools option and then click Install.**

You don't need to install anything more than the default features. The Installation Details pane on the right side of the Visual Studio Installer window contains a confusing array of options that you won't need for this book. The download process of approximately 1.1GB begins immediately. You can get a cup of coffee while you wait. The Visual Studio Installer window displays the progress of the download and installation. At some point, you see a message saying that the installation succeeded.

5. **Close the Visual Studio Installer window.**

Your copy of the Visual C++ Build Tools is ready for use. You may need to restart your system after performing the installation, especially if you had Visual Studio installed previously.

Accessing your new environment in Notebook

When you open Notebook, it automatically selects the base or root environment — the default environment for the Anaconda tools. However, you need to access the DL4Denv environment to work with the code in this book. To make this happen, open Anaconda Navigator, rather than Jupyter Notebook as usual. In the resulting window, shown in Figure 4-3, you see an Applications On drop-down list. Choose the DL4Denv option from the drop-down list. You can then click Launch in the Jupypter Notebook panel to start Notebook using the DL4Denv environment.

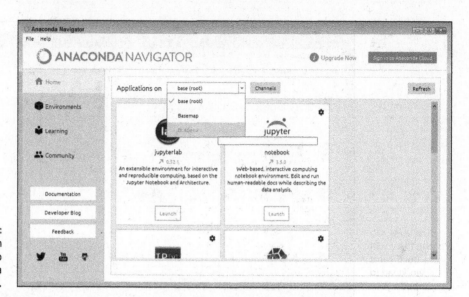

FIGURE 4-3:
Select an environment to use in Anaconda Navigator.

2
Considering Deep Learning Basics

IN THIS PART . . .

Perform essential matrix math tasks.

Work with linear regression.

Consider neural network essentials.

Move to deep learning basics.

Work with CNNs and RNNs.

Chapter 5

Reviewing Matrix Math and Optimization

hapter 1 of this book tells you about the basis of deep learning and why it's important today. In Chapter 2, you delve a little deeper into the process of learning something from data through machine learning. A key point from both those chapters is that your computer doesn't understand anything, but you can provide it with data and, in turn, it can help you understand something new from that data. For example, you can describe a math operation to it that helps you gain insight or understand your data in a way that you couldn't otherwise. The computer becomes a tool for performing truly advanced math far faster than you could ever do it manually. The basis of these math operations is the use of specific data structures, including the matrix.

You need to understand scalar, vector, and matrix operations as part of discovering how deep learning can make a significant difference in how you view the data that describes the world today. Combining data found in specific kinds of structures with algorithms designed to work with these structures is a basic element of deep learning. This chapter helps you understand the data, data structures used to contain it, and the manner in which you can perform simple tasks with those structures.

So far, you haven't really seen anything that looks like learning of any kind. Just having data structures and appropriate operations to interact with them isn't enough to consider the process learning. The final section of this chapter helps you make the connection between performing these operations and performing them quickly using optimization. The act of optimizing operations performed on data is what constitutes learning: The computer is learning to avoid unnecessary delays in performing the analysis you need to complete your tasks.

REMEMBER

You don't have to type the source code for this chapter manually. Using the downloadable source is a lot easier. The source code for this chapter appears in the DL4D_05_Reviewing_Matrix_Math_and_Optimization.ipynb source code file (see the Introduction for details on how to find that source file).

Revealing the Math You Really Need

The world is an incredibly complex place, and trying to represent it using data and math makes this fact very clear. *Data* expresses the real world as an abstraction using numeric or other values as the means to quantify the abstraction. For example, the color blue may become the value 1. *Math* is the means by which you manipulate these values to understand them better and to recognize patterns that might otherwise be unclear. For example, you might find that a larger proportion of people living in a particular area prefer the color blue to any other color. The following sections help you understand the data and the math from the perspective of AI, which allows you to interact with the world in an automated fashion (such as by cleaning your carpet with a robot or asking your car's navigation system to provide directions to a place you haven't been before).

Working with data

Without data, it's impossible to represent real world entities in a form that a computer can help you understand and manage. The computer doesn't understand the data; it simply stores the data and enables you to manipulate the data using math. The computer doesn't understand the output, either. The output of the manipulation requires interpretation by a human to have meaning. So data begins and ends with human interpretation of the real world presented as an abstraction.

When creating data, you must provide some consistent measure of the abstraction or else communication becomes impossible. For example, if one dataset presents the color blue as the integer 1, another dataset presents the color blue as the real number 2.0, and a third presents the color blue as the string blue, you can't combine the information unless you create another dataset containing the same values for each blue entry. Because humans are inconsistent, data can be inconsistent as well (assuming that it's correct in the first place). The transformation of values between datasets doesn't change the fact that the humans interpreting it still see the color blue encoded in the abstraction that is data.

After you collect enough data, you can manipulate it in ways that allows a computer to present you with patterns that you may not have seen before. As always, the computer has no understanding of the data or its interpretation, or even that it has created a pattern for you. The math defined by incredibly smart scientists manipulates the data into a pattern using math expressions.

From a deep learning perspective, then, what you have is a human interpreter providing data abstractions of real-world objects, a computer performing one or more manipulations of that data, and an output that again requires human interpretation to have any meaning at all. *Deep learning,* for the purposes of this chapter, is simply the act of automating the data manipulation process using the same techniques that a human might use matched with the speed that a computer can provide. The act of learning means to discover how to perform manipulations successfully so that useful patterns appear as part of the output.

REMEMBER

Automation isn't useful unless it's controlled, and deep learning provides that control through matrix computations. A *matrix computation* is a series of multiplications and summations of ordered sets of numbers. You need to understand how deep learning works mathematically so that you can

>> Dispel any fantasy that deep learning operates in the same way as a human brain

>> Define the tools needed later to create an example of a deep neural network

Creating and operating with a matrix

Ensuring that all the abstractions used for specific real-world objects are the same isn't sufficient to create a meaningful model. Simply deciding that the integer value 1 represents the color blue doesn't provide the necessary structure to perform math manipulation unless such manipulation is on a single value (a *scalar*). A group of related values can appear in a list (a *vector*), but only if each of the values represents the same kind of object. For example, you could create a list of colors, each of which has a specific value. To be truly useful, data must appear in a form that groups like entries in a form that enhances automated processing. Generally, the preferred form is a table (a *matrix*) that has specific object value types in the column and individual entries in rows.

You see matrixes used a lot in this book because they provide a convenient means of moving complex entries as a unit. A matrix of properties in Boston might include all sorts of related information, such as the price, number of rooms, and environmental characteristics for each house. In fact, you can find such a *dataset* (a file containing the essential data to present real-world entries) description at `https://www.cs.toronto.edu/~delve/data/boston/bostonDetail.html`. Even though you obtain the data in another form, an importing process that transforms it into a matrix is the first step in using the dataset to see useful patterns by applying deep learning.

The math you need then comes down to these things:

>> The process, including math, used to transform all data elements into like form

>> The process, including math, used to place the data elements into a structure, such as a matrix, to aid in automatically processing the data

>> The math needed to manipulate the matrix so that useful patterns appear

>> The methodology, including math, uses to provide output for human interpretation of the patterns

Understanding Scalar, Vector, and Matrix Operations

To perform useful work with Python, you often need to work with larger amounts of data that comes in specific forms. These forms have odd-sounding names, but the names are quite important. The three terms you need to know for this chapter are as follows:

>> **Scalar:** A single base data item. For example, the number 2 shown by itself is a scalar.

>> **Vector:** A one-dimensional array (essentially a list) of data items. For example, an array containing the numbers 2, 3, 4, and 5 would be a vector. You access items in a vector using a zero-based *index,* a pointer to the item you want. The item at index 0 is the first item in the vector, which is 2 in this case.

>> **Matrix:** An array of two or more dimensions (essentially a table) of data items. For example, an array containing the numbers 2, 3, 4, and 5 in the first row and 6, 7, 8, and 9 in the second row is a matrix. You access items in a matrix using a zero-based row-and-column index. The item at row 0, column 0 is the first item in the matrix, which is 2 in this case.

REMEMBER

Deep learning relies on matrices. The data sources you use have a row-and-column format to describe the attributes of a particular data element. For example, to describe a person, the matrix may include attributes such as name, age, address, and number of a particular item purchased each year. By knowing these attributes, you can perform an analysis that yields new types of information and helps you make generalizations about a particular population.

Python provides an interesting assortment of features on its own, but you'd still need to do a lot of work to perform some tasks. To reduce the amount of work you do, you can rely on code written by other people and found in libraries. The following sections describe how to use the NumPy library to perform various tasks on matrixes.

Creating a matrix

Before you can do anything with a matrix, you must create it, which includes filling it with data. The easiest way to perform this task is to use the NumPy library, which you import as np using the following code:

```
import numpy as np
```

To create a basic matrix, you simply use the NumPy array function as you would with a vector, but you define additional dimensions. A *dimension* is a direction in the matrix. For example, a two-dimensional matrix contains rows (one direction) and columns (a second direction). The array call myMatrix = np.array([[1,2,3], [4,5,6], [7,8,9]]) produces a matrix containing three rows and three columns, like this:

```
array([[1, 2, 3],
       [4, 5, 6],
       [7, 8, 9]])
```

Note how you embed three lists within a container list to create the two dimensions. To access a particular array element, you provide a row and column index value, such as myMatrix[0, 0] to access the first value of 1. You can produce matrixes with any number of dimensions using a similar technique. For example, myMatrix = np.array([[[1,2], [3,4]], [[5,6], [7,8]]]) produces a three-dimensional matrix with x, y, and z axis that looks like this:

```
array([[[1, 2],
        [3, 4]],

       [[5, 6],
        [7, 8]]])
```

In this case, you embed two lists, within two container lists, within a single container list that holds everything together. In this case, you must provide an x, y, and z index value to access a particular value. For example, myMatrix[0, 1, 1] accesses the value 4.

In some cases, you need to create a matrix that has certain start values. For example, if you need a matrix filled with ones at the outset, you can use the ones function. The call to myMatrix = np.ones([4,4], dtype=np.int32) produces a matrix containing four rows and four columns filled with int32 values like this:

```
array([[1, 1, 1, 1],
       [1, 1, 1, 1],
       [1, 1, 1, 1],
       [1, 1, 1, 1]])
```

Likewise, a call to myMatrix = np.ones([4,4,4], dtype=np.bool) will create a three-dimensional array. This time, the matrix will contain Boolean values of True. Functions are also available for creating a matrix filled with zeros, the identity matrix, and for meeting other needs. You can find a full listing of vector and matrix array-creation functions at https://docs.scipy.org/doc/numpy/reference/routines.array-creation.html.

The NumPy library supports an actual matrix class. The matrix class supports special features that make performing matrix-specific tasks easier. You discover these features later in the chapter. For now, all you really need to know is how to create a matrix of the matrix data type. The easiest method is to make a call similar to the one you use for the array function, but using the mat function instead, such as myMatrix = np.mat([[1,2,3], [4,5,6], [7,8,9]]), which produces the following matrix:

```
matrix([[1, 2, 3],
        [4, 5, 6],
        [7, 8, 9]])
```

You can also convert an existing array to a matrix using the asmatrix function. Use the asarray function to convert a matrix object back to an array form.

The only problem with the matrix class is that it works on only two-dimensional matrixes. If you attempt to convert a three-dimensional matrix to the matrix class, you see an error message telling you that the shape is too large to be a matrix.

Performing matrix multiplication

Two common methods of multiplying a matrix are element by element and dot product. The element-by-element approach is straightforward. The following code produces an element-by-element multiplication of two matrixes:

```
a = np.array([[1,2,3],[4,5,6]])
b = np.array([[1,2,3],[4,5,6]])

print(a*b)
```

What you get in return is an array of the sort shown here:

```
[[ 1  4  9]
 [16 25 36]]
```

WARNING Note that a and b are the same shape: two rows and three columns. To perform an element-by-element multiplication, the two matrixes must be the same shape. Otherwise, you see an error message telling you that the shapes are wrong. As with vectors, the multiply function also produces an element-by-element result.

WARNING Unfortunately, an element-by-element multiplication can produce incorrect results when working with algorithms. In many cases, what you really need is a *dot product,* which is the sum of the products of two number sequences. The discussion at https://www.mathsisfun.com/algebra/vectors-dot-product.html tells you about dot products and helps you understand where they might fit in with algorithms. You can learn more about the linear algebra manipulation functions for numpy at https://docs.scipy.org/doc/numpy/reference/routines.linalg.html.

When performing a dot product with a matrix, the number of columns in matrix a must match the number of rows in matrix b. However, the number of rows in matrix a can be any number, and the number of columns in matrix b can be any number as long as you create of dot product of a by b. For example, the following code produces a correct dot product:

```
a = np.array([[1,2,3],[4,5,6]])
b = np.array([[1,2,3],[3,4,5],[5,6,7]])

print(a.dot(b))
```

Here is what you receive as output in this case:

```
[[22 28 34]
 [49 64 79]]
```

Note that the output contains the number of rows found in matrix a and the number of columns found in matrix b. So how does this all work? To obtain the value found in the output array at index [0,0] of 22, you sum the values of a[0,0]*b[0,0] (which is 1), a[0,1]*b[1,0] (which is 6), and a[0,2]*b[2,0] (which is 15) to obtain the value of 22. The other entries work in precisely the same way.

TIP

An advantage of using the numpy matrix class is that some tasks become more straightforward. For example, multiplication works precisely as you expect it should. The following code produces a dot product using the matrix class:

```
a = np.mat([[1,2,3],[4,5,6]])
b = np.mat([[1,2,3],[3,4,5],[5,6,7]])

print(a*b)
```

The output with the * operator is the same as using the dot function with an array. However, even though the output looks the same as when using the dot function, it's not precisely the same. The output of the previous code is an array, while the output of this code is a matrix. This example also points out that you must know whether you're using an array or a matrix object when performing tasks such as multiplying two matrixes.

TIP

To perform an element-by-element multiplication using two matrix objects, you must use the numpy multiply function.

Executing advanced matrix operations

This book takes you through all sorts of interesting matrix operations, but you use some of them commonly, which is why they appear in this chapter. When working with arrays, you sometimes get data in a shape that doesn't work with the algorithm. Fortunately, numpy comes with a special reshape function that lets you put the data into any shape needed. In fact, you can use it to reshape a vector into a matrix, as shown in the following code:

```
changeIt = np.array([1,2,3,4,5,6,7,8])

print(changeIt)

print(changeIt.reshape(2,4))

print(changeIt.reshape(2,2,2))
```

This code produces the following outputs, which show the progression of changes produced by the reshape function:

```
[1 2 3 4 5 6 7 8]

[[1 2 3 4]
 [5 6 7 8]]

[[[1 2]
  [3 4]]

 [[5 6]
  [7 8]]]
```

REMEMBER

The starting shape of changeIt is a vector, but using the reshape function turns it into a matrix. In addition, you can shape the matrix into any number of dimensions that work with the data. However, you must provide a shape that fits with the required number of elements. For example, calling changeIt.reshape(2,3,2) will fail because there aren't enough elements to provide a matrix of that size.

You may encounter two important matrix operations in some algorithm formulations. They are the transpose and inverse of a matrix. *Transposition* occurs when a matrix of shape n x m is transformed into a matrix m x n by exchanging the rows with the columns. Most texts indicate this operation by using the superscript *T*, as in A^T. You see this operation used most often for multiplication in order to obtain the right dimensions. When working with numpy, you use the transpose function to perform the required work. For example, when starting with a matrix that has two rows and four columns, you can transpose it to contain four rows with two columns each, as shown in this example:

```
changeIt = np.array([[1, 2, 3, 4], [5, 6, 7, 8]])

print(np.transpose(changeIt))
```

The output shows the effects of the transposition:

```
[[1 5]
 [2 6]
 [3 7]
 [4 8]]
```

You apply *matrix inversion* to matrixes of shape m x m, which are square matrixes that have the same number of rows and columns. This operation is quite important because it allows the immediate resolution of equations involving matrix multiplication, such as y=bX, where you have to discover the values in the vector b. Because most scalar numbers (exceptions include zero) have a number whose multiplication results in a value of 1, the idea is to find a matrix inverse whose multiplication will result in a special matrix called the *identity matrix*. To see an identity matrix in numpy, use the identity function, like this:

```
print(np.identity(4))
```

Here's the output from this function:

```
[[1. 0. 0. 0.]
 [0. 1. 0. 0.]
 [0. 0. 1. 0.]
 [0. 0. 0. 1.]]
```

Note that an identity matrix contains all ones on the diagonal. Finding the inverse of a scalar is quite easy (the scalar number n has an inverse of n^{-1} that is 1/n). It's a different story for a matrix. Matrix inversion involves quite a large number of computations. The inverse of a matrix A is indicated as A^{-1}. When working with numpy, you use the linalg.inv function to create an inverse. The following example shows how to create an inverse, use it to obtain a dot product, and then compare that dot product to the identity matrix by using the allclose function:

```
a = np.array([[1,2], [3,4]])
b = np.linalg.inv(a)

print(np.allclose(np.dot(a,b), np.identity(2)))
```

The output from this code is

```
True
```

REMEMBER

Sometimes, finding the inverse of a matrix is impossible. When a matrix cannot be inverted, it is referred to as a *singular matrix* or a *degenerate matrix*. Singular matrixes aren't the norm; they're quite rare.

Extending analysis to tensors

A simple way of starting to look at tensors is that they begin as a generalized matrix that can be any number of dimensions. They can be 0-D (scalar), 1-D (a vector), or 2-D (a matrix). In fact, tensors can have more dimensions than imaginable. Tensors have the number of dimensions needed to convey the meaning behind some object using data. Even though most humans view data as a 2-D matrix having rows containing individual objects and columns that have individual data elements that define those objects, in many cases a 2-D matrix won't be enough.

For instance, you may need to process data that has a time element, creating a 2-D matrix for every observed instant. All these sequences of 2-D matrixes require a 3-D structure to store because the third dimension is time.

REMEMBER

However, tensors are more than simply a fancy sort of matrix. They represent a mathematical entity that lives in a structure filled with other mathematical entities. All these entities interact with each other such that transforming the entities as a whole means that individual tensors must follow a particular transformation rule. The dynamic nature of tensors distinguishes them from standard matrixes. Every tensor within a structure responds to changes in every other tensor that occurs as part of a transformation.

To think about how tensors work with regard to deep learning, consider that an algorithm could require three inputs to function, as expressed by this vector:

```
inputs = np.array([5, 10, 15])
```

These are single values based on a single event. Perhaps they represent a query about which detergent is best on Amazon. However, before you can feed these values into the algorithm, you must weight their values based on the training performed on the model. In other words, given the detergents bought by a large group of people, the matrix represents which one is actually best given specific inputs. It's not that the detergent is best in every situation, just that it represents the best option given certain inputs.

The act of weighting the values helps reflect what the deep learning application has learned from analyzing huge datasets. For the sake of argument, you could see the weights in the matrix that follows as learned values:

```
weights = np.array([[.5,.2,-1], [.3,.4,.1], [-.2,.1,.3]])
```

Now that weighting is available for the inputs, you can transform the inputs based on the learning the algorithm performed in the past:

```
result = np.dot(inputs, weights)
```

The output of

```
[2.5 6.5 0.5]
```

transforms the original inputs so that they now reflect the effects of learning. The vector, inputs, is a hidden layer in a neural network and the output, result, is the next hidden layer in the same neural network. The transformations or other actions that occur at each layer determine how each hidden layer contributes to the whole neural network, which was weighting, in this case. Later chapters help you understand the concepts of layers, weighting, and other activities within a neural network. For now, simply consider that each tensor interacts with the structure based on the activities of every other tensor.

Using vectorization effectively

Vectorization is a process in which an application processes multiple scalar values simultaneously, rather than one at a time. The main reason to use vectorization is to save time. In many cases, a processor will include a special instruction related to vectorization, such as the SSE instruction in x86 systems (https://docs. oracle.com/cd/E26502_01/html/E28388/eojde.html). Instead of performing single instructions within a loop, a vectorization approach will perform them as a group, making the process considerably faster.

When working with huge amounts of data, vectorization becomes important because you perform the same operation many different times. Anything you can do to keep the process out of a loop will make the code as a whole execute faster. Here is an example of a simple vectorization:

```
def doAdd(a, b):
    return a + b

vectAdd = np.vectorize(doAdd)

print(vectAdd([1, 2, 3, 4], [1, 2, 3, 4]))
```

When you execute this code, you get the following output:

```
[2 4 6 8]
```

The vectAdd function worked on all the values at one time, in a single call. Consequently, the doAdd function, which allows only two scalar inputs, was extended to allow four inputs at one time. In general, vectorization offers these benefits:

>> Code that is concise and easier to read

>> Reduced debugging time because of fewer lines of code

>> The means to represent mathematical expressions more closely in code

>> A reduced number of inefficient loops

Interpreting Learning as Optimization

So far, the chapter has discussed data as an abstraction, the transformation of data into useful forms, storage of the data in a matrix, and the basics of manipulating that matrix once constructed. All these things lead toward the ability to automate data processing so that you can find useful patterns. For example, a set of pixels, the smallest element of an image, is simply a series of numbers within a matrix. Locating a specific face within that image requires manipulation of those numbers to find the specific sequences that equate to a face.

REMEMBER

Before long, you realize that finding a pattern and then interpreting it correctly takes time, even for a computer, to perform with any accuracy. Of course, time is always a factor. Discovering that a criminal has entered an airport an hour after the fact isn't useful — the discovery must occur as soon as possible. To make this happen, the data manipulation and pattern recognition must occur as quickly as possible, which means optimizing the process. *Optimization* simply means to find ways to perform the task faster without losing much or anything in the way of accuracy.

Learning, from the perspective of a computer, occurs when an application finds the means to perform optimization successfully. You have to keep in mind that computer learning is different from human learning in that a computer doesn't actually understand anything new when learning takes place. The computer simply can manipulate data with greater speed and accuracy to locate patterns of interest. The rest of this book explores the concept of optimization in detail, but the following sections give you a quick overview of what optimizing the manipulation means.

Exploring cost functions

Humans understand the idea of cost quite well. You go to one store and find that a product costs a certain amount. However, you know that another store sells precisely the same product for less. The products are the same in both cases, so you purchase the item from the store that sells it for less. The same cost principle applies to computer learning. A computer can provide multiple methods of finding the patterns you want, but only one of those methods will produce output of the desired accuracy in the required time frame. The method that performs best, the one that you'll ultimately use, has the lowest *cost.*

For instance, you may need to predict a number or a class to solve a problem. It's possible to transform each of these problems into a cost that the deep learning algorithm can use to determine whether its prediction is correct. This task is done using the *cost function* (also called the *loss function*) that measures the difference between the correct answer and the answer provided by the deep learning algorithm. The output of the cost function is the difference between the correct value and the predicted value as a number. The cost function is what truly drives the success of a deep learning, because it determines what the algorithm learns. You must choose the right cost function for your problem wisely. Here are the cost functions that you frequently see used with deep learning:

>> **Mean squared error:** Takes the square of the difference between a correct value and the value predicted by the algorithm. When the difference is great, the squared value is even greater, highlighting the algorithm error.

>> **Cross entropy or log loss:** Evaluates prediction errors employing a logarithm. Deep learning algorithms use probabilities to provide answers. (They don't output the probability, but the output has a certain probability.) Probabilities are based on their correctness and are transformed into a numeric measure that represents the error.

Knowing the cost that a deep learning algorithm produces when guessing an output is just one part of the process. Just as humans learn from errors when made aware of them, deep learning learns through the output of the cost function. Cost implies finding a method that performs tasks in an optimal manner. The word *optimum* is purposely imprecise because what may seem optimal in one situation may not be optimal in another. The *optimal solution* is the one that will continue to locate the required patterns in the minimum time with the specified accuracy over a large number of data items. Creating a method that works with the data you know about doesn't pay. What you want is an optimal method for dealing with the data that you don't know about today.

Descending the error curve

When a human makes a mistake and someone sees it, the other person provides feedback to help the first person understand the nature of the mistake and the correct resolution for it. A single feedback session may not suffice to help a person correct the error; therefore, repeating the feedback may be necessary to help a person gradually correct the mistake. Likewise, the automation provided by deep learning requires correction by subsequent corrections.

After detecting an error, the automation provides correction to the algorithms performing the processing. This feedback loop improves the responses given by the deep learning solution over time, which makes the solution more accurate in finding the correct patterns. As this process continues the error level measured by the cost function decreases, thus drawing a *descending curve*. The cost function drives the process just described, but it needs other algorithms, such as optimization and the error correction, to make actual changes. The cost function reports the error level only when a deep learning model outputs a prediction.

For the purposes of this book, different algorithms achieve different kinds of optimization. Gradient Descent, Stochastic Gradient Descent, Momentum, Adagrad, RMSProp, Adadelta, and Adam are all variants of the same optimization concept that the book explores later. Error correction relies on a different algorithm called *backpropagation*. An error function sends feedback through the neural network in the form of weights that affect how the solution transforms data inputs to ensure the correct output.

Learning the right direction

Gradient descent is a widely used approach to determine what corrections are needed make a deep learning model perform better given a certain error. It always starts with an initial deep learning network configuration and translates the feedback of the cost function into a general correction to distribute to the deep learning network nodes. This process requires a number of iterations to complete — until the cost function output is in the desired range.

Figuratively, you can see gradient descent as the captain of a boat that has to navigate a waterway to avoid numerous obstacles, such as rocks or icebergs. As the captain sees a danger (an error reported by the cost function), it provides a correction for the ship's wheel that avoids the collision. Naturally, the captain transmits the correction to the crew. The crew uses this information to control the ship's engines and rudders, the part of the story played by the backpropagation algorithm (see Chapter 7, which also details the deep learning network internals).

Based on the cost function, the network also requires optimization to minimize the error. However, optimization occurs only on the training data. Unfortunately, a perfect training data optimization can lead to overfitting. Recognizing issues such as overfitting is where the art aspect of deep learning occurs; you have to optimize using the training data, but not optimize completely (overfitting) to make the resulting model perform well on test data as well. This balancing act of finding the right level of optimization is *generalization*. Fixing a limited number of optimization iterations or stopping the optimization when you notice that the model starts to perform poorly on test data that you separate from the training data (a process called early stopping) are common strategies to achieve deep learning optimization.

One interesting point is that the series of corrections provided by the gradient descent algorithm may not be optimal in the end. Determining how to correct a single error successfully is simple; correcting many errors simultaneously may prove difficult. In many cases, the optimization algorithm gets stuck in a dead end and can't find the correct way to improve neural network performance, as shown in Figure 5-1. This situation is a *local minima*, in which it the solution appears to be performing optimally even though it really isn't because further corrections could continue to improve performance.

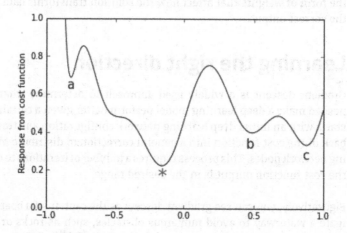

FIGURE 5-1:
Optimization
driving toward
the global
minimum.

Figure 5-1 shows an example of an optimization process with many local minima (the minimum points on the curved marked with letters) where the optimization process may get struck and can't continue its descent toward the deep minimum marked with an asterisk. In an optimization process for a deep learning model, you distinguish between different optimization outcomes. You can have a *global minimum*, a good model that outputs predictions with the lowest possible error for the problem, and many *local minima*, solutions that seem to provide the best error correction but actually don't.

REMEMBER

Apart from local minima, saddle points are other problems that you can encounter during optimization. In *saddle points*, you don't have a minimum but your optimization slows down abruptly, inducing you to believe that the algorithm has reached a minimum. In reality, saddle points represent only an optimization pause. By insisting that the algorithm goes in a particular optimization direction, you ensure that it can easily escape saddle points and proceed with error reduction. Here are ways to improve your chances of obtaining algorithms that are optimized and perform well:

>> Prepare the learning data as needed to reflect the problem

>> Choose different optimization variants and set their learning as needed

>> Set other deep learning network key characteristics

Updating

Updating a neural network with weights can take one of two forms: stochastic and batch. When performing *stochastic updates,* each input generates a weight adjustment individually. This approach has the advantage of reducing the risk that the algorithm could get stuck in a local minima. When performing *batch updates,* the error accumulates in some manner and the weight adjustment occurs when the batch is complete. The advantage of this approach is that learning occurs faster because the impact of the weight adjustments is greater.

TIP

The best way for a deep neural network to learn is to try to minimize the errors of all the examples at one time. This goal is not always possible because the data could be too large to fit into memory. Batch updates are the best strategy possible in many cases, with batch sizes being the largest possible for the hardware you are using.

Chapter **6**

Laying Linear Regression Foundations

The term *linear regression* may seem complicated, but it's not, as you see in this chapter. A *linear regression* is essentially a straight line drawn through a series of x/y coordinates that determine the location of a *data point*. The data points may not always lie directly on the line, but the line shows where the data points would fall in a perfect world of linear coordinates. By using the line, you can predict a value of y (the *criterion* variable) given a value of x (the *predictor* variable). When you have just one predictor variable, you have a *simple linear regression*. As a contrast, when you have many predictors, you have a *multiple linear regression*, which doesn't rely on a line but rather on a plane extending through multiple dimensions. Deep learning uses data inputs to guess the nonlinear plane that will most correctly go through the middle of a set of data points in a more sophisticated manner than linear regression. It does share some key characteristics with linear regression, which is the main topic of this chapter: To tell you about linear regression and provide you with useful ideas that you can later transfer to deep learning. The first part of this chapter discusses variables and how you work with them to create a linear regression.

Moving on, say that you've created a linear regression model, but that the line is separating two categories. Data points on one side of the line are one thing and data points on the other side of the line are another thing. A neural network can use linear regression to determine the probability of a data point's being on one side of the line or the other. By knowing what sort of *object* (as expressed by the data point) you're dealing with, you can *categorize* the object — that is, determine what group of objects that it belongs to.

The essence of performing all this work is to develop a solution to a problem. For example, you may have a whole list of data points and need to know which group each data point belongs to, which would be an arduous task without some sort of automation. However, to create a valid solution to any given problem, you must have the right data, which means determining the correct inputs, or *features*, to use. The third part of this chapter discusses how to select features that will best answer the questions that you must consider.

Finally, this chapter uses what you've discovered so far to solve a simple problem using stochastic gradient descent (SGD). Putting everything together will make the use of linear regression in solving problems clear.

Combining Variables

Regression boasts a long history in different domains: statistics, economics, psychology, social sciences, and political sciences. Apart from being capable of a large range of predictions involving numeric values, binary and multiple classes, probabilities, and count data, linear regression also helps you understand group differences, model consumer preferences, and quantify the importance of a feature in a model.

Stripped of most of its statistical properties, linear regression remains a simple, understandable, yet effective algorithm for the prediction of values and classes. Fast to train, easy to explain to nontechnical people, and simple to implement in any programming language, linear and logistic regression are the first choice of most deep learning practitioners when building models to compare with more sophisticated solutions (a baseline model). People also use them to determine the key features in a problem, to experiment, and to obtain insight into feature creation.

Working through simple linear regression

You need to differentiate between the statistical write-ups of linear regression that involve plotting coordinates and drawing a line through them from the algorithm that deep learning uses to predict the location of that line in a plot. Linear regression works by combining numeric features through summation. Adding a constant number, called the *bias*, completes the summation. The bias represents the prediction baseline when all the features have values of zero. Bias can play an important role in producing default predictions, especially when some of your features are missing (and so have a zero value). Here's the common formula for a linear regression:

$$y = \beta X + \alpha$$

In this expression, y is the vector of the response values. Possible response vectors are the prices of houses in a city or the sales of a product, which is simply any answer that is numeric, such as a measure or a quantity. The X symbol states the matrix of features to use to guess the y vector. X is a matrix that contains only numeric values. The Greek letter alpha (α) represents the bias, which is a constant, whereas the letter beta (β) is a vector of coefficients that a linear regression model uses with the bias to create the prediction.

REMEMBER

Using Greek letters alpha and beta in regression is widespread to the point that most practitioners call the vector of coefficients the *regression beta*.

You can make sense of this expression in different ways. To simplify, you can imagine that X is actually composed of a single feature (described as a *predictor* in statistical practice), so you can represent it as a vector named x. When only one predictor is available, the calculation is a *simple linear regression*. Now that you have a simpler formulation, your high school algebra and geometry tell you that the formulation *y=bx+a* is a line in a coordinate plane made of an x axis (the *abscissa*) and a y axis (the *ordinate*).

Advancing to multiple linear regression

The world seldom offers problems that have just one feature. When predicting house prices, you must consider all sorts of issues, such as the neighborhood and the number of rooms in the house. Otherwise, people could solve most problems without using automation such as deep learning. When you have more than one feature (a *multiple linear regression*), you can't use a simple coordinate plane made of x and y anymore. The space now spans multiple dimensions, with each dimension being a feature. Now your formula is more intricate, composed of multiple x values, each weighted by its own beta. For instance, if you have four features (so that the space is four dimensional), the regression formulation, as explicated from matrix form, is

$$y = x_1 b_1 + x_2 b_2 + x_3 b_3 + x_4 b_4 + a$$

This complex formula, which exists in a multidimensional space, isn't a line anymore, but rather a plane with as many dimensions as the space. This is a *hyperplane,* and its surface individuates the response values for every possible combination of values in the feature dimensions.

This discussion explains regression in its geometrical meaning, but you can also view it as just a large weighted summation. You can decompose the response into many parts, each one referring to a feature and contributing to a certain portion. The geometric meaning is particularly useful for discussing regression properties, but the weighted summation meaning helps you understand practical examples better. For instance, if you want to predict a model for advertising expenditures, you can use a regression model and create a model like this:

```
sales = advertising*b_adv + shops*b_shop + price*b_price + a
```

In this formulation, sales are the sum of advertising expenditures, the number of shops distributing the product, and the product's price. You can quickly demystify linear regression by explaining its components. First, you have the bias, the constant a, which acts as a starting point. Then you have three feature values, each one expressed in a different scale (advertising is a lot of money, price is some affordable value, and shops is a positive number), each one rescaled by its respective beta coefficient.

Each beta presents a numeric value that describes the intensity of the relationship to the response. It also has a sign that shows the effect of a change in feature. When a beta coefficient is near zero, the effect of the feature on the response is weak, but if its value is far from zero, either positive or negative, the effect is significant and the feature is important to the regression model.

TIP

To obtain an estimate of the target value, you scale each beta to the measure of the feature. A high beta provides more or less effect on the response depending on the scale of the feature. A good habit is to standardize the features (by subtracting the mean and dividing by standard deviation) to avoid being fooled by high beta values on small-scale features and to compare different beta coefficients. The resulting beta values are comparable, allowing you to determine which ones have the most impact on the response (those with the largest absolute value).

If beta is positive, increasing the feature will increase the response, whereas decreasing the feature will decrease the response. Conversely, if beta is negative, the response will act contrary to the feature: When one is increasing, the other is decreasing. Each beta in a regression represents an impact.

Including gradient descent

Using the gradient descent algorithm discussed later in this chapter, linear regression can find the best set of beta coefficients (and bias) to minimize a cost function given by the squared difference between the predictions and the real values:

$$J(w) = \frac{1}{2n}\sum (Xw - y)^2$$

This formula tells you the cost J as a function of w, the vector of coefficients of the linear model. The cost is the summed, squared difference of response values from predicted values (the multiplication Xw) divided by two times the number of observations (n). The algorithm strives to find the minimum possible solution values for the difference between the real target values and the predictions derived from the linear regression.

You can express the result of the optimization graphically as the vertical distances between the data points and the regression line. The regression line represents the response variable well when the distances are small, as shown in Figure 6-1 (with a simple linear regression on the left and a multiple linear regression on the right). If you sum the squares of the distances (the length of the line connecting the data point to the regression line in the figure), the sum is always the minimum possible when you calculate the regression line correctly. (No other combination of beta will result in a lower error.)

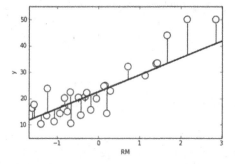
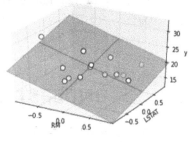

FIGURE 6-1:
An example of visualizing errors of a regression line and plane.

REMEMBER

In statistics, practitioners often indicate estimating the solution of a linear regression based on matrix calculus (that's called *solving by closed form*). Using this approach isn't always feasible, and computations are quite slow when the input matrix is large. In deep learning, you obtain the same results using the Gradient Descent Optimization (GDO), which handles larger amounts of data easier and faster, thus estimating a solution from any input matrix.

Seeing linear regression in action

The following Python example uses the Boston dataset from Scikit-learn to try to guess the Boston housing prices using a linear regression. The example also tries to determine which variables influence the result more. Beyond computational issues, standardizing the predictors proves quite useful if you want to determine the influential variables:

```
from sklearn.datasets import load_boston
from sklearn.preprocessing import scale
boston = load_boston()
X, y = scale(boston.data), boston.target
```

The regression class in Scikit-learn is part of the `linear_model` module. Because you previously scaled the X variables, you don't need to decide any other preparations or special parameters when using this algorithm:

```
from sklearn.linear_model import LinearRegression
regression = LinearRegression()
regression.fit(X, y)
```

Now that the algorithm is fitted, you can use the `score` method to report the R^2 measure:

```
print('R2 %0.3f' % regression.score(X, y))

R2 0.741
```

UNDERSTANDING R^2 A LITTLE BETTER

R^2, also known as coefficient of determination, is a measure ranging from 0 to 1. It shows how using a regression model is better in predicting the response than using a simple mean. The coefficient of determination is derived from statistical practice and directly relates to the sum of squared errors. You can also understand R^2 as the quantity of information explained by the model (the same as the squared correlation), so getting near 1 means being able to explain most of the data using the model.

Calculating the R^2 on the same set of data used for the training is common in statistics. In data science and deep learning, you're always better off to test scores on data not used for training. Complex algorithms can memorize the data rather than learn from it. In certain circumstances, this problem can also happen when you use simpler models, such as linear regression.

To understand what drives the estimates in the multiple regression model, you have to look at the coefficients_ attribute, which is an array containing the regression beta coefficients. By printing the boston.DESCR attribute, you can understand the variable reference:

```
print([a + ':' + str(round(b, 1)) for a, b in
       zip(boston.feature_names, regression.coef_)])

['CRIM:-0.9', 'ZN:1.1', 'INDUS:0.1', 'CHAS:0.7',
 'NOX:-2.1', 'RM:2.7', 'AGE:0.0', 'DIS:-3.1',
 'RAD:2.7', 'TAX:-2.1', 'PTRATIO:-2.1',
 'B:0.9', 'LSTAT:-3.7']
```

The DIS variable, which contains the weighted distances to five employment centers, has the largest absolute unit change. In real estate, a house that's too far away from people's interests (such as work) lowers the value. Instead, AGE or INDUS, which are both proportions that describe the building's age and whether nonretail activities are available in the area, don't influence the result as much; the absolute value of their beta coefficients is much lower.

REMEMBER

You may wonder why the chapter's examples don't use Keras and TensorFlow. Using these libraries is possible, but deep learning packages are most suited for deep learning solutions. Using them for simpler models means overcomplicating the solution. Scikit-learn offers clear and simple implementations of linear regression models that help you understand how these algorithms work better.

Mixing Variable Types

Quite a few problems arise with the effective, yet simple, linear regression tool. Sometimes, depending on the data you use, the problems are greater than the benefits of using this tool. The best way to determine whether linear regression will work is to use the algorithm and test its efficacy on your data.

Modeling the responses

Linear regression can model responses only as quantitative data. When you need to model categories as a response, you must turn to logistic regression. When working with predictors, you do best by using continuous numeric variables; although you can fit both ordinal numbers and, with some transformations, qualitative categories.

A qualitative variable might express a color feature, such as the color of a product, or a feature that indicates the profession of a person. You have a number of options for transforming a qualitative variable by using a technique such as binary encoding (the most common approach). When making a qualitative variable binary, you create as many features as classes in the feature. Each feature contains zero values unless its class appears in the data, when it takes the value of one. This procedure is called *one-hot encoding*. A simple Python example using the Scikit-learn preprocessing module shows how to perform one-hot encoding:

```
from sklearn.preprocessing import OneHotEncoder
from sklearn.preprocessing import LabelEncoder
lbl = LabelEncoder()
enc = OneHotEncoder()
qualitative = ['red', 'red', 'green', 'blue',
               'red', 'blue', 'blue', 'green']
labels = lbl.fit_transform(qualitative).reshape(8,1)
print(enc.fit_transform(labels).toarray())

[[ 0.  0.  1.]
 [ 0.  0.  1.]
 [ 0.  1.  0.]
 [ 1.  0.  0.]
 [ 0.  0.  1.]
 [ 1.  0.  0.]
 [ 1.  0.  0.]
 [ 0.  1.  0.]]
```

In this case, you see what appears to be three columns: blue, green, and red. For example, notice that in array element [0, 2] you see a value of 1., which equates to a value of red in that position. Now look at the original array, where you see that qualitative[0] is indeed 'red'.

Modeling the features

In statistics, because you solve the linear regression using the closed form, when you want to make a binary variable out of a categorical one, you transform all the levels but one because you use the inverse matrix computation formula, which has quite a few limitations. In deep learning, you use gradient descent, so you instead transform all the levels.

If a data matrix is missing data and you don't deal with it properly, the model will stop working. Consequently, you need to impute the missing values (for instance, by replacing a missing value with the mean value calculated from the feature itself). Another solution is to use a zero value for the missing case, and to create an additional binary variable whose unit values point out missing values in the feature. In addition, *outliers* (values outside the normal range) disrupt linear regression because the model tries to minimize the square value of the errors (also called *residuals*). Outliers have large residuals, thus forcing the algorithm to focus more on them than on regular points.

Dealing with complex relations

The greatest linear regression limitation is that the model is a summation of independent terms, because each feature stands alone in the summation, multiplied only by its own beta. This mathematical form is perfect for expressing a situation in which the features are unrelated. For instance, a person's age and eye color are unrelated terms because they do not influence each other. Thus, you can consider them to be independent terms, and in a regression summation, having them stay separated makes sense.

Contrast unrelated terms with related terms. For example, a person's age and hair color relate because aging causes hair to whiten. When you put these features in a regression summation, it's like summing the same information. Because of this limitation, you can't determine how to represent the effect of variable combinations on the outcome. In other words, you can't represent complex situations with your data. Because the model is made of simple combinations of weighted features, its predictions are more affected by bias than variance. In fact, after fitting the observed outcome values, the solution proposed by linear models is always a proportionally rescaled mix of features.

Unfortunately, you can't represent some relations between a response and a feature faithfully by using a proportionally rescaled mix of features. On many occasions, the response depends on features in a nonlinear way: Some feature values act as hurdles, after which the response suddenly increases or decreases, strengthens or weakens, or even reverses. As an example, consider how human beings grow in height from childhood. If observed in a specific age range, the relationship between age and height is somehow linear: the child gets taller as age increases. However, some children grow more (overall height) and some grow faster (growth in a certain amount of time). This observation holds when you expect a linear model to find an average answer. However, after a certain age, children stop growing and the height remains constant for a long part of life, slowly decreasing in older age. Clearly, a linear regression can't grasp such a nonlinear relationship. (In the end, you can represent it as a kind of parabola.)

Because the relation between the target and each predictor variable is based on a single coefficient, you don't have a way to represent complex relations like a parabola (a unique value of x maximizing or minimizing the response), an exponential growth, or a more complex nonlinear curve unless you enrich the feature.

The easiest way to model complex relations is by employing mathematical transformations of the predictors using polynomial expansion. *Polynomial expansion*, given a certain degree d, creates powers of each feature up to the d-power and d-combinations of all the terms. For instance, if you start with a simple linear model such as the following:

```
y = b1x1 + b2x2 + a
```

and then use a polynomial expansion of the second degree, that model becomes

```
y = b1x1 + b2x2 + a + b3x1**2+b4x2**2+b5x1x2
```

You make the addition to the original formulation (the expansion) using powers and combinations of the existing predictors. As the degree of the polynomial expansion grows, so does the number of derived terms.

REMEMBER

When using polynomial expansion, you start putting the variables in relation to each other. That's exactly what neural networks and deep learning do at a different scale; they relate each variable to each other.

The following Python example uses the Boston dataset to check the technique's effectiveness. If successful, the polynomial expansion will catch nonlinear relationships in data that require a curve, not a line, to predict correctly and overcome any difficulty in prediction at the expense of an increased number of predictors.

```
from sklearn.preprocessing import PolynomialFeatures
from sklearn.model_selection import train_test_split
from sklearn.metrics import r2_score

pf = PolynomialFeatures(degree=2)
poly_X = pf.fit_transform(X)
X_train, X_test, y_train, y_test = (
    train_test_split(poly_X,
                     y, test_size=0.33, random_state=42))

from sklearn.linear_model import Ridge
reg_regression = Ridge(alpha=0.1, normalize=True)
reg_regression.fit(X_train,y_train)
print ('R2: %0.3f'
    % r2_score(y_test,reg_regression.predict(X_test)))

R2: 0.819
```

TIP

Because feature scales are enlarged by power expansion, standardizing the data after a polynomial expansion is a good practice.

Polynomial expansion doesn't always provide the advantages demonstrated by the previous example. By expanding the number of features, you reduce the bias of the predictions at the expense of potentially overfitting.

Switching to Probabilities

Up to now, the chapter has considered only regression models, which express numeric values as outputs from data learning. Most problems, however, also require classification. The following sections discuss how you can address both numeric and classification output.

Specifying a binary response

A solution to a problem involving a binary response (the model has to choose from between two possible classes) would be to code a response vector as a sequence of ones and zeros (or positive and negative values). The following Python code proves both the feasibility and limits of using a binary response:

```
import numpy as np

a = np.array([0, 0, 0, 0, 1, 1, 1, 1])
b = np.array([1, 2, 3, 4, 5, 6, 7, 8]).reshape(8,1)
from sklearn.linear_model import LinearRegression
regression = LinearRegression()
regression.fit(b,a)
print (regression.predict(b)>0.5)

[False False False False  True  True  True  True]
```

In statistics, linear regression can't solve classification problems because doing so would create a series of violated statistical assumptions. So, for statistics, using regression models for classification purposes is mainly a theoretical problem, not a practical one. In deep learning, the problem with linear regression is that it serves as a linear function that's trying to minimize prediction errors; therefore, depending on the slope of the computed line, it may not be able to solve the data problem.

When a linear regression is given the task of predicting two values, such as 0 and +1, which represent two classes, it tries to compute a line that provides results close to the target values. In some cases, even though the results are precise, the output is too far from the target values, which forces the regression line to adjust in order to minimize the summed errors. The change results in fewer summed deviance errors but more misclassified cases.

Linear regression doesn't produce acceptable results when the priority is classification accuracy, as shown in Figure 6-2 on the left. Therefore, it won't work satisfactorily in many classification tasks. Linear regression works best on a continuum of numeric estimates. However, for classification tasks, you need a more suitable measure, such as the probability of class ownership.

FIGURE 6-2: Probabilities do not work as well with a straight line as they do with a sigmoid curve.

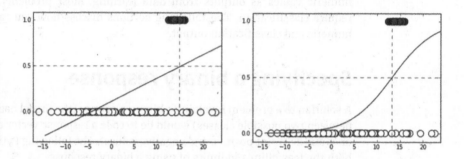

Transforming numeric estimates into probabilities

Thanks to the following formula, you can transform linear regression numeric estimates into probabilities that are more apt to describe how a class fits an observation:

$$p(y=1) = \frac{\exp(r)}{(1+\exp(r))}$$

In this formula, the target is the probability that the response y will correspond to the class 1. The letter r is the *regression result*, the sum of the variables weighted by their coefficients. The exponential function, exp(r), corresponds to Euler's number e elevated to the power of r. A linear regression using this transformation formula (also called a *link function*) for changing its results into probabilities is a logistic regression.

Logistic regression (shown on the right in Figure 6-2) is the same as a linear regression except that the y data contains integer numbers indicating the class relative to the observation. So, using the Boston dataset from the Scikit-learn datasets module, you can try to guess what makes houses in an area overly expensive (median values >= 40):

```
from sklearn.linear_model import LogisticRegression
from sklearn.model_selection import train_test_split

binary_y = np.array(y >= 40).astype(int)
X_train, X_test, y_train, y_test = train_test_split(X,
            binary_y, test_size=0.33, random_state=5)
logistic = LogisticRegression()
logistic.fit(X_train,y_train)
from sklearn.metrics import accuracy_score
print('In-sample accuracy: %0.3f' %
        accuracy_score(y_train, logistic.predict(X_train)))
print('Out-of-sample accuracy: %0.3f' %
        accuracy_score(y_test, logistic.predict(X_test)))


In-sample accuracy: 0.973
Out-of-sample accuracy: 0.958
```

The example splits the data into training and testing sets, enabling you to check the efficacy of the logistic regression model on data that the model hasn't used for learning. The resulting coefficients tell you the probability of a particular class's being in the target class (which is any class encoded using a value of 1). If a coefficient increases the likelihood, it will have a positive coefficient; otherwise, the coefficient is negative.

```
for var,coef in zip(boston.feature_names,
                logistic.coef_[0]):
        print ("%7s : %7.3f" %(var, coef))

   CRIM :  -0.006
     ZN :   0.197
  INDUS :   0.580
   CHAS :  -0.023
    NOX :  -0.236
     RM :   1.426
    AGE :  -0.048
    DIS :  -0.365
    RAD :   0.645
    TAX :  -0.220
PTRATIO :  -0.554
      B :   0.049
  LSTAT :  -0.803
```

Reading the results on your screen, you can see that in Boston, criminality (CRIM) has some effect on prices. However, the level of poverty (LSTAT), distance from work (DIS), and pollution (NOX) all have much greater effects. Moreover, contrary to linear regression, logistic regression doesn't simply output the resulting class (in this case a 1 or a 0) but also estimates the probability of the observation's being part of one of the two classes:

```
print('\nclasses:',logistic.classes_)
print('\nProbs:\n',logistic.predict_proba(X_test)[:3,:])

classes: [0 1]

Probs:
 [[ 0.39022779  0.60977221]
  [ 0.93856655  0.06143345]
  [ 0.98425623  0.01574377]]
```

In this small sample, only the first case has a 61 percent probability of being an expensive housing area. When you perform predictions using this approach, you also know the probability that your forecast is accurate and act accordingly, choosing only predictions with the right level of accuracy. (For instance, you might pick only predictions that exceed an 80 percent likelihood.)

Guessing the Right Features

Having many features to work with may seem to address the need for deep learning to understand a problem fully. However, just having features doesn't solve anything; you need the right features to solve problems. The following sections discuss how to select the right features when performing deep learning tasks.

Defining the outcome of incompatible features

Unless you use cross-validation, error measures such as R^2 can be misleading because the number of features can easily inflate it, even if the feature doesn't contain relevant information. The following example shows what happens to R^2 when you add just random features:

```
from sklearn.model_selection import train_test_split
from sklearn.metrics import r2_score
```

```
X_train, X_test, y_train, y_test = train_test_split(X,
                y, test_size=0.33, random_state=42)
check = [2**i for i in range(8)]
for i in range(2**7+1):
    X_train = np.column_stack((X_train,np.random.random(
        X_train.shape[0])))
    X_test = np.column_stack((X_test,np.random.random(
        X_test.shape[0])))
    regression.fit(X_train, y_train)
    if i in check:
        print ("Random features: %i -> R2: %0.3f" % (i,
            r2_score(y_train,regression.predict(X_train))))


Random features: 1 -> R2: 0.739
Random features: 2 -> R2: 0.740
Random features: 4 -> R2: 0.740
Random features: 8 -> R2: 0.743
Random features: 16 -> R2: 0.746
Random features: 32 -> R2: 0.762
Random features: 64 -> R2: 0.797
Random features: 128 -> R2: 0.859
```

What seems like an increased predictive capability is really just an illusion. You can reveal what happened by checking the test set and discovering that the model performance has decreased:

```
regression.fit(X_train, y_train)
print ('R2 %0.3f'
    % r2_score(y_test,regression.predict(X_test)))
# Please notice that the R2 result may change from run to
# run due to the random nature of the experiment

R2 0.474
```

Solving overfitting using selection and regularization

Regularization is an effective, fast, and easy solution to implement when you have many features and want to reduce the variance of the estimates because of multi-collinearity between your predictors. It can also help if you have outliers and noise in your data. Regularization works by adding a penalty to the cost function. The penalization is a summation of the coefficients. If the coefficients are squared (so that positive and negative values can't cancel each other), it's an *L2 regularization* (also called the *Ridge*). When you use the coefficient absolute value, it's an *L1 regularization* (also called the *Lasso*).

However, regularization doesn't always work perfectly. L2 regularization keeps all the features in the model and balances the contribution of each of them. In an L2 solution, if two variables correlate well, each one contributes equally to the solution for a portion, whereas without regularization, their shared contribution would have been unequally distributed.

Alternatively, L1 brings highly correlated features out of the model by making their coefficient zero, thus proposing a real selection among features. In fact, setting the coefficient to zero is just like excluding the feature from the model. When multicollinearity is high, the choice of which predictor to set to zero becomes a bit random, and, depending on your sample, you can get various solutions characterized by differently excluded features. Such solution instability may prove a nuisance, making the L1 solution less than ideal.

TIP

Scholars have found a fix by creating various solutions based on L1 regularization and then looking at how the coefficients behave across solutions. In this case, the algorithm picks only the stable coefficients (the ones that are seldom set to zero). You can read more about this technique on the Scikit-learn website at `https://scikit-learn.org/0.15/auto_examples/linear_model/plot_sparse_recovery.html`. The following example modifies the polynomial expansions example using L2 regularization (Ridge regression) and reduces the influence of redundant coefficients created by the expansion procedure:

```
from sklearn.preprocessing import PolynomialFeatures
from sklearn.model_selection import train_test_split

pf = PolynomialFeatures(degree=2)
poly_X = pf.fit_transform(X)
X_train, X_test, y_train, y_test =
    train_test_split(poly_X,
                     y, test_size=0.33, random_state=42)

from sklearn.linear_model import Ridge
reg_regression = Ridge(alpha=0.1, normalize=True)
reg_regression.fit(X_train,y_train)
print ('R2: %0.3f'
    % r2_score(y_test,reg_regression.predict(X_test)))

R2: 0.819
```

Learning One Example at a Time

Finding the right coefficients for a linear model is just a matter of time and memory. However, sometimes a system won't have enough memory to store a huge dataset. In this case, you must resort to other means, such as learning from one example at a time, rather than having all of them loaded into memory. The following sections demonstrate the one-example-at-a-time approach to learning.

Using gradient descent

The gradient descent finds the right way to minimize the cost function one iteration at a time. After each step, it checks all the model's summed errors and updates the coefficients to make the error even smaller during the next data iteration. The efficiency of this approach derives from considering all the examples in the sample. The drawback of this approach is that you must load all the data into memory.

Unfortunately, you can't always store all the data in memory because some datasets are huge. In addition, learning using simple learners requires large amounts of data to build effective models (more data helps to correctly disambiguate multicollinearity). Getting and storing chunks of data on your hard disk is always possible, but it's not feasible because of the need to perform matrix multiplication, which requires data swapping from disk to select rows and columns. Scientists who have worked on the problem have found an effective solution. Instead of learning from all the data after having seen it all (which is called an *iteration*), the algorithm learns from one example at a time, as picked from storage using sequential access, and then goes on to learn from the next example. When the algorithm has learned all the examples, it starts from the beginning unless it meets some stopping criterion (such as completing a predefined number of iterations).

Understanding how SGD is different

Stochastic gradient descent (SGD) is a slight variation on the gradient descent algorithm. It provides an update procedure for estimating beta coefficients. Linear models are perfectly at ease with this approach.

In SGD, the formulation remains the same as in the standard version of gradient descent (called the batch version, in contrast to the online version), except for the update. In SGD, the update is executed a single instance at a time, allowing the algorithm to leave core data in storage and place just the single observation needed to change the coefficient vector in memory:

$$w_j = w_j - \alpha(wx - y)x_j$$

As with the gradient descent algorithm, the algorithm updates the coefficient, w, of feature j by subtracting the difference between the prediction and the real response. It then multiplies the difference by the value of the feature j and by a learning factor alpha (which can reduce or increase the effect of the update on the coefficient).

SGD offers other subtle differences. The most important difference is the stochastic term in the name of this online learning algorithm. In fact, SGD expects an example at a time, drawn randomly from the available examples (random sampling). The problem with online learning is that example ordering changes the way the algorithm guesses beta coefficients. With partial optimization, one example can change the way the algorithm reaches the optimum value, creating a different set of coefficients than would have happened without that example. As a practical example, SGD can learn the order in which it sees the examples. If the algorithm performs any kind of ordering (historical, alphabetical, or, worse, related to the response variable), it invariably learns it. Only random sampling allows you to obtain a reliable online model that works effectively on unseen data. When streaming data, you need to randomly re-order your data (data shuffling).

The SGD algorithm, contrary to batch learning, needs a much larger number of iterations to obtain the right global direction in spite of the contrary indications that come from single examples. In fact, the algorithm updates after each new example, and the consequent journey toward an optimum set of parameters is more erratic in comparison to an optimization made on a batch, which immediately tends to get the right direction because it's derived from data as a whole, as shown in Figure 6-3.

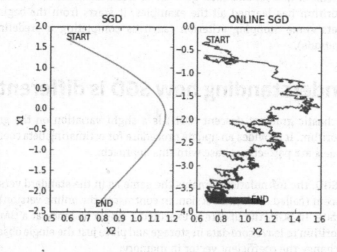

FIGURE 6-3: Visualizing the different optimization paths on the same data problem.

In this case, the learning rate has even more importance because it dictates how the SGD optimization procedure can resist bad examples. In fact, if the learning rate is high, an outlying example could derail the algorithm completely, preventing it from reaching a good result. On the other hand, high learning rates help to keep the algorithm learning from examples. A good strategy is to use a flexible learning rate, that is, starting with a flexible learning rate and making it rigid as the number of examples it has seen grows.

Both SGD classification and regression implementations in Scikit-learn feature different loss functions that you can apply to the stochastic gradient descent optimization. Only two of those functions refer to the methods dealt with in this chapter:

» `loss='squared_loss'`: Ordinary least squares (OLS) for linear regression

» `loss='log'`: Classical logistic regression

To demonstrate the effectiveness of out-core learning, the following example sets up a brief experiment in Python using regression and squared_loss as the cost function. It relies on the Boston dataset after shuffling it and separating it into training and testing sets. The example demonstrates how beta coefficients change as the algorithm sees more examples. The example also passes the same data multiple times to reinforce data pattern learning. Using a test set guarantees a fair evaluation, providing measures of the capability of the algorithm to generalize to out-of-sample data. The output shows how long it takes before R^2 increases and the value of coefficients stabilize:

```
from sklearn.model_selection import train_test_split
from sklearn.linear_model import SGDRegressor

X_train, X_test, y_train, y_test = train_test_split(X,
                    y, test_size=0.33, random_state=42)
SGD = SGDRegressor(penalty=None,
                    learning_rate='invscaling',
                    eta0=0.01, power_t=0.25,
                    max_iter=5, tol=None)

power = 17
check = [2**i for i in range(power+1)]
for i in range(400):
    for j in range(X_train.shape[0]):
        SGD.partial_fit(X_train[j,:].reshape(1,13),
                    y_train[j].reshape(1,))
        count = (j+1) + X_train.shape[0] * i
```

```
    if count in check:
        R2 = r2_score(y_test,SGD.predict(X_test))
        print ('Example %6i R2 %0.3f coef: %s' %
        (count, R2, ' '.join(map(
            lambda x:'%0.3f' %x, SGD.coef_))))

Example 131072 R2 0.724 coef: -1.098 0.891 0.374 0.849
    -1.905 2.752 -0.371 -3.005 2.026 -1.396 -2.011
    1.102 -3.956
```

No matter the amount of data, you can always fit a simple but effective linear regression model using SGD online learning capabilities.

Chapter **7**

Introducing Neural Networks

You may have heard the term *neural network* in reference to artificial intelligence. The first thing you need to know is that the correct term is *Artificial Neural Network (ANN)* because no one has discovered any method of recreating a real brain, which is where the concept of a neural network comes from. Chapter 2 of this book describes the various approaches to deep learning, of which ANNs are one. You find the term shortened in this book because everyone else is using the short term, but you need to know that ANN is actually the correct term and that they're the work of the connectionist tribe. (See the "Discovering the five main approaches" section of Chapter 2 for a discussion of the five tribes of machine learning and the approaches they've developed to solving problems.)

After you get past the whole idea that your computer lacks a brain — at least a *real* brain — you can begin to appreciate the perceptron, which is the simplest type of neural network. The perceptron is the focus of many of the neural network pictures you see online, but not all neural networks mimic the perceptron.

A neural network can work with complex data because of how it allows multiple inputs to flow through multiple layers of processing to produce myriad outputs. (The perceptron can only actually choose between two outputs.) The idea is that each of the paths fires only when it actually has a chance of answering whatever question you pose with your inputs, based on the algorithms you choose. The next section of the chapter discusses some of these methods of dealing with complex data.

Because neural networks can model incredibly complex data in a manner that amazes some people, you might think it can correct for errors in processing, such as overfitting (see the "Looking for generalization" section of Chapter 2 for details). Unfortunately, computers really don't have real brains, so overfitting is a problem that you need to solve. The final section of this chapter looks at some solutions for overfitting and discusses why it's such a big problem in the first place.

Discovering the Incredible Perceptron

Even though this book is about deep learning, you still need to know something about the previous implementation levels of machine learning and AI. The perceptron is actually a type (implementation) of machine learning for most people, but other sources will tell you that it's a true form of deep learning. You can start the journey toward discovering how machine learning algorithms work by looking at models that figure out their answers using lines and surfaces to divide examples into classes or to estimate value predictions. These are *linear models*, and this chapter presents one of the earliest linear algorithms used in machine learning: the perceptron. Later chapters will help you discover other sorts of modeling significantly more advanced than the perceptron. However, before you can advance to these other topics, you should understand the interesting history of the perceptron.

Understanding perceptron functionality

Frank Rosenblatt, of the Cornell Aeronautical Laboratory, devised the perceptron in 1957 under the sponsorship of the United States Naval Research. Rosenblatt was a psychologist and pioneer in the field of artificial intelligence. Proficient in cognitive science, his idea was to create a computer that could learn by trial and error, just as a human does.

The idea was successfully developed, and at the beginning, the perceptron wasn't conceived as just a piece of software; it was created as software running on dedicated hardware. You can see it at https://blogs.umass.edu/comphon/2017/06/15/did-frank-rosenblatt-invent-deep-learning-in-1962/. Using that combination allowed faster and more precise recognition of complex images than any other computer could do at the time. The new technology raised great expectations and caused a huge controversy when Rosenblatt affirmed that the perceptron was the embryo of a new kind of computer that would be able to walk, talk, see, write, and even reproduce itself and be conscious of its existence. If true, it would have been a powerful tool, and it introduced the world to AI.

Needless to say, the perceptron didn't realize the expectations of its creator. It soon displayed a limited capacity, even in its image-recognition specialization. The general disappointment ignited the first *AI winter* (a period of reduced funding and interest due to overhyping, for the most part) and the temporary abandonment of connectionism until the 1980s.

Connectionism is the approach to machine learning that is based on neuroscience as well as the example of biologically interconnected networks. You can retrace the root of connectionism to the perceptron.

The perceptron is an iterative algorithm that strives to determine, by successive and reiterative approximations, the best set of values for a vector, w, which is also called the *coefficient vector*. When the perceptron has achieved a suitable coefficient vector, it can predict whether an example is part of a class. For instance, one of the tasks the perceptron initially performed was to determine whether an image received from visual sensors resembled a boat (an image recognition example required by the United States Office of Naval Research, the sponsor of the research on the perceptron). When the perceptron saw the image as part of the boat class, it meant that it classified the image as a boat.

Vector w can help predict the class of an example when you multiply it by the matrix of features, X, containing the information in numeric valuesexpressed in numeric values relative to your example, and then add the result of the multiplication to a constant term, called the bias, b. If the result of the sum is zero or positive, perceptron classifies the example as part of the class. When the sum is negative, the example isn't part of the class. Here's the perceptron formula, in which the sign function outputs 1 (when the example is part of the class) when the value inside the parenthesis is equal or above zero; otherwise, it outputs 0:

```
y = sign(Xw + b)
```

Note that this algorithm contains all the elements that characterize a deep neural network, meaning that all the building blocks enabling the technology were present since the beginning:

>> **Numeric processing of the input:** X contains numbers, and no symbolic values are used as input until you process it as a number. For instance, you can't input symbolic information such as red, green, or blue until you convert these color values to numbers.

- **Weights and bias:** The perceptron transforms X by multiplying by the weights and adding the bias.

- **Summation of results:** Uses matrix multiplication when multiplying X by the w vector (an aspect of matrix multiplication covered in Chapter 5).

- **Activation function:** The perceptron activates a result of the input being part of the class when the summation exceeds a threshold — in this case, when the resulting sum is zero or more.

- **Iterative learning of the best set of values for the vector w:** The solution relies on successive approximations based on the comparison between the perceptron output and the expected result.

Touching the nonseparability limit

The secret to perceptron calculations is in how the algorithm updates the vector w values. Such updates happen by randomly picking one of the misclassified examples. You have a misclassified example when the perceptron determines that an example is part of the class, but it isn't, or when the perceptron determines an example isn't part of the class, but it is. The perceptron handles one misclassified example at a time (call it x_t) and operates by changing the w vector using a simple weighted addition:

```
w = w + η(x_t * y_t)
```

This formula is called the update strategy of the perceptron, and the letters stand for different numerical elements:

- The letter w is the *coefficient vectors*, which is updated to correctly show whether the misclassified example t is part of the class or not.

- The Greek letter eta (η) is the *learning rate*. It's a floating number between 0 and 1. When you set this value near zero, it can limit the capability of the formula to update the vector w almost completely, whereas setting the value near one makes the update process fully impact the w vector values. Setting different learning rates can speed up or slow down the learning process. Many other algorithms use this strategy, and lower eta is used to improve the optimization process by reducing the number of sudden w value jumps after an update. The trade-off is that you have to wait longer before getting the concluding results.

- The x_t variable refers to the vector of numeric features for the example t.

- The y_t variable refers to the ground truth of whether the example t is part of the class or not. For the perceptron algorithm, y_t is numerically expressed with

+1 when the example is part of the class and with –1 when the example is not part of the class.

The update strategy provides intuition about what happens when using a perceptron to learn the classes. If you imagine the examples projected on a Cartesian plane, the perceptron is nothing more than a line trying to separate the positive class from the negative one. As you may recall from linear algebra, everything expressed in the form of y = xb+a is actually a line in a plane. The perceptron uses a formula of y = xw + b, which uses different letters but expresses the same form, the line in a Cartesian plane.

Initially, when w is set to zero or to random values, the separating line is just one of the infinite possible lines found on a plane, as shown in Figure 7-1. The updating phase defines it by forcing it to become nearer to the misclassified point. As the algorithm passes through the misclassified examples, it applies a series of corrections. In the end, using multiple iterations to define the errors, the algorithm places the separating line at the exact border between the two classes.

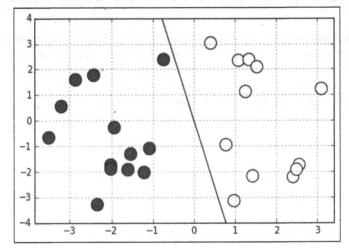

FIGURE 7-1: The separating line of a perceptron across two classes.

In spite of being such a smart algorithm, the perceptron showed its limits quite soon. Apart from being capable of guessing two classes using only quantitative features, it had an important limit: If two classes had no border because of mixing, the algorithm couldn't find a solution and kept updating itself infinitively.

REMEMBER

If you can't divide two classes spread on two or more dimensions by any line or plane, they're *nonlinearly separable*. Overcoming data's being nonlinearly separable is one of the challenges that machine learning has to overcome in order to become effective against complex problems based on real data, not just on artificial data created for academic purposes.

When the nonlinearly separability matter came under scrutiny and practitioners started losing interest in the perceptron, experts quickly theorized that they could fix the problem by creating a new feature space in which previously inseparable classes are tuned to become separable. Thus, the perceptron would be as fine as before. Unfortunately, creating new feature spaces is a challenge because it requires computational power that's only partially available to the public today. Creating a new feature space is an advanced topic discussed later in the book when studying the learning strategies of algorithms, such as neural networks and support vector machines.

In recent years, the algorithm has had a revival thanks to big data: the perceptron, in fact, doesn't need to work with all the data in memory, but it can do fine using single examples (updating its coefficient vector only when a misclassified case makes it necessary). It's therefore a perfect algorithm for online learning, such as learning from big data an example at a time.

Hitting Complexity with Neural Networks

The previous section of the chapter helped you discover the neural network from the perspective of the perceptron. Of course, there is more to neural networks than that simple beginning. The capacity and other issues that plague the perceptron see at least partial resolution in newer algorithms. The following sections help you understand neural networks as they exist today.

Considering the neuron

The core neural network component is the *neuron* (also called a *unit*). Many neurons arranged in an interconnected structure make up a neural network, with each neuron linking to the inputs and outputs of other neurons. Thus, a neuron can input features from examples or the results of other neurons, depending on its location in the neural network.

When the psychologist Rosenblatt conceived the perceptron, he thought of it as a simplified mathematical version of a brain neuron. A perceptron takes values as inputs from the nearby environment (the dataset), weights them (as brain cells do, based on the strength of the in-bound connections), sums all the weighted values, and activates when the sum exceeds a threshold. This threshold outputs a value of 1; otherwise, its prediction is 0. Unfortunately, a perceptron can't learn when the classes it tries to process aren't linearly separable. However, scholars discovered that even though a single perceptron couldn't learn the logical operation XOR shown in Figure 7-2 (the exclusive or, which is true only when the inputs are dissimilar), two perceptrons working together could.

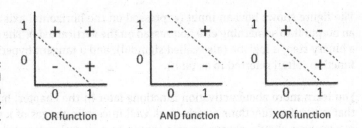

FIGURE 7-2:
Learning logical
XOR using a
single separating
line isn't possible.

OR function   AND function   XOR function

Neurons in a neural network are a further evolution of the perceptron: they take many weighted values as inputs, sum them, and provide the summation as the result, just as a perceptron does. However, they also provide a more sophisticated transformation of the summation, something that the perceptron can't do. In observing nature, scientists noticed that neurons receive signals but don't always release a signal of their own. It depends on the amount of signal received. When a neuron acquires enough stimuli, it fires an answer; otherwise, it remains silent. In a similar fashion, algorithmic neurons, after receiving weighted values, sum them and use an *activation function* to evaluate the result, which transforms it in a non-linear way. For instance, the activation function can release a zero value unless the input achieves a certain threshold, or it can dampen or enhance a value by nonlinearly rescaling it, thus transmitting a rescaled signal.

A neural network has different activation functions, as shown in Figure 7-3. The linear function (labeled Binary step) doesn't apply any transformation, and it's seldom used because it reduces a neural network to a regression with polynomial transformations. Neural networks commonly use the sigmoid (labeled Logistic) or the hyperbolic tangent (labeled TanH), or the ReLU (which is by far the more common today) activation functions. (The "Choosing the right activation function" section of Chapter 8 describes activation functions in more detail.)

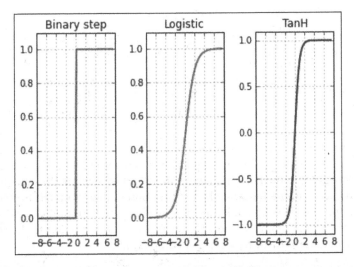

FIGURE 7-3:
Plots of different
activation
functions.

The figure shows how an input (expressed on the horizontal axis) can transform an output into something else (expressed on the vertical axis). The examples show a binary step, a logistic (also called sigmoid), and a tangent hyperbolic activation function (often referred to as tanh).

TIP

You learn more about activation functions later in the chapter, but note for now that activation functions clearly work well in certain ranges of x values. For this reason, you should always rescale inputs to a neural network using statistical standardization (zero mean and unit variance) or normalize the input in the range from 0 to 1 or from −1 to 1.

REMEMBER

Activation functions are what make a neural network perform in a classification or regression; yet, the initial choice of the sigmoid or tanh activations for most networks pose a critical limit when using networks that are more complex, because both activations work optimally for a very restricted range of values.

Pushing data with feed-forward

In a neural network, you must consider the architecture, which is how the neural network components are arranged. Contrary to other algorithms, which have a fixed pipeline that determines how algorithms receive and process data, neural networks require you to decide how information flows by fixing the number of units (the neurons) and their distribution in layers, as shown in Figure 7-4.

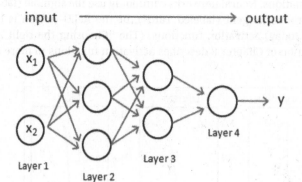

FIGURE 7-4:
An example of the architecture of a neural network.

The figure shows a simple neural architecture. Note how the layers filter information in a progressive way. This is a feed-forward input because data feeds one way forward into the network. Connections exclusively link the units in one layer with the units in the following layer (information flow from left to right). No connections exist between units in the same layer or with units outside the next layer. Moreover, the information pushes forward (from the left to the right). Processed data never returns to previous neuron layers.

Using a neural network is like using a stratified filtering system for water: You pour the water from above and the water is filtered at the bottom. The water has no way to go back; it just goes forward and straight down, and never laterally. In the same way, neural networks force data features to flow through the network and mix with each other only according to the network's architecture. By using the best architecture to mix features, the neural network creates new composed features at every layer and helps achieve better predictions. Unfortunately, there is no way to determine the best architecture without empirically trying different solutions and testing whether the output data helps predict your target values after flowing through the network.

The first and last layers play an important role. The first layer, called the *input layer*, picks ups the features from each data example processed by the network. The last layer, called the *output layer*, releases the results.

A neural network can process only numeric, continuous information; it can't be constrained to work with qualitative variables (for example, labels indicating a quality such as red, blue, or green in an image). You can process qualitative variables by transforming them into a continuous numeric value, such as a series of binary values. When a neural network processes a binary variable, the neuron treats the variable as a generic number and turns the binary values into other values, even negative ones, by processing across units.

Note the limitation of dealing only with numeric values, because you can't expect the last layer to output a nonnumeric label prediction. When dealing with a regression problem, the last layer is a single unit. Likewise, when you're working with a classification and you have output that must choose from a number *n* of classes, you should have *n* terminal units, each one representing a score linked to the probability of the represented class. Therefore, when classifying a multiclass problem such as iris species, the final layer has as many units as species. For instance, in the archetypal Iris classification example, created by the famous statistician Fisher, you have three classes: setosa, versicolor, and virginica. In a neural network based on the Iris dataset, you therefore have three units representing one of the three Iris species. For each example, the predicted class is the one that gets the higher score at the end.

TIP

Some neural networks have special final layers, collectively called softmax, which can adjust the probability of each class based on the values received from a previous layer. In classification, the final layer may represent both a partition of probabilities thanks to softmax (a multiclass problem in which total probabilities sum to 100 percent) or an independent score prediction (because an example can have more classes, which is a multilabel problem in which summed probabilities can be more than 100 percent). When the classification problem is a binary classification, a single output suffices. Also, in regression, you can have multiple output units, each one representing a different regression problem. (For instance, in forecasting, you can have different predictions for the next day, week, month, and so on.)

Going even deeper into the rabbit hole

Neural networks have different layers, each one having its own weights. Because the neural network segregates computations by layers, knowing the reference layer is important because you can account for certain units and connections. You can refer to every layer using a specific number and generically talk about each layer using the letter l.

Each layer can have a different number of units, and the number of units located between two layers dictates the number of connections. By multiplying the number of units in the starting layer with the number in the following layer, you can determine the total number of connections between the two: *number of connections*$^{(l)}$ = *units*$^{(l)}$ * *units*$^{(l+1)}$.

A matrix of weights, usually named with the uppercase Greek letter Theta (θ), represents the connections. For ease of reading, the book uses the capital letter W, which is a fine choice because it is a matrix or a multi-dimensional array. Thus, you can use W^1 to refer to the connection weights from layer 1 to layer 2, W^2 for the connections from layer 2 to layer 3, and so on.

Weights represent the strength of the connection between neurons in the network. When the weight of the connection between two layers is small, it means that the network dumps values flowing between them and signals that taking this route won't likely influence the final prediction. Alternatively, a large positive or negative value affects the values that the next layer receives, thus changing certain predictions. This approach is analogous to brain cells, which don't stand alone but connect with other cells. As someone grows in experience, connections between neurons tend to weaken or strengthen to activate or deactivate certain brain network cell regions, causing other processing or an activity (a reaction to a danger, for instance, if the processed information signals a life-threatening situation).

HIDDEN LAYERS

Outside this book, the layers between the input and the output are sometimes called *hidden layers,* and the layer count starts from the first hidden layer. This is just a different convention from the one used in this book. The examples in the book always start counting from the input layer, so the first hidden layer is layer number 2.

Now that you know some conventions regarding layers, units, and connections, you can start examining the operations that neural networks execute in detail. To begin, you can call inputs and outputs in different ways:

» **a:** The result stored in a unit in the neural network after being processed by the activation function (called g). This is the final output that is sent further along the network.

» **z:** The multiplication between a and the weights from the W matrix. z represents the signal going through the connections, analogous to water in pipes that flows at a higher or lower pressure depending on the pipe diameter. In the same way, the values received from the previous layer get higher or lower values because of the connection weights used to transmit them.

Each successive layer of units in a neural network progressively processes the values taken from the features (picture a conveyor belt). As data transmits in the network, it arrives at each unit as a value produced by the summation of the values present in the previous layer and weighted by connections represented in the matrix W. When the data with added bias exceeds a certain threshold, the activation function increases the value stored in the unit; otherwise, it extinguishes the signal by reducing it. After processing by the activation function, the result is ready to push forward to the connection linked to the next layer. These steps repeat for each layer until the values reach the end and you have a result, as shown in Figure 7-5.

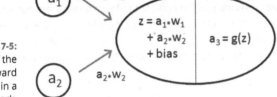

FIGURE 7-5:
A detail of the feed-forward process in a neural network.

The figure shows a detail of the process that involves two units pushing their results to another unit. This event happens in every part of the network. When you understand the passage from two neurons to one, you can understand the entire feed-forward process, even when more layers and neurons are involved. For more explanation, here are the seven steps used to produce a prediction in a neural network made of four layers (refer to Figure 7-4):

1. The first layer (notice the superscript 1 on a) loads the value of each feature in a different unit:

$$a^{(1)} = X$$

2. The weights of the connections bridging the input layer with the second layer are multiplied by the values of the units in the first layer. A matrix multiplication weights and sums the inputs for the second layer together.

$$z^{(2)} = W^{(1)}a^{(1)}$$

3. The algorithm adds a bias constant to layer two before running the activation function. The activation function transforms the second layer inputs. The resulting values are ready to pass to the connections.

$$a^{(2)} = g(z^{(2)} + bias^{(2)})$$

4. The third layer connections weigh and sum the outputs of layer two.

$$z^{(3)} = W^{(2)}a^{(2)}$$

5. The algorithm adds a bias constant to layer three before running the activation function. The activation function transforms the layer-three inputs.

$$a^{(3)} = g(z^{(3)} + bias^{(3)})$$

6. The layer-three outputs are weighted and summed by the connections to the output layer.

$$z^{(4)} = W^{(3)}a^{(3)}$$

7. Finally, the algorithm adds a bias constant to layer four before running the activation function. The output units receive their inputs and transform the input using the activation function. After this final transformation, the output units are ready to release the resulting predictions of the neural network.

$$a^{(4)} = g(z^{(4)} + bias^{(4)})$$

The activation function plays the role of a signal filter, helping to select the relevant signals and avoid the weak and noisy ones (because it discards values below a certain threshold). Activation functions also provide nonlinearity to the output because they enhance or damp the values passing through them in a nonproportional way.

REMEMBER

The weights of the connections provide a way to mix and compose the features in a new way, creating new features in a way not too different from a polynomial expansion. The activation renders nonlinear the resulting recombination of the features by the connections. Both of these neural network components enable the algorithm to learn complex target functions that represent the relationship between the input features and the target outcome.

Using backpropagation to adjust learning

From an architectural perspective, a neural network does a great job of mixing signals from examples and turning them into new features to achieve an approximation of complex nonlinear functions (functions that you can't represent as a straight line in the features' space). To create this capability, neural networks work as *universal approximators* (for more details, go to https://www.techleer.com/articles/449-the-universal-approximation-theorem-for-neural-networks/), which means that they can guess any target function. However, you have to consider that one aspect of this feature is the capacity to model complex functions *(representation capability),* and another aspect is the capability to learn from data effectively. Learning occurs in a brain because of the formation and modification of synapses between neurons, based on stimuli received by trial-and-error experience. Neural networks provide a way to replicate this process as a mathematical formulation called *backpropagation.*

Since its early appearance in the 1970s, the backpropagation algorithm has been given many fixes. Each neural network learning process improvement resulted in new applications and a renewed interest in the technique. In addition, the current deep learning revolution, a revival of neural networks, which were abandoned at the beginning of the 1990s, is due to key advances in the way neural networks learn from their errors. As seen in other algorithms, the cost function activates the necessity to learn certain examples better (large errors correspond to high costs). When an example with a large error occurs, the cost function outputs a high value that is minimized by changing the parameters in the algorithm. The optimization algorithm determines the best action for reducing the high outputs from the cost function.

In linear regression, finding an update rule to apply to each parameter (the vector of beta coefficients) is straightforward. However, in a neural network, things are a bit more complicated. The architecture is variable and the parameter coefficients (the connections) relate to each other because the connections in a layer depend on how the connections in the previous layers recombined the inputs. The solution to this problem is the backpropagation algorithm. Backpropagation is a smart way to propagate the errors back into the network and make each connection adjust its weights accordingly. If you initially feed-forward propagated information to the network, it's time to go backward and give feedback on what went wrong in the forward phase.

REMEMBER

Backpropagation is how adjustments required by the optimization algorithm are propagated through the neural network. Distinguishing between optimization and backpropagation is important. In fact, all neural networks use backpropagation, but the next chapter discusses many different optimization algorithms.

Discovering how backpropagation works isn't complicated, even though demonstrating how it works using formulas and mathematics requires derivatives and the proving of some formulations, which is quite tricky and beyond the scope of this book. To get a sense of how backpropagation operates, start from the end of the network, just at the moment when an example has been processed and you have a prediction as an output. At this point, you can compare it with the real result and, by subtracting the two results, get an offset, which is the error. Now that you know the mismatch of the results at the output layer, you can progress backward in order to distribute it along all the units in the network.

TIP

The cost function of a neural network for classification is based on cross-entropy (as seen in logistic regression):

$$Cost = y * \log(h_w(X)) + (1 - y)*\log(1 - h_w(X))$$

This is a formulation involving logarithms. It refers to the prediction produced by the neural network and expressed as $h_w(X)$ (which reads as the result of the network given connections W and X as input). To make things easier, when thinking of the cost, it helps to think of it as computing the offset between the expected results and the neural network output.

The first step in transmitting the error back into the network relies on backward multiplication. Because the values fed to the output layer are made of the contributions of all units, proportional to the weight of their connections, you can redistribute the error according to each contribution. For instance, the vector of errors of a layer n in the network, a vector indicated by the Greek letter delta (δ), is the result of the following formulation:

$$\delta^{(n)} = W^{(n)T} * \delta^{(n+1)}$$

This formula says that, starting from the final delta, you can continue redistributing delta going backward in the network and using the weights you used to push forward the value to partition the error to the different units. In this way, you can get the terminal error redistributed to each neural unit, and you can use it to recalculate a more appropriate weight for each network connection to minimize the error. To update the weights W of layer l, you just apply the following formula:

$$W^{(1)} = W^{(1)} + \eta * \delta^{(1)} * g'(z^{(1)}) *a^{(1)}$$

The formula may appear puzzling at first sight, but it is a summation, and you can discover how it works by looking at its elements. First, look at the function g'. It's the first derivative of the activation function g, evaluated by the input values z. In fact, this is the gradient descent method. Gradient descent determines how to reduce the error measure by finding, among the possible combinations of values, the weights that most reduce the error.

The Greek letter eta (η), sometimes also called alpha (α) or epsilon (ε) depending on the textbook you consult, is the learning rate. As found in other algorithms, it reduces the effect of the update suggested by the gradient descent derivative. In fact, the direction provided may be only partially correct or just roughly correct. By taking multiple small steps in the descent, the algorithm can take a more precise direction toward the global minimum error, which is the target you want to achieve (that is, a neural network producing the least possible prediction error).

Different methods are available for setting the right eta value, because the optimization largely depends on it. One method sets the eta value starting high and reduces it during the optimization process. Another method variably increases or decreases eta based on the improvements obtained by the algorithm: large improvements call a larger eta (because the descent is easy and straight); smaller improvements call a smaller eta so that the optimization will move slower, looking for the best opportunities to descend. Think of it as being on a tortuous path in the mountains: You slow down and try not to be struck or thrown off the road as you descend.

TIP

Most implementations offer an automatic setting of the correct eta. You need to note this setting's relevance when training a neural network because it's one of the important parameters to tweak to obtain better predictions, together with the layer architecture. Weight updates can happen in different ways with respect to the training set of examples:

>> **Online mode:** The weight update happens after every example traverses the network. In this way, the algorithm treats the learning examples as a stream from which to learn in real time. This mode is perfect when you have to learn *out of core,* that is, when the training set can't fit into RAM memory. However, this method is sensitive to outliers, so you have to keep your learning rate low. (Consequently, the algorithm is slow to converge to a solution.)

>> **Batch mode:** The weight update happens after processing all the examples in the training set. This technique makes optimization fast and less subject to having variance appear in the example stream. In batch mode, the backpropagation considers the summed gradients of all examples.

>> **Mini-batch (or stochastic) mode:** The weight update happens after the network has processed a subsample of randomly selected training set examples. This approach mixes the advantages of online mode (low memory usage) and batch mode (a rapid convergence) while introducing a random element (the subsampling) to avoid having the gradient descent stuck in a *local minima* (a drop in value that isn't the true minimum).

Struggling with Overfitting

Given the neural network architecture, you can imagine how easily the algorithm could learn almost anything from data, especially if you added too many layers. In fact, the algorithm does so well that its predictions are often affected by a high estimate variance called *overfitting*. Overfitting causes the neural network to learn every detail of the training examples, which makes replicating them in the prediction phase possible. But, apart from the training set, the network won't ever correctly predict anything different. The following sections discuss some of the issues with overfitting in more detail.

Understanding the problem

When you use a neural network for a real problem, you become stricter and more cautious in an implementation than you do with other algorithms. Neural networks are frailer and more prone to relevant errors than other machine learning solutions.

You carefully split your data into training, validation, and test sets. Before the algorithm learns from data, you must evaluate the goodness of your parameters:

>> Architecture (the number of layers and nodes in them)

>> Activation functions

>> Learning parameter

>> Number of iterations

In particular, the architecture offers great opportunities to create powerful predictive models at a high risk of overfitting. The learning parameter controls how fast a network learns from data, but it may not suffice in preventing overfitting the training data. (See the "Looking for generalization" section of Chapter 2 for more details about why overfitting can cause problems.)

Opening the black box

You have two possible solutions to the problem of overfitting. The first is regularization, as in linear and logistic regression. You can sum all connection coefficients, squared or in absolute value, to penalize models with too many coefficients with high values (achieved by L2 regularization) or with values different from zero (achieved by L1 regularization). The second solution is also effective because it controls when overfitting happens. It's called *early stop* and works by checking the cost function on the validation set as the algorithm learns from the training set. (The "Learning the right direction" section of Chapter 5 provides more details about early stopping.)

TIP

You may not realize when your model starts overfitting. The cost function calculated using the training set keeps improving as optimization progresses. However, as soon as you start recording noise from the data and stop learning general rules, you can check the cost function on an out-of-sample data (the validation sample). At some point, you'll notice that it stops improving and starts worsening, which means that your model has reached its learning limit.

Chapter **8**

Building a Basic Neural Network

C hapter 7 introduces neural networks using the simplest and most basic neural network of all: the perceptron. However, neural networks come in a number of forms, each of which has advantages. Fortunately, all the forms of neural networks follow a basic architecture and rely on certain strategies to accomplish what they need to do. If you learn how a basic neural network works, you can figure out how more complex architectures operate. The first part of this chapter discusses the basics of neural network functionality — that is, what you need to know to understand how a neural network performs useful work. It explains neural network functionality using a basic neural network that you can build from scratch using Python.

The second part of the chapter delves into some differences between neural networks. For example, you discover in Chapter 7 that individual neurons fire after reaching a particular threshold. An activation function determines when the input is sufficient for the neuron to fire, so knowing which activator functions are available is important to differentiate between neural networks. In addition, you need to know about the optimizer used to ensure that you get fast results that actually model the problem you want to solve. Finally, you need to decide how fast your neural network learns.

Save yourself the time and mistakes of typing the code manually. You can find the downloadable source for this chapter in the DL4D_08_NN_From_Scratch.ipynb file. (The Introduction tells you where to download the source code for this book.)

Understanding Neural Networks

You can find many discussions about neural network architectures online (such as the one at https://www.kdnuggets.com/2018/02/8-neural-network-architectures-machine-learning-researchers-need-learn.html). The problem, however, is that they all quickly become insanely complex, making normal people want to pull out their hair. Some unwritten law seems to say that math has to become instantly abstract and so complicated that no mere mortal can understand it, but anyone can understand a neural network. The material in Chapter 7 gives you a good start. Even though Chapter 7 does rely a little on math to get its point across, the math is relatively simple. Now, in this chapter you learn by putting into Python code all the essential functionalities of a neural network.

What a neural network truly represents is a kind of filter. You pour data into the top, that data percolates through the various layers you create, and an output appears at the bottom. The things that differentiate neural networks are the same sorts of things you might look for in a filter. For example, the kind of algorithm you choose determines the kind of filtering the neural network will perform. You may want to filter the lead out of the water but leave the calcium and other beneficial minerals intact, which means choosing a kind of filter to do that.

However, filters can come with controls. For example, you might choose to filter particles of one size but let particles of another size pass. The use of weights and biases in a neural network are simply a kind of control. You adjust the control to fine-tune the filtering you receive. In this case, because you're using electrical signals modeled after those found in the brain, a signal is allowed to pass when it meets a particular condition — a threshold defined by an activation function. To keep things simple for now, though, just think about it as you would adjustments to any filter's basic operation.

You can monitor the activity of your filter. However, unless you want to stand there all day looking at it, you probably rely on some sort of automation to ensure that the filter's output remains constant. This is where an optimizer comes into play. By optimizing the output of the neural network, you see the results you need without constantly tuning it manually.

Finally, you want to allow a filter to work at a speed and capacity that allows it to perform its tasks correctly. Pouring water or some other substance through the filter too quickly would cause it to overflow. If you don't pour fast enough, the filter might clog or work erratically. Adjusting the learning rate of the optimizer of a neural network enables you to ensure that the neural network produces the output you want. It's like adjusting the pouring rate of a filter.

Neural networks can seem hard to understand. The fact that much of what they do is shrouded in mathematical complexity doesn't help matters. However, you don't have to be a rocket scientist to understand what neural networks are all about. All you really need to do is break them down into manageable pieces and use the right perspective to look at them. The following sections demonstrate how to code each part of a basic neural network from scratch.

Defining the basic architecture

A neural network relies on numerous computation units, the *neurons*, arranged into hierarchical layers. Each neuron accepts inputs from all its predecessors and provides outputs to its successors until the neural network as a whole satisfies a requirement. At this point, the network processing ends and you receive the output.

All these computations occur singularly in a neural network. The network passes over each of them using loops for loop iterations. You can also leverage the fact that most of these operations are plain multiplications, followed by addition, and take advantage of the matrix calculations shown in the "Performing matrix multiplication" section of Chapter 5.

The example in this section creates a network with an input layer (whose dimensions are defined by the input), a hidden layer with three neurons, and a single output layer that tells whether the input is part of a class (basically a binary 0/1 answer). This architecture implies creating two sets of weights represented by two matrices (when you're actually using matrices):

>> The first matrix uses a size determined by the number of inputs x 3, represents the weights that multiply the inputs, and sums them into three neurons.

>> The second matrix uses a size of 3 x 1, gathers all the outputs from the hidden layer, and makes that layer converge into the output.

Here's the required Python script (which may take a while to complete running, depending on the speed of your system):

```
import numpy as np
from sklearn.datasets import make_moons
from sklearn.model_selection import train_test_split
```

```
import matplotlib.pyplot as plt
%matplotlib inline

def init(inp, out):
    return np.random.randn(inp, out) / np.sqrt(inp)

def create_architecture(input_layer, first_layer,
                        output_layer, random_seed=0):
    np.random.seed(random_seed)
    layers = X.shape[1], 3 , 1
    arch = list(zip(layers[:-1], layers[1:]))
    weights = [init(inp, out) for inp, out in arch]
    return weights
```

The interesting point of this initialization is that it uses a sequence of matrices to automate the network calculations. How the code initializes them matters because you can't use numbers that are too small — there will be too little signal for the network to work. However, you must also avoid numbers that are too big because the calculations become too cumbersome to handle. Sometimes they fail, which causes the exploding gradient problem or, more often, causes *saturation of the neurons*, which means that you can't correctly train a network because all the neurons are always activated.

Initializing your network using all zeros is always a bad idea because if all the neurons have the same value, they will react in the same way to the training input. No matter how many neurons the architecture contains, they operate as a single neuron.

The simpler solution is to start with initial random weights which are in the range required for the *activation functions*, which are the transformation functions that add flexibility to solving problems using the network. A possible simple solution is to set the weights to zero mean and one standard deviation, which in statistics is called the *standard normal distribution* and in the code appears as the np.random. radn command.

There are, however, smarter weight initializations for more complex networks, such as those found in this article: https://towardsdatascience.com/weight-initialization-techniques-in-neural-networks-26c649eb3b78.

Moreover, because each neuron accepts the inputs of all previous neurons, the code rescales the random normal distributed weights using the square root of the number of inputs. Consequently, the neurons and their activation functions always compute the right size for everything to work smoothly.

Documenting the essential modules

The architecture is just one part of a neural network. You can imagine it as the structure of the network. Architecture explains how the network processes data and provides results. However, for any processing to happen, you also need to code the neural network's core functionalities.

The first building block of the network is the activation function. Chapter 7 details a few activation functions used in neural networks without explaining them in much in detail. The example in this section provides code for the sigmoid function, one of the basic neural network activation functions. The sigmoid function is a step up from the *Heaviside step* function, which acts as a switch that activates at a certain threshold. A Heaviside step function outputs 1 for inputs above the threshold and 0 for inputs below it.

The sigmoid functions outputs 0 or 1, respectively, for small input values below zero or high values above zero. For input values in the range between −5 and +5, the function outputs values in the range 0–1, slowly increasing the output of released values until it reaches around 0.2 and then growing fast in a linear way until reaching 0.8. It then decreases again as the output rate approaches 1. Such behavior represents a logistic curve, which is useful for describing many natural phenomena, such as the growth of a population that starts growing slowly and then fully blossoms and develops until it slows down before hitting a resource limit (such as available living space or food).

In neural networks, the sigmoid function is particularly useful for modeling inputs that resemble probabilities, and it's *differentiable*, which is a mathematical aspect that helps reverse its effects and works out the best backpropagation phase mentioned in the "Going even deeper into the rabbit hole" section of Chapter 7.

```
def sigmoid(z):
    return 1/(1 + np.exp(-z))

def sigmoid_prime(s):
    return s * (1 -s)
```

After you have an activation function, you can create a *forward procedure*, which is a matrix multiplication between the input to each layer and the weights of the connection. After completing the multiplication, the code applies the activation function to the results to transform them in a nonlinear way. The following code embeds the sigmoid function into the network's feed-forward code. Of course, you can use any other activation function if desired.

```
def feed_forward(X, weights):
    a = X.copy()
    out = list()
    for W in weights:
        z = np.dot(a, W)
        a = sigmoid(z)
        out.append(a)
    return out
```

By applying the feed forward to the complete network, you finally arrive at a result in the output layer. Now you can compare the output against the real values you want the network to obtain. The accuracy function determines whether the neural network is performing predictions well by comparing the number of correct guesses to the total number of predictions provided.

```
def accuracy(true_label, predicted):
    correct_preds = np.ravel(predicted)==true_label
    return np.sum(correct_preds) / len(true_label)
```

The backpropagation function comes next because the network is working, but all or some of the predictions are incorrect. Correcting predictions during training enables you to create a neural network that can take on new examples and provide good predictions. The training is incorporated into its connection weights as patterns present in data that can help predict the results correctly.

To perform backpropagation, you first compute the error at the end of each layer (this architecture has two). Using this error, you multiply it by the derivative of the activation function. The result provides you with a gradient, that is, the change in weights necessary to compute predictions more correctly. The code starts by comparing the output with the correct answers (12_error), and then computes the gradients, which are the necessary weight corrections (12_delta). The code then proceeds to multiply the gradients by the weights the code must correct. The operation distributes the error from the output layer to the intermediate one (11_error). A new gradient computation (11_delta) also provides the weight corrections to apply to the input layer, which completes the process for a network with an input layer, a hidden layer, and an output layer.

```
def backpropagation(11, 12, weights, y):
    12_error = y.reshape(-1, 1) - 12
    12_delta = 12_error * sigmoid_prime(12)
    11_error = 12_delta.dot(weights[1].T)
    11_delta = 11_error * sigmoid_prime(11)
    return 12_error, 11_delta, 12_delta
```

REMEMBER

This is a Python code translation, in simplified form, of the formulas in Chapter 7. The cost function is the difference between the network's output and the correct answers. The example doesn't add biases during the feed forward phase, which reduces the complexity of the backpropagation process and makes it easier to understand.

After backpropagation assigns each connection its part of the correction that should be applied over the entire network, you adjust the initial weights to represent an updated neural network. You do so by adding to the weights of each layer, the multiplication of the input to that layer, and the delta corrections for the layer as a whole. This is a gradient descent method step in which you approach the solution by taking repeated small steps in the right direction, so you may need to adjust the step size used to solve the problem. The alpha parameters help make changing the step size possible. Using a value of 1 won't affect the impact of the previous weight correction, but values smaller than 1 effectively reduce it.

```
def update_weights(X, l1, l1_delta, l2_delta, weights,
   alpha=1.0):
    weights[1] = weights[1] + (alpha * l1.T.dot(l2_delta))
    weights[0] = weights[0] + (alpha * X.T.dot(l1_delta))
    return weights
```

A neural network is not complete if it can only learn from data, but not predict. The last `predict` function pushes new data using feed forward, reads the last output layer, and transforms its values to problem predictions. Because the sigmoid activation function is so adept at modeling probability, the code uses a value halfway between 0 and 1, that is, 0.5, as the threshold for having a positive or negative output. Such a binary output could help in classifying two classes or a single class against all the others if a dataset has three or more types of outcomes to classify.

```
def predict(X, weights):
    _, l2 = feed_forward(X, weights)
    preds = np.ravel((l2 > 0.5).astype(int))
    return preds
```

At this point, the example has all the parts that make a neural network work. You just need a problem that demonstrates how the neural network works.

Solving a simple problem

In this section, you test the neural network code you wrote by asking it to solve a simple, but not banal, data problem. The code uses the Scikit-learn package's `make_moons` function to create two interleaving circles of points shaped as two half moons. Separating these two circles requires an algorithm capable of defining a nonlinear separation function that generalizes to new cases of the same kind. A neural network, such as the one presented earlier in the chapter, can easily handle the challenge.

```
np.random.seed(0)

coord, cl = make_moons(300, noise=0.05)
X, Xt, y, yt = train_test_split(coord, cl,
                                test_size=0.30,
                                random_state=0)

plt.scatter(X[:,0], X[:,1], s=25, c=y, cmap=plt.cm.Set1)
plt.show()
```

The code first sets the random seed to produce the same result anytime you want to run the example. The next step is to produce 300 data examples and split them into a train and a test dataset. (The test dataset is 30 percent of the total.) The data consists of two variables representing the x and y coordinates of points on a Cartesian graph. Figure 8-1 shows the output of this process.

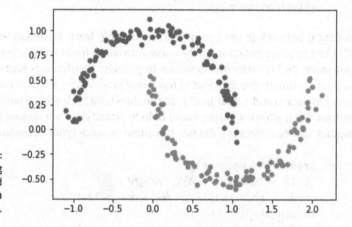

FIGURE 8-1: Two interleaving moon-shaped clouds of data points.

Because learning in a neural network happens in successive iterations (called *epochs*), after creating and initializing the sets of weights, the code loops 30,000 iterations of the two half moons data (each passage is an epoch). On each iteration, the script calls some of the previously prepared core neural network functions:

>> Feed forward the data through the entire network.

>> Backpropagate the error back into the network.

» Update the weights of each layer in the network, based on the backpropagated error.

» Compute the training and validation errors.

The following code uses comments to detail when each function operates:

```python
weights = create_architecture(X, 3, 1)

for j in range(30000 + 1):

    # First, feed forward through the hidden layer
    l1, l2 = feed_forward(X, weights)

    # Then, error backpropagation from output to input
    l2_error, l1_delta, l2_delta = backpropagation(l1,
                                          l2, weights, y)

    # Finally, updating the weights of the network
    weights = update_weights(X, l1, l1_delta, l2_delta,
                             weights, alpha=0.05)

    # From time to time, reporting the results
    if (j % 5000) == 0:
        train_error = np.mean(np.abs(l2_error))
        print('Epoch {:5}'.format(j), end=' - ')
        print('error: {:0.4f}'.format(train_error),
                end= ' - ')
        train_accuracy = accuracy(true_label=y,
                                  predicted=(l2 > 0.5))
        test_preds = predict(Xt, weights)
        test_accuracy = accuracy(true_label=yt,
                                 predicted=test_preds)
        print('acc: train {:0.3f}'.format(train_accuracy),
                end= ' | ')
        print('test {:0.3f}'.format(test_accuracy))
```

Variable j counts the iterations. At each iteration, the code tries to divide j by 5,000 and check whether the division leaves a module. When the module is zero, the code infers that 5,000 epochs have passed since the previous check, and summarizing the neural network error is possible by examining its accuracy (how many times the prediction is correct with respect to the total number of predictions) on the training set and on the test set. The accuracy on the training set shows how well the neural network is fitting the data by adapting its parameters by the backpropagation process. The accuracy on the test set provides an idea of how well the solution generalized to new data and thus whether you can reuse it.

TIP

The test accuracy should matter the most because it shows the potential usability of the neural network with other data. The training accuracy just tells you how the network scores with the present data you are using.

Looking Under the Hood of Neural Networks

After you know how neural networks basically work, you need a better understanding of what differentiates them. Beyond the different architectures, the choice of the activation functions, the optimizers and the neural network's learning rate can make the difference. Knowing basic operations isn't enough because you won't get the results you want. Looking under the hood helps you understand how you can tune your neural network solution to model specific problems. In addition, understanding the various algorithms used to create a neural network will help you obtain better results with less effort and in a shorter time. The following sections focus on three areas of neural network differentiation.

Choosing the right activation function

An activation function simply defines when a neuron fires. Consider it a sort of tipping point: Input of a certain value won't cause the neuron to fire because it's not enough, but just a little more input *can* cause the neuron to fire. A neuron is defined in a simple manner as follows:

```
y = Σ (weight * input) + bias
```

The output, y, can be any value between + infinity and − infinity. The problem, then, is to decide on what value of y is the firing value, which is where an activation function comes into play. The activation function determines which value is high or low enough to reflect a decision point in the neural network for a particular neuron or group of neurons.

As with everything else in neural networks, you don't have just one activation function. You use the activation function that works best in a particular scenario. With this in mind, you can break the activation functions into these categories:

» **Step:** A step function (also called a binary function) relies on a specific threshold for making the decision about activating or not. Using a step function means that you know which specific value will cause an activation. However, step functions are limited in that they're either fully activated or fully deactivated —no shades of gray exist. Consequently, when attempting to determine which class is most likely correct based in a given input, a step function won't work.

» **Linear:** A linear function (A = cx) provides a straight-line determination of activation based on input. Using a linear function helps you determine which output to activate based on which output is most correct (as expressed by weighting). However, linear functions work only as a single layer. If you were to stack multiple linear function layers, the output would be the same as using a single layer, which defeats the purpose of using neural networks. Consequently, a linear function may appear as a single layer, but never as multiple layers.

» **Sigmoid:** A sigmoid function (A = 1 / 1 + e⁻ˣ), which produces a curve shaped like the letter C or S, is nonlinear. It begins by looking sort of like the step function, except that the values between two points actually exist on a curve, which means that you can stack sigmoid functions to perform classification with multiple outputs. The range of a sigmoid function is between 0 and 1, not – infinity to + infinity as with a linear function, so the activations are bound within a specific range. However, the sigmoid function suffers from a problem called *vanishing gradient,* which means that the function refuses to learn after a certain point because the propagated error shrinks to zero as it approaches far away layers.

» **Tanh:** A tanh function (A = (2 / 1 + e⁻²ˣ) – 1) is actually a scaled sigmoid function. It has a range of –1 to 1, so again, it's a precise method for activating neurons. The big difference between sigmoid functions and tanh functions is that the tanh function gradient is stronger, which means that detecting small differences is easier, making classification more sensitive. Like the sigmoid function, tanh suffers from vanishing gradient issues.

» **ReLU:** A ReLU, or Rectified Linear Units, function (A(x) = max(0, x)) provides an output in the range of 0 to infinity, so it's similar to the linear function except that it's also nonlinear, enabling you to stack ReLU functions. An advantage of ReLU is that it requires less processing power because fewer neurons fire. The lack of activity as the neuron approaches the 0 part of the line means that there are fewer potential outputs to look at. However, this advantage can also become a disadvantage when you have a problem called the dying ReLU. After a while, the neural network weights don't provide the desired effect any longer (it simply stops learning) and the affected neurons die — they don't respond to any input.

Also, the ReLU has some variants that you should consider:

>> **ELU (Exponential Linear Unit):** Differs from ReLU when the inputs are negative. In this case, the outputs don't go to zero but instead slowly decrease to –1 exponentially.

>> **PReLU (Parametric Rectified Linear Unit):** Differs from ReLU when the inputs are negative. In this case, the output is a linear function whose parameters are learned using the same technique as any other parameter of the network.

>> **LeakyReLU:** Similar to PReLU but the parameter for the linear side is fixed.

Relying on a smart optimizer

An optimizer serves to ensure that your neural network performs fast and correctly models whatever problem you want to solve by modifying the neural network's biases and weights. It turns out that an algorithm performs this task, but you must choose the correct algorithm to obtain the results you expect. As with all neural network scenarios, you have a number of optional algorithm types from which to choose (see https://keras.io/optimizers/):

>> Stochastic gradient descent (SGD)

>> RMSProp

>> AdaGrad

>> AdaDelta

>> AMSGrad

>> Adam and its variants, Adamax and Nadam

An optimizer works by minimizing or maximizing the output of an objective function (also known as an error function) represented as E(x). This function is dependent on the model's internal learnable parameters used to calculate the target values (Y) from the predictors (X). Two internal learnable parameters are weights (W) and bias (b). The various algorithms have different methods of dealing with the objective function.

You can categorize the optimizer functions by the manner in which they deal with the derivative (dy/dx), which is the instantaneous change of y with respect to x. Here are the two levels of derivative handling:

>> **First order:** These algorithms minimize or maximize the objective function using gradient values with respect to the parameters.

>> **Second order:** These algorithms minimize or maximize the object function using the second-order derivative values with respect to the parameters. The second-order derivative can give a hint as to whether the first-order derivative is increasing or decreasing, which provides information about the curvature of the line.

You commonly use first-order optimization techniques, such as Gradient Descent, because they require fewer computations and tend to converge to a good solution relatively fast when working on large datasets.

Setting a working learning rate

Each optimizer has completely different parameters to tune. One constant is fixing the *learning rate*, which represents the rate at which the code updates the network's weights (such as the alpha parameter used in the example for this chapter). The learning rate can affect both the time the neural network takes to learn a good solution (the number of epochs) and the result. In fact, if the learning rate is too low, your network will take forever to learn. Setting the value too high causes instability when updating the weights, and the network won't ever converge to a good solution.

Choosing a learning rate that works is daunting because you can effectively try values in the range from 0.000001 to 100. The best value varies from optimizer to optimizer. The value you choose depends on what type of data you have. Theory can be of little help here; you have to test different combinations before finding the most suitable learning rate for training your neural network successfully.

REMEMBER

In spite of all the math surrounding them, tuning neural networks and having them work best is mostly a matter of empirical efforts in trying different combinations of architectures and parameters.

Chapter **9**

Moving to Deep Learning

Chapters 7 and 8 look at AI from a machine learning perspective, with a little added information for deep learning. This chapter looks exclusively at deep learning, because you actually need deep learning solutions to work with today's overabundance of data in a smart way. Although machine learning adds the capability to learn to the AI arsenal, it's essential to realize from the outset that computers have limitations — they don't actually understand what humans are doing. Algorithms, which are mathematical representations of various data interpretation processes, control everything. So the first part of this chapter looks at data from a deep learning perspective because you need huge amounts of data to perform pattern matching effectively.

As you move from AI to machine learning to deep learning, the computational requirements increase. In fact, one of the major reasons for AI winters in the past was a lack of processing power. Today, you can use GPUs, such as the NVIDIA Titan V (https://www.nvidia.com/en-us/titan/titan-v/), with 5,120 Compute Unified Device Architecture (CUDA) cores, to process data in ways that weren't possible even a few years ago. Therefore, the second part of this chapter discusses how you can improve your deep learning experience by throwing more hardware at it or using other strategies currently employed by data scientists (among many others).

The third part of the chapter focuses on precisely how deep learning differs from machine learning — a difference that's a constant source of problems for many people. Finding a precise definition that everyone can agree with is nearly impossible, so if you're already a deep learning expert, you may not completely agree with everything this chapter has to say. Even so, this book relies on this definition to present deep learning principles and examples, so you need to know this book's particular way of viewing deep learning.

Finally, the fourth part of the chapter takes all the essentials that you discover in the first three parts and improves on them. You begin to realize that deep learning comes in many forms and that some forms are especially suited to solving particular problems. Currently, no single solution exists that solves every problem, even inadequately, so knowing the right set of solutions to solve a particular problem can save you a great deal of time and frustration.

Seeing Data Everywhere

Big data is more than a buzzword used by vendors to propose new ways to store data and analyze it. The big data revolution is an everyday reality and a driving force of our times. You may have heard big data mentioned in many specialized scientific and business publications and wondered what the term really means. From a technical perspective, *big data* refers to large and complex amounts of computer data, so large and intricate that applications can't deal with the data by using additional storage or increasing computer power. The following sections help you understand what makes data a universal resource today.

Considering the effects of structure

Big data implies a revolution in data storage and manipulation. It affects what you can achieve with data in more qualitative terms (meaning that, in addition to doing more, you can perform tasks better). Computers store big data in different formats from a human perspective, but the computer sees data as a stream of ones and zeros (the core language of computers). You can view data as being one of two types, depending on how you produce and consume it:

>> **Structured:** You know exactly what it contains and where to find every piece of data. Typical examples of structured data are database tables, in which information is arranged into columns and each column contains a specific type of information. Data is often structured by design. You gather it selectively and record it in its correct place. For example, you might want to place a count of the number of people buying a certain product in a specific column, in a specific table, in a specific database. As with a library, if you know what data you need, you can find it immediately.

>> **Unstructured:** You have an idea of what it contains, but you don't know exactly how it is arranged. Typical examples of unstructured data are images, videos, and sound recordings. You may use an unstructured form for text so that you can tag it with characteristics, such as size, date, or content type. Usually you don't know exactly where data appears in an unstructured dataset because the data appears as sequences of ones and zeros that an application must interpret or visualize.

REMEMBER

Transforming unstructured data into a structured form can cost lots of time and effort and can involve the work of many people. Most of the data of the big data revolution is unstructured and stored as it is unless someone renders it in structured form.

This copious and sophisticated data store didn't appear suddenly overnight. The technology to store this amount of data took time to develop. Spreading the technology that generates and delivers data, namely computers, sensors, smart mobile phones, the Internet, and its World Wide Web services, took time as well.

Understanding Moore's implications

In 1965, Gordon Moore, cofounder of Intel and Fairchild Semiconductor, wrote in an article entitled "Cramming More Components Onto Integrated Circuits" (https://ieeexplore.ieee.org/document/4785860/) that the number of components found in integrated circuits would double every year for the next decade. At that time, transistors dominated electronics. Being able to stuff more transistors into an Integrated Circuit (IC) meant being able to make electronic devices more capable and useful. This process is called *integration* and implies a strong process of electronics miniaturization (making the same circuit much smaller). Today's computers aren't all that much smaller than computers of a decade ago, yet they are decisively more powerful. The same goes for mobile phones. Even though they're the same size as their predecessors, they have become able to perform more tasks.

What Moore stated in that article has actually been true for many years. The semiconductor industry calls it Moore's Law (see http://www.mooreslaw.org/ for details). Doubling did occur for the first ten years, as predicted. In 1975, Moore corrected his statement, forecasting a doubling every two years. Figure 9-1 shows the effects of this doubling. This rate of doubling is still valid, although now common opinion holds that it won't persist beyond the end of the present decade (up to about 2020). Starting in 2012, a mismatch began to occur between expected speed increases and what semiconductor companies can achieve with regard to miniaturization.

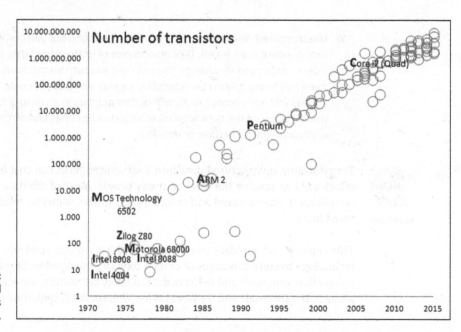

FIGURE 9-1:
Stuffing more and
more transistors
into a CPU.

Physical barriers exist to integrating more circuits on an IC using the present silica components because you can make things only so small. However, innovation continues, as described at https://www.nature.com/news/the-chips-are-down-for-moores-law-1.19338. In the future, Moore's Law may not apply. That will happen because industry will switch to a new technology, such as making components by using optical lasers instead of transistors (see the article at https://www.extremetech.com/extreme/187746-by-2020-you-could-have-an-exascale-speed-of-light-optical-computeron-your-desk for details about optical computing). Eventually, people will disregard Moore's Law because industry won't be able to keep up the pace as it did in the past (see the story on the MIT Technology Review at https://www.technologyreview.com/s/601441/mooreslaw-is-dead-now-what/).

Considering what Moore's Law changes

What matters to the data scientist and others interested in deep learning is that, since 1965, the doubling of components every two years has ushered in great advancements in digital electronics that have had far-reaching consequences in the acquisition, storage, manipulation, and management of data.

Moore's Law has a direct effect on data. It begins with smarter devices. The smarter the device, the more people rely on it to interact with data in new ways (as evidenced by electronics being everywhere today). The greater the diffusion of this computing power, the lower the price becomes, creating an endless loop that drives the use of powerful computing machines and small sensors everywhere. With large amounts of computer memory available and larger storage disks for data, the consequences are an expansion of data availability, such as websites, transaction records, measurements, digital images, and other sorts of data. Without these advancements, the Internet of today, wouldn't be possible because its flow of data depends on such smarter devices.

The Internet now generates and distributes new data in large amounts, thanks to computers, mobile devices, and sensors interconnected with it. Some sources estimate the current daily data production at about 2.5 quintillion (a number with 18 zeros) bytes, with the lion's share going to unstructured data such as videos and audios (see the article at https://www.forbes.com/sites/bernardmarr/ 2018/05/21/how-much-data-do-we-create-every-day-the-mind- blowing-stats-everyone-should-read/ for details). Most of this data relates to common human activities, feelings, experiences, and relations, accompanied by a growing share of data relative to the functioning of connected machines that range from complex industrial machineries to simple smart home lamps (lamps that you can control remotely through the Internet).

Discovering the Benefits of Additional Data

With the explosion of data availability on digital devices, data assumes new nuances of value and usefulness beyond its initial scope of instructing (training) and transmitting knowledge (transferring data). The abundance of data, when considered as part of data analysis, acquires new functions that distinguish it from the informative ones:

>> Data describes the world better by presenting a wide variety of facts and in more detail by providing nuances for each fact. It has become so abundant that it covers every aspect of reality. You can use it to unveil how even apparently unrelated things and facts actually relate to each other.

>> Data shows how facts associate with events. You can derive general rules and learn how the world will change or transform, given certain premises. When people act in a certain fashion, data provides a certain predictive capability as well.

The following sections discuss how having more data is usually better. By having more data to work with, your deep learning project can become more accurate, reliable, and, in some cases, feasible.

Defining the ramifications of data

In some respects, data provides us with new superpowers. Chris Anderson, *Wired*'s previous editor-in-chief, discusses how large amounts of data can help scientific discoveries outside the scientific method (see the article at https://www.wired.com/2008/06/pb-theory/). The author relies on the example of achievements of Google in the advertising and translation business sectors, in which Google achieved prominence not by using specific models or theories but rather by applying algorithms to learn from data.

As in advertising, scientific data (such as from physics or biology) can support innovation that allows scientists to approach problems without hypotheses, instead considering the variations found in large amounts of data and using discovery algorithms. Galileo Galilei relied on the scientific method to create the foundations of modern physics and astronomy (see https://www.biography.com/people/galileo-9305220). Most early advances rely on observations and controlled experiments that define reasons for how and why things happen. The capability to innovate by using data alone is a major breakthrough in the way we understand the world.

In the past, scientists took uncountable observations and made a multitude of deductions to describe the physics of the universe. This manual process allowed people to find underlying laws of the world we live in. Data analysis, by pairing observations expressed as inputs and outputs, allows you to determine how things work and to define, thanks to deep learning, approximate rules, or laws, of the world without having to resort to using manual observations and deductions. The process is now faster and more automatic.

Considering data timeliness and quality

More than simply powering deep learning, data makes deep learning possible. Some people would say that deep learning is the output of sophisticated algorithms of elevated mathematical complexity, and that's certainly true. Activities like vision and language understanding require algorithms that aren't easily explained in layman's terms and necessitate millions of computations to work. (Hardware plays a role here, too.)

Deep learning is more than algorithms, though. Dr. Alexander Wissner-Gross, an American research scientist, entrepreneur, and fellow at the Institute for Applied Computation Science at Harvard, offers his insights on deep learning in a recent interview at Edge (https://www.edge.org/response-detail/26587). The interview reflects on why deep learning technology took so long to take off. Wissner-Gross concludes that quality and availability of data might have been key factors rather than simply algorithmic availability. In other words, having powerful algorithms is necessary but not sufficient if you don't have the right data to run them.

Wissner-Gross reviews the timing of most breakthrough deep learning achievements in recent years, showing how data and algorithms contribute to the success of each breakthrough and highlighting how each of them was fresh at the time the AI community reached the milestone. Wissner-Gross shows how data is relatively new and always updated, whereas algorithms aren't new discoveries but rather rely on consolidation of older technology.

For instance, when you consider recent deep learning achievements, the near-human performance of the GoogleLeNet network in correctly classifying images into classes relies on an old algorithm run on recent data. It uses Convolutional Neural Networks for Visual Recognition, an algorithm developed in 1989 that could show its real effectiveness only after being trained using the ImageNet corpus (http://www.image-net.org/) of more than 1.5 million images, spread over 1,000 categories (the ImageNet corpus became available in 2010).

Another achievement to consider is the result of the team at Google DeepMind. The team deployed a deep neural network that achieves the same skillfulness as humans in playing 29 different Atari games. They relied on a 1992 algorithm, Q-Learning, which they could apply to Atari games only after 2013 when convolutional neural networks become more common and a complete dataset of 50 Atari 2600 games, called the Arcade Learning Environment (https://github.com/mgbellemare/Arcade-Learning-Environment), became available.

Wissner-Gross provides other examples of the same kind of deep learning achievement, such as when IBM Deep Blue defeated Garry Kasparov and when IBM Watson become the world *Jeopardy!* champion. In all these cases, Wissner-Gross concludes that, on average, the algorithm is usually 15 years older than the data. He points out that data is pushing deep learning's achievements forward and leaves the reader wondering what could happen if feeding the presently available algorithms with better data in terms of quality and quantity is possible.

Improving Processing Speed

When you look inside deep learning, you may be surprised to find a lot of old technology, but amazingly, everything works as it never has before. Because researchers finally figured out how to make some simple, good-ol' solutions work together, big data can automatically filter, process, and transform data. For instance, new activations such as ReLU aren't all that new; they've been known since the perceptron (which dates back to 1957; see Chapter 7).

The image-recognition capabilities that initially made deep learning so popular aren't new, either. Initially, deep learning achieved great momentum thanks to

Convolutional Neural Networks (CNN). Discovered in the 1980s by the French scientist Yann LeCun (whose personal home page is at http://yann.lecun.com/), such networks now bring about astonishing results because they use many neural layers and lots of data.

The same goes for technology that allows a machine to understand human speech or translate from one language to another. In every case, the solution relies on decades old technology that a researcher revisited and got to work in the new deep learning paradigm. The only problem is that all this data processing requires a great many processing cycles, so the sections that follow discuss how to improve processing speed so that you can actually see the result of analyzing data in a reasonable amount of time.

Leveraging powerful hardware

The use of incredible amounts of data makes the difference in algorithm performance today. To process so much data, scientists of various types rely on the increased usage of GPUs and computer networking to get answers quickly. Together with parallelism (more computers put in clusters and operating in parallel), GPUs allow you to create larger networks and successfully train them on more data. In fact, a GPU can perform certain operations 70 times faster than any CPU, allowing a cut in training times for neural networks from weeks to days or even hours. (The article at https://www.quora.com/Why-are-CPUs-still-being-made-when-GPUs-are-so-much-faster tells you why you need both CPUs and GPUs to create an effective deep learning system.)

GPUs are powerful matrix and vector calculation computing units necessary for backpropagation. These technologies make training neural networks achievable in a shorter time and accessible to more people. Research also opened a world of new applications. Neural networks can learn from huge amounts of data and take advantage of big data (images, text, transactions, and social media data), creating models that continuously perform better, depending on the flow of data you feed them.

TECHNICAL STUFF

For more information about how much a GPU can empower machine learning by using a neural network, peruse this technical paper on the topic: https://icml.cc/2009/papers/218.pdf.

Making other investments

Big players such as Google, Facebook, Microsoft, and IBM spotted the new trend and since 2012 have started acquiring companies and hiring experts in the new fields of deep learning. Two of these experts are Geoffrey Hinton, who is most noted for his work on applying the backpropagation algorithm to multilayer neural networks and now works with Google, and Yann LeCun, the creator of Convolutional Neural Networks, who now leads Facebook AI research.

Today, everyone can access networks, and people can access tools that help create deep learning networks as well. This access goes beyond reading publicly available scientific papers that explain how deep learning works; it also includes the tools for programming networks.

In the early days of deep learning, scientists built every network from scratch using languages such as C++. Unfortunately, developing applications in such a low-level language limits data access to a few well-trained specialists. Scripting capabilities today (for instance, using Python; go to https://www.python.org) are better because of a large array of open source deep learning frameworks, such as TensorFlow by Google (https://www.tensorflow.org/) or PyTorch by Facebook (https://pytorch.org/). These frameworks allow the replication of the most recent advances in deep learning using straightforward commands.

Explaining Deep Learning Differences from Other Forms of AI

Given the embarrassment of riches that pertain to AI as a whole, such as large amounts of data, new and powerful computational hardware available to everyone, and plenty of private and public investments, you may be skeptical about the technology behind *deep learning*, which consists of neural networks that have more neurons and hidden layers than in the past. Deep networks contrast with the simpler, shallower networks of the past, which featured one or two hidden layers at best. Many solutions that render deep learning today possible are not at all new, but deep learning uses them in new ways.

REMEMBER

Deep learning isn't simply a rebranding of an old technology, the perceptron, discovered in 1957 by Frank Rosenblatt at the Cornell Aeronautical Laboratory (see Chapter 7 for more details about the perceptron). Deep learning works better because of the extra sophistication it adds through the full use of powerful computers and the availability of better (not just more) data. Deep learning also implies a profound qualitative change in the capabilities offered by the technology along with new and astonishing applications. The presence of these capabilities modernizes old but good neural networks, transforming them into something new. The following sections describe just how deep learning achieves its task.

Adding more layers

You may wonder why deep learning has blossomed only now when the technology used as the foundation of deep learning existed long ago. As mentioned earlier in this chapter, computers are more powerful today, and deep learning can access huge amounts of data. However, these answers point only to important problems with deep learning in the past, and lower computing power along with less data weren't the only insurmountable obstacles. Until recently, deep learning also suffered from a key technical problem that kept neural networks from having enough layers to perform truly complex tasks.

Because it can use many layers, deep learning can solve problems that are out of reach of machine learning, such as image recognition, machine translation, and speech recognition. When fitted with only a few layers, a neural network is a perfect *universal function approximator*, which is a system that can recreate any possible mathematical function. When fitted with many more layers, a neural network becomes capable of creating, inside its internal chain of matrix multiplications, a sophisticated system of representations to solve complex problems. To understand how a complex task like image recognition works, consider this process:

1. A deep learning system trained to recognize images (such as a network capable of distinguishing photos of dogs from those featuring cats) defines internal weights that have the capability to recognize a picture topic.

2. After detecting each single contour and corner in the image, the deep learning network assembles all such basic traits into composite characteristic features.

3. The network matches such features to an ideal representation that provides the answer.

In other words, a deep learning network can distinguish dogs from cats using its internal weights to define a representation of what, ideally, a dog and a cat should resemble. It then uses these internal weights to match any new image you provide it with.

REMEMBER

One of the earliest achievements of deep learning that made the public aware of its potentiality is the *cat neuron*. The Google Brain team, run at that time by Andrew Ng and Jeff Dean, put together 16,000 computers to calculate a deep learning network with more than a billion weights, thus enabling unsupervised learning from YouTube videos. The computer network could even determine by itself, without any human intervention, what a cat is, and Google scientists managed to dig out of the network a representation of how the network itself expected a cat should look (see the *Wired* article at https://www.wired.com/2012/06/google-x-neural-network/).

During the time that scientists couldn't stack more layers into a neural network because of the limits of computer hardware, the potential of the technology remained buried, and scientists ignored neural networks. The lack of success added to the profound skepticism that arose around the technology during the last AI winter. However, what really prevented scientists from creating something more sophisticated was the problem with vanishing gradients.

A *vanishing gradient* occurs when you try to transmit a signal through a neural network and the signal quickly fades to near zero values; it can't get through the activation functions. This happens because neural networks are chained multiplications. Each below-zero multiplication decreases the incoming values rapidly, and activation functions need large enough values to let the signal pass. The farther neuron layers are from the output, the higher the likelihood that they'll get locked out of updates because the signals are too small and the activation functions will stop them. Consequently, your network stops learning as a whole, or it learns at an incredibly slow pace.

Every attempt at putting together and testing complex networks ended in failure because the backpropagation algorithm couldn't update the layers nearer the input, thus rendering any learning from complex data, even when such data was available at the time, almost impossible. Today, deep networks are possible thanks to the studies of scholars from the University of Toronto in Canada, such as Geoffrey Hinton (https://www.utoronto.ca/news/artificial-intelligence-u-t), who insisted on working on neural networks even when they seemed to most to be an old-fashioned machine learning approach.

Professor Hinton, a veteran of the field of neural networks (he contributed to defining the backpropagation algorithm), and his team in Toronto devised a few methods to circumvent the problem of vanishing gradients. He opened the field to rethinking new solutions that made neural networks a crucial tool in machine learning and AI again.

REMEMBER

Professor Hinton and his team are memorable also for being among the first to test GPU usage in order to accelerate the training of a deep neural network. In 2012, they won an open competition, organized by the pharmaceutical company Merck and Kaggle (the latter a website for data science competitions), using their most recent deep learning discoveries. This event brought great attention to their work. You can read all the details of the Hinton team's revolutionary achievement with neural network layers from this Geoffrey Hinton interview: http://blog.kaggle.com/2012/11/01/deep-learning-how-i-did-it-merck-1st-place-interview/.

Changing the activations

Geoffrey Hinton's team (see preceding section) was able to add more layers to a neural architecture because of two solutions that prevented trouble with backpropagation:

>> They prevented the exploding gradients problem by using smarter network initialization. An *exploding gradient* differs from a vanishing gradient because it can make a network blow up as the exploding gradient becomes too large to handle.

TIP

Your network can explode unless you correctly initialize the network to prevent it from computing large weight numbers. Then you solve the problem of vanishing gradients by changing the network activations.

>> The team realized that passing a signal through various activation layers tended to damp the backpropagation signal until it becomes too faint to pass anymore after examining how a sigmoid activation worked. They used a new activation as the solution for this problem. The choice of which algorithm to use fell toward an old activation type of ReLU, which stands for rectified linear units (see Chapter 7 for more about RELU). An ReLU activation stopped the received signal if it was below zero assuring the non-linearity characteristic of neural networks and letting the signal pass as it was if above zero. (Using this type of activation is an example of combining old but still good technology with current technology.) Figure 9-2 shows how this process works.

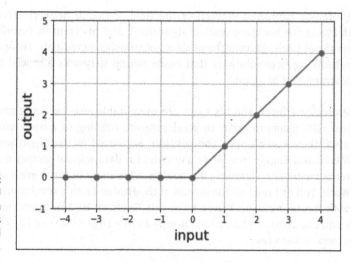

FIGURE 9-2:
How the ReLU activation function works receiving and releasing signals.

The ReLU worked incredibly well and let the backpropagation signal arrive at the initial deep network layers. When the signal is positive, its derivative is 1. You can also find proof of the ReLU derivative in looking at Figure 9-2. Note that the rate of change is constant and equivalent to a unit when the input signal is positive (whereas when the signal is negative, the derivative is 0, thus preventing the signal from passing).

TIP

You can calculate the ReLU function using `f(x)=max(0,x)`. The use of this algorithm increased training speed a lot, allowing fast training of even deeper networks without incurring any dead neurons. A *dead neuron* is one that the network can't activate because the signals are too faint.

Adding regularization by dropout

The other introduction to deep learning made by Hinton's team (see preceding sections in this chapter) to complete the initial deep learning solution aimed at regularizing the network. A *regularized network* limits the network weights, which keeps the network from memorizing the input data and generalizing the witnessed data patterns.

Previous discussions in this chapter note that certain neurons memorize specific information and force the other neurons to rely on this stronger neuron, causing the weak neurons give up learning anything useful themselves (a situation called *co-adaptation*). To prevent co-adaptation, the code temporary switches off the activation of a random portion of neurons in the network.

As you see from the left side of Figure 9-3, the weights normally operate by multiplying their inputs into outputs for the activations. To switch off activation, the code multiplies a mask made of a random mix of ones and zeros with the results. If the neuron is multiplied by one, the network passes its signal. When a neuron is multiplied by zero, the network stops its signal, forcing others neurons not to rely on it in the process.

TECHNICAL STUFF

Dropout works only during training and doesn't touch any part of the weights. It simply masks and hides part of the network, forcing the unmasked part to take a more active role in learning data patterns. During prediction time, dropout doesn't operate, and the weights are numerically rescaled to take into account the fact that they didn't work all together during training.

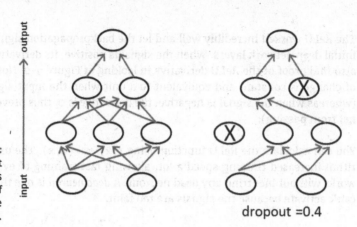

FIGURE 9-3:
Dropout
temporarily rules
out 40 percent of
neurons from the
training.

dropout =0.4

Finding Even Smarter Solutions

Deep learning influences AI's effectiveness in solving problems in image recognition, machine translation, and speech recognition. These problems were initially tackled by classic AI and machine learning. In addition, deep learning presents new and advantageous solutions in the following areas:

» Continuous learning using online learning

» Reusable solutions using transfer learning

» Simple straightforward solutions using end-to-end learning

The following sections help you understand what online learning, transfer learning, and end-to-end learning are all about.

Using online learning

Neural networks are more flexible than other machine learning algorithms, and they can continue to train as they work on producing predictions and classifications. This capability comes from optimization algorithms that allow neural networks to learn, which can work repeatedly on small samples of examples (called *batch learning*) or even on single examples (called *online learning*). Deep learning networks can build their knowledge step by step and remain receptive to new information that may arrive (like a baby's mind, which is always open to new stimuli and to learning experiences).

For instance, a deep learning application on a social media website can train on cat images. As people post photos of cats, the application recognizes them and tags them with an appropriate label. When people start posting photos of dogs on the social network, the neural network doesn't need to restart training; it can continue by learning images of dogs as well. This capability is particularly useful for coping with the variability of Internet data. A deep learning network can be open to novelty and adapt its weights to deal with it.

Transferring learning

Flexibility is handy even when a network completes its training, but you must reuse it for purposes different from the initial learning. Networks that distinguish objects and correctly classify them require a long time and a lot of computational capacity to learn what to do. Extending a network's capability to new kinds of images that weren't part of the previous learning means transferring the knowledge to this new problem (*transfer learning*).

For instance, you can transfer a network that's capable of distinguishing between dogs and cats to perform a job that involves spotting dishes of macaroni and cheese. You use the majority of the layers of the network as they are (you freeze them) and then work on the final, output layers (fine-tuning). In a short time, and with fewer examples, the network will apply what it learned in distinguishing dogs and cats to macaroni and cheese. It will perform even better than a neural network trained only to recognize macaroni and cheese.

Transfer learning is something new to most machine learning algorithms and opens up a possible market for transferring knowledge from one application to another, from one company to another. Google is already doing that, actually sharing its immense data repository by making public the networks that it built on it (as detailed in this post: https://techcrunch.com/2017/06/16/object-detection-api/). This is a step in democratizing deep learning by allowing everyone to access its potentiality.

Learning end to end

Finally, deep learning allows end-to-end learning, which means that it solves problems in an easier and more straightforward way than previous deep learning solutions. This flexibility might result in a greater impact when solving problems.

You may want to solve a difficult problem, such as having the AI recognize known faces or drive a car. When using the classical AI approach, you had to split the problem into more manageable subproblems to achieve an acceptable result in a feasible time. For instance, if you wanted to recognize faces in a photo, previous AI systems arranged the problem into parts, as follows:

1. Find the faces in the photo.
2. Crop the faces from the photo.
3. Process the cropped faces to have a pose similar to an ID card photo.
4. Feed the processed cropped faces as learning examples to a neural network for image recognition.

Today, you can feed the photo to a deep learning architecture, guide it to learn to find faces in the images, and then use the deep learning architecture to classify them. You can use the same approach for language translation, speech recognition, or even self-driving cars. In all cases, you simply pass the input to a deep learning system and obtain the wanted result.

Chapter **10**

Explaining Convolutional Neural Networks

W hen you look inside deep learning, you may be surprised to find a lot of old technology, but amazingly, everything works as it never has before because researchers finally know how to make some simple, older solutions work together. As a result, big data can automatically filter, process, and transform data.

For instance, novel activations like Rectified Linear Units (ReLU), discussed in previous chapters, aren't new, but you see them used in new ways. ReLU is a neural networks function that leaves positive values untouched and turns negative ones into zero; you can find a first reference to ReLU in a scientific paper by Hahnloser and others from 2000. Also, the image recognition capabilities that made deep learning so popular a few years ago aren't new, either.

In recent years, deep learning achieved great momentum thanks to the ability to code certain properties into the architecture using Convolutional Neural Networks (CNNs), which are also called ConvNets. The French scientist Yann LeCun and other notable scientists devised the idea of CNNs at the end of the 1980s, and they fully developed their technology during the 1990s. But only now, about 25 years later, are such networks starting to deliver astonishing results, even achieving better performance than humans do in particular recognition tasks. The change has come because it's possible to configure such networks into complex architectures that can refine their learning from lots of useful data.

CNNs have strongly fueled the recent deep learning renaissance. The following sections discuss how CNNs help in detecting image edges and shapes for tasks such as deciphering handwritten text, exactly locating a certain object in an image, or separating different parts of a complex image scene.

REMEMBER

Save yourself the time and mistakes of typing this chapter's example code by hand. You can find the downloadable source for this chapter in the DL4D_10_ LeNet5.ipynb file. (The Introduction tells you where to download the source code for this book.)

Beginning the CNN Tour with Character Recognition

CNNs aren't a new idea. They appeared at the end of the 1980s as the solution for character recognition problems. Yann LeCun devised CNNs when he worked at AT&T Labs Research, together with other scientists such as Yoshua Bengio, Leon Bottou, and Patrick Haffner on a network named LeNet5. Before delving into the technology of these specialized neural networks, this chapter spends time understanding the problem of image recognition.

Digital images are everywhere today because of the pervasive presence of digital cameras, webcams, and mobile phones with cameras. Because capturing images has become so easy, a new, huge stream of data is provided by images. Being able to process images opens the doors to new applications in fields such as robotics, autonomous driving, medicine, security, and surveillance.

Understanding image basics

Processing an image for use by a computer transforms it into data. Computers send images to a monitor as a data stream composed of pixels, so computer images are best represented as a matrix of pixels values, with each position in the matrix corresponding to a point in the image.

Modern computer images represent colors using a series of 32 bits (8 bits apiece for red, blue, green, and transparency — the alpha channel). You can use just 24 bits to create a true color image, however. The article at http://www.rit-mcsl. org/fairchild/WhyIsColor/Questions/4-5.html explains this process in more detail. Computer images represent color using three overlapping matrices, each one providing information relative to one of three colors: Red, Green, or Blue (also called RGB). Blending different amounts of these three colors enables you to represent any standard human-viewable color, but not those seen by people with extraordinary perception. (Most people can see a maximum of 1,000,000 colors, which is well within the color range of the 16,777,216 colors offered by 24-bit color. Tetrachromats can see 100,000,000 colors, so you couldn't use a computer to analyze what they see. The article at `http://nymag.com/scienceofus/2015/02/what-like-see-a-hundred-million-colors.html` tells you more about tetrachromats.)

Generally, an image is therefore manipulated by a computer as a three-dimensional matrix consisting of height, width, and the number of channels — which is three for an RGB image, but could be just one for a black-and-white image. (Grayscale is a special sort of RGB image for which each of the three channels is the same number; see `https://introcomputing.org/image-6-grayscale.html` for a discussion of how conversions between color and grayscale occurs.) With a grayscale image, a single matrix can suffice by having a single number represent the 256-grayscale colors, as demonstrated by the example in Figure 10-1. In that figure, each pixel of an image of a number is quantified by its matrix values.

255	255	170	34	102	238	255	255
255	255	34	0	85	0	170	255
255	204	0	221	255	68	119	255
255	187	51	255	255	119	119	255
255	170	119	255	255	102	119	255
255	187	68	255	238	51	136	255
255	221	17	170	85	51	255	255
255	255	153	34	85	255	255	255

FIGURE 10-1: Each pixel is read by the computer as a number in a matrix.

Given the fact that images are pixels (represented as numeric inputs), neural network practitioners initially achieved good results by connecting an image directly to a neural network. Each image pixel connected to an input node in the network. Then one or more following hidden layers completed the network, finally resulting in an output layer. The approach worked acceptably for small images and to solve small problems, giving way to different approaches for solving image recognition. As an alternative, researchers used other machine learning algorithms or applied intensive feature creation to transform an image into newly processed data that could help algorithms recognize the image better. An example of image feature creation is the Histograms of Oriented Gradients (HOG), which is a computational way to detect patterns in an image and turn them into a numeric matrix. (You can explore how HOG works by viewing this tutorial from the Skimage package: `http://scikit-image.org/docs/dev/auto_examples/features_detection/plot_hog.html`.)

Neural network practitioners found image feature creation to be computationally intensive and often impractical. Connecting image pixels to neurons was difficult because it required computing an incredibly large number of parameters and the network couldn't achieve translation invariance, which is the capability to decipher a represented object under different conditions of size, distortion, or position in the image, as shown in Figure 10-2.

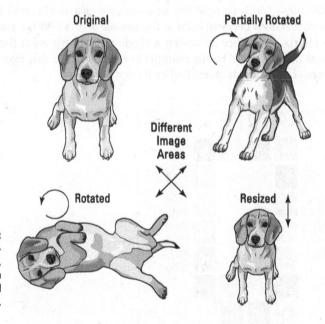

Original   Partially Rotated

Different
Image
Areas

Rotated   Resized

FIGURE 10-2:
Only by transla-
tion invariance,
an algorithm can
spot the dog and
its variations.

A neural network, which is made of dense layers as described in the previous chapters, can detect only images that are similar to those used for training — those that it has seen before — because it learns by spotting patterns at certain image locations. Also, a neural network can make many mistakes. Transforming an image before feeding it to the neural network can partially solve the problem by resizing, moving, cleaning the pixels, and creating special chunks of information for better network processing. This technique, called feature creation, requires expertise on the necessary image transformations, as well as many computations in terms of data analysis. Because of the intense level of custom work required, image recognition tasks are more the work of an artisan than a scientist. However, the amount of custom work has decreased over time as the base of libraries automating certain tasks has increased.

Explaining How Convolutions Work

Convolutions easily solve the problem of translation invariance because they offer a different image-processing approach inside the neural network. The idea started from a biological point of view by observing what happens in the human visual cortex.

A 1962 experiment by Nobel Prize winners David Hunter Hubel and Torsten Wiesel demonstrated that only certain neurons activate in the brain when the eye sees certain patterns, such as horizontal, vertical, or diagonal edges. In addition, the two scientists found that the neurons organize vertically, in a hierarchy, suggesting that visual perception relies on the organized contribution of many single, specialized neurons. (You can find out more about this experiment by reading the article at https://knowingneurons.com/2014/10/29/hubel-and-wiesel-the-neural-basis-of-visual-perception/.) Convolutions simply take this idea and, by using mathematics, apply it to image processing in order to enhance the capabilities of a neural network to recognize different images accurately.

Understanding convolutions

To understand how convolutions work, you start from the input. The input is an image composed of one or more pixel layers, called channels, and the image uses values from 0, which means that the individual pixel is fully switched off, to 255, which means that the individual pixel is switched on. (Usually, the values are stored as integers to save memory.) As mentioned in the preceding section of this chapter, RGB images have individual channels for red, green, and blue colors. Mixing these channels generates the palette of colors as you see them on the screen.

A convolution works by operating on small image chunks across all image channels simultaneously. (Picture a slice of layer cake, with, each piece showing all the layers). Image chunks are simply a moving image window: The convolution window can be a square or a rectangle, and it starts from the upper left of the image and moves from left to right and from top to bottom. The complete tour of the window over the image is called a *filter* and implies a complete transformation of the image. Also important to note is that when a new chunk is framed by the window, the window then shifts a certain number of pixels; the amount of the slide is called a *stride*. A stride of 1 means that the window is moving one pixel toward right or bottom; a stride of 2 implies a movement of two pixels; and so on.

Every time the convolution window moves to a new position, a filtering process occurs to create part of the filter described in the previous paragraph. In this process, the values in the convolution window are multiplied by the values in the *kernel* (a small matrix used for blurring, sharpening, embossing, edge detection, and more — you choose the kernel you need for the task in question). (The article at http://setosa.io/ev/image-kernels/ tells you more about various kernel types.) The kernel is the same size as the convolution window. Multiplying each part of the image with the kernel creates a new value for each pixel, which in a sense is a new processed feature of the image. The convolution outputs the pixel value and when the sliding window has completed its tour across the image, you have *filtered* the image. As a result of the convolution, you find a new image having the following characteristics:

>> If you use a single filtering process, the result is a transformed image of a single channel.

>> If you use multiple kernels, the new image has as many channels as the number of filters, each one containing specially processed new feature values. The number of filters is the *filter depth* of a convolution.

>> If you use a stride of 1, you get an image of the same dimensions as the original.

>> If you use strides of a size above 1, the resulting convoluted image is smaller than the original (a stride of size two implies halving the image size).

>> The resulting image may be smaller depending on the kernel size, because the kernel has to start and finish its tour on the image borders. When processing the image, a kernel will eat up its size minus one. For instance, a kernel of 3 x 3 pixels processing a 7-x-7-pixel image will eat up 2 pixels from the height and width of the image, and the result of the convolution will be an output of size 5 x 5 pixels. You have the option to pad the image with zeros at the border (meaning, in essence, to put a black border on the image) so that the convolution process won't reduce the final output size. This strategy is called *same padding*. If you just let the kernel reduce the size of your starting image, it's called *valid padding*.

Image processing has relied on the convolution process for a long time. Convolution filters can detect an edge or enhance certain characteristics of an image. Figure 10-3 provides an example of some convolutions transforming an image.

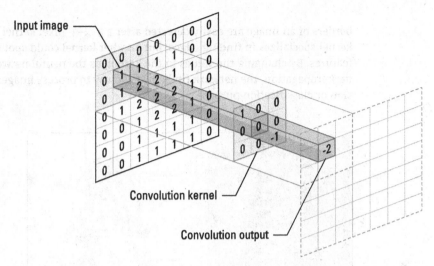

FIGURE 10-3:
A convolution processes a chunk of an image by matrix multiplication.

Input image

Convolution kernel

Convolution output

The problem with using convolutions is that they are human made and require effort to figure out. When using a neural network convolution instead, you just set the following:

>> The number of filters (the number of kernels operating on an image that is its output channels)

>> The kernel size (set just one side for a square; set width and height for a rectangle)

>> The strides (usually 1- or 2-pixel steps)

>> Whether you want the image black bordered (choose valid padding or same padding)

After determining the image-processing parameters, the optimization process determines the kernel values used to process the image in a way to allow the best classification of the final output layer. Each kernel matrix element is therefore a neural network neuron and modified during training using backpropagation for the best performance of the network itself.

Another interesting aspect of this process is that each kernel specializes in finding specific aspects of an image. For example, a kernel specialized in filtering features typical of cats can find a cat no matter where it is in an image and, if you use enough kernels, every possible variant of an image of a kind (resized, rotated, translated) is detected, rendering your neural network an efficient tool for image classification and recognition.

borders of an image are easily detected after a 3-x-3-pixel kernel is applied. This kernel specializes in finding edges, but another kernel could spot different image features. By changing the values in the kernel, as the neural network does during backpropagation, the network finds the best way to process images for its regression or classification purpose.

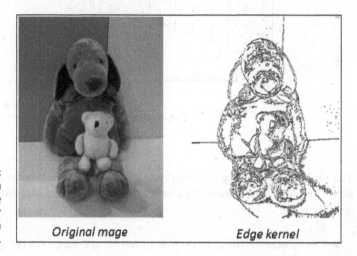

FIGURE 10-4:
The borders of an image are detected after applying a 3-x-3-pixel kernel.

Original mage   *Edge kernel*

TECHNICAL STUFF

The kernel is a matrix whose values are defined by the neural network optimization, multiplied by a small patch of the same size moving across the image, but it can be intended as a neural layer whose weights are shared across the different input neurons. You can see the patch as an immobile neural layer connected to the many parts of the image always using the same set of weights. It is exactly the same result.

Keras offers a convolutional layer, Conv2D, out of the box. This Keras layer can take both the input directly from the image (in a tuple, you have to set the input_shape the width, height, and number of channels of your image) or from another layer (such as another convolution). You can also set filters, kernel_size, strides, and padding, which are the basic parameters for any convolutional layers, as described earlier in the chapter.

TIP

When setting a Conv2D layer, you may also set many other parameters, which are actually a bit too technical and maybe not necessary for your first experiments with CNNs. The only other parameters you may find useful now are activation, which can add an activation of your choice, and name, which sets a name for the layer.

Simplifying the use of pooling

Convolutional layers transform the original image using various kinds of filtering. Each layer finds specific patterns in the image (particular sets of shapes and colors that make the image recognizable). As this process continues, the complexity of the neural network grows because the number of parameters grows as the network gains more filters. To keep the complexity manageable, you need to speed the filtering and reduce the number of operations.

Pooling layers can simplify the output received from convolutional layers, thus reducing the number of successive operations performed and using fewer convolutional operations to perform filtering. Working in a fashion similar to convolutions (using a window size for the filter and a stride to slide it), pooling layers operate on patches of the input they receive and reduce a patch to a single number, thus effectively downsizing the data flowing through the neural network.

Figure 10-5 represents the operations done by a pooling layer, receiving as input the filtered data represented by the left 4-x-4 matrix: operating on it using a window of size 2 pixels and moving by a stride of 2 pixels. As a result, the pooling layer produces the right output: a 2-x-2 matrix. The network applies the pooling operation on four patches represented by four different colored parts of the matrix. For each patch, the pooling layer computes the maximum value and saves it as an output.

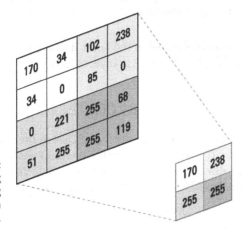

FIGURE 10-5:
A max pooling layer operating on chunks of a reduced image.

The current example relies on the max pooling layer because it uses the max transformation on its sliding window. You actually have access to four principal types of pooling layers:

» Max pooling

» Average pooling

» Global max pooling

» Global average pooling

In addition, these four pooling layer types have different versions, depending on the dimensionality of the input they can process:

» **1-D pooling:** Works on vectors. Thus, 1-D pooling is ideal for sequence data such as temporal data (data representing events following each other in time) or text (represented as sequences of letters or words). It takes the maximum or the average of contiguous parts of the sequence.

» **2-D pooling:** Fits spatial data that fits a matrix. You can use 2-D pooling for a grayscale image or each channel of an RBG image separately. It takes the maximum or the average of small patches (squares) of the data.

» **3-D pooling:** Fits spatial data represented as spatial-temporal data. You could use 3-D pooling for images taken across time. A typical example is to use magnetic resonance imagining (MRI) for a medical examination. Radiologists use an MRI to examine body tissues with magnetic fields and radio waves. (See the article from Stanford AI for healthcare to learn more about the contribution of deep learning: `https://medium.com/stanford-ai-for-healthcare/dont-just-scan-this-deep-learning-techniques-for-mri-52610e9b7a85`.) This kind of pooling takes the maximum or the average of small chunks (cubes) from the data.

You can find all these layers described in the Keras documentation, together with all their parameters, at `https://keras.io/layers/pooling/`.

Describing the LeNet architecture

You may have been amazed by the description of a CNN in the preceding section, and about how its layers (convolutions and max pooling) work, but you may be even more amazed at discovering that it's not a new technology; instead, it appeared in the 1990s. The following sections describe the LeNet architecture in more detail.

Considering the underlying functionality

The key person behind this innovation was Yann LeCun, who was working at AT&T Labs Research as head of the Image Processing Research Department. LeCun specialized in optical character recognition and computer vision. Yann LeCun is a

French computer scientist who created convolutional neural networks with Léon Bottou, Yoshua Bengio, and Patrick Haffner. At present, he is the Chief AI Scientist at Facebook AI Research (FAIR) and a Silver Professor at New York University (mainly affiliated with the NYU Center for Data Science). His personal home page is at http://yann.lecun.com/.

In the late 1990s, AT&T implemented LeCun's LeNet5 to read ZIP codes for the United States Postal Service. The company also used LeNet5 for ATM check readers, which can automatically read the check amount. The system doesn't fail, as reported by LeCunn at https://pafnuty.wordpress.com/2009/06/13/yann-lecun/. However, the success of the LeNet passed almost unnoticed at the time because the AI sector was undergoing an *AI winter:* both the public and investors were significantly less interested and attentive to improvements in neural technology than they are now.

REMEMBER

Part of the reason for an AI winter is that many researchers and investors lost their faith in the idea that neural networks would revolutionize AI. Data of the time lacked the complexity for such a network to perform well. (ATMs and the USPS were notable exceptions because of the quantities of data they handled.) With a lack of data, convolutions only marginally outperform regular neural networks made of connected layers. In addition, many researchers achieved results comparable to LeNet5 using brand-new machine learning algorithms such as Support Vector Machines (SVMs) and Random Forests, which were algorithms based on mathematical principles different from those used for neural networks.

You can see the network in action at http://yann.lecun.com/exdb/lenet/ or in this video, in which a younger LeCun demonstrates an earlier version of the network: https://www.youtube.com/watch?v=FwFduRA_L6Q. At that time, having a machine able to decipher both typewritten and handwritten numbers was quite a feat.

As shown in Figure 10-6, the LeNet5 architecture consists of two sequences of convolutional and average pooling layers that perform image processing. The last layer of the sequence is then flattened; that is, each neuron in the resulting series of convoluted 2-D arrays is copied into a single line of neurons. At this point, two fully connected layers and a softmax classifier complete the network and provide the output in terms of probability. The LeNet5 network is really the basis of all the CNNs that follow. Recreating the architecture using Keras will explain it layer-by-layer and demonstrate how to build your own convolutional networks.

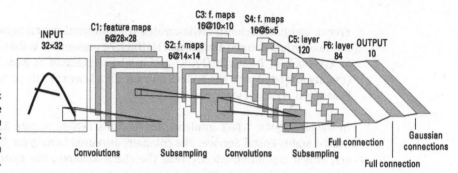

C3: f. maps
16@10×10

S4: f. maps
16@5×5

INPUT
32×32

C1: feature maps
6@28×28

S2: f. maps
6@14×14

C5: layer
120

F6: layer
84

OUTPUT
10

FIGURE 10-6:
The architecture
of LeNet5, a
neural network
for handwritten
digits recognition.

Convolutions   Subsampling   Convolutions   Subsampling

Full connection   Gaussian
connections

Full connection

Building your own LeNet5 network

This network will be trained on a relevant amount of data (the digits dataset provided by Keras, consisting of more than 60,000 examples). You could therefore have an advantage if you run it on Colab, as explained in Chapter 3, or on your local machine if you have a GPU available. After opening a new notebook, you start by importing the necessary packages and functions from Keras using the following code:

```
import keras
import numpy as np
from keras.datasets import mnist
from keras.models import Sequential
from keras.layers import Conv2D, AveragePooling2D
from keras.layers import Dense, Flatten
from keras.losses import categorical_crossentropy
```

After importing the necessary tools, you need to collect the data:

```
(X_train, y_train), (X_test, y_test) = mnist.load_data()
```

The first time you execute this command, the `mnist` command will download all the data from the Internet, which could take a while. The downloaded data consists of single-channel 28-x-28-pixel images representing handwritten numbers from zero to nine. As a first step, you need to convert the response variable (`y_train` for the training phase and `y_test` for the test after the model is completed) into something that the neural network can understand and work on:

```
num_classes = len(np.unique(y_train))
print(y_train[0], end=' => ')
y_train = keras.utils.to_categorical(y_train, 10)
y_test = keras.utils.to_categorical(y_test, 10)
print(y_train[0])
```

This code snippet translates the response from numbers to vectors of numbers, where the value at the position corresponding to the number the network will guess is 1 and the others are 0. The code will also output the transformation for the first image example in the train set:

```
5 => [0. 0. 0. 0. 0. 1. 0. 0. 0. 0.]
```

TIP

Notice that the output is 0 based and that the 1 appears at the position corresponding to the number 5. This setting is used because the neural network needs a response layer, which is a set of neurons (hence the vector) that should become activated if the provided answer is correct. In this case, you see ten neurons, and in the training phase, the code activates the correct answer (the value at the correct position is set to 1) and turns the others off (their values are 0). In the test phase, the neural network uses its database of examples to turn the correct neuron on, or at least turn on more than the correct one. In the following code, the code prepares the training and test data:

```
X_train = X_train.astype(np.float32) / 255
X_test = X_test.astype(np.float32) / 255
img_rows, img_cols = X_train.shape[1:]
X_train = X_train.reshape(len(X_train),
                          img_rows, img_cols, 1)
X_test = X_test.reshape(len(X_test),
                        img_rows, img_cols, 1)
input_shape = (img_rows, img_cols, 1)
```

The pixel numbers, which range from 0 to 255, are transformed into a decimal value ranging from 0 to 1. The first two lines of code optimize the network to work properly with large numbers that could cause problems. The lines that follow reshape the images to have height, width, and channels.

The following line of code defines the LeNet5 architecture. You start by calling the `sequential` function that provides an empty model:

```
lenet = Sequential()
```

The first layer added is a convolutional layer, named "":

```
lenet.add(Conv2D(6, kernel_size=(5, 5), activation='tanh',
        input_shape=input_shape, padding='same', name='C1'))
```

The convolution operates with a filter size of 6 (meaning that it will create six new channels made by convolutions) and a kernel size of 5 x 5 pixels.

The activation for all the layers of the network but the last one is *tanh* (Hyperbolic Tangent function), a nonlinear function that was the state of the art for activation at the time Yann LeCun created LetNet5. The function is outdated today, but the example uses it in order to build a network that resembles the original LetNet5 architecture. To use such a network for your own projects, you should replace it with a modern ReLU (see https://www.kaggle.com/dansbecker/rectified-linear-units-relu-in-deep-learning for details). The example adds a pooling layer, named S2, which uses a 2-x-2-pixel kernel:

```
lenet.add(AveragePooling2D(pool_size=(2, 2), strides=(1, 1),
    padding='valid'))
```

At this point, the code proceeds with the sequence, always performed with a convolution and a pooling layer but this time using more filters:

```
lenet.add(Conv2D(16, kernel_size=(5, 5), strides=(1, 1),
                 activation='tanh', padding='valid'))
lenet.add(AveragePooling2D(pool_size=(2, 2), strides=(1, 1),
    padding='valid'))
```

The LeNet5 closes incrementally using a convolution with 120 filters. This convolution doesn't have a pooling layer but rather a flattening layer, which projects the neurons into the last convolution layer as a dense layer:

```
lenet.add(Conv2D(120, kernel_size=(5, 5), activation='tanh',
    name='C5'))
lenet.add(Flatten())
```

The closing of the network is a sequence of two dense layers that process the convolution's outputs using the tanh and softmax activation. These two layers provide the final output layers where the neurons activate an output to signal the predicted answer. The softmax layer is actually the output layer as specified by name='OUTPUT':

```
lenet.add(Dense(84, activation='tanh', name='FC6'))
lenet.add(Dense(10, activation='softmax', name='OUTPUT'))
```

When the network is ready, you need Keras to compile it. (Behind all the Python code is some C language code.) Keras compiles it based on the SGD optimizer:

```
lenet.compile(loss=categorical_crossentropy, optimizer='SGD',
    metrics=['accuracy'])
lenet.summary()
```

At this point, you can run the network and wait for it to process the images:

```
batch_size = 64
epochs = 50
history = lenet.fit(X_train, y_train,
                    batch_size=batch_size,
                    epochs=epochs,
                    validation_data=(X_test,
                                     y_test))
```

Completing the run takes 50 epochs, each epoch processing batches of 64 images at one time. (An *epoch* is the passing of the entire dataset through the neural network one time, while a *batch* is a part of the dataset, which means breaking the dataset into 64 chunks in this case.) With each epoch (lasting about 8 seconds if you use Colab), you can monitor a progress bar telling you the time required to complete that epoch. You can also read the accuracy measures for both the training set (the optimistic estimate of the goodness of your model, see https://towardsdatascience.com/measuring-model-goodness-part-1-a24ed4d62f71 for details on what precisely goodness means) and the test set (the more realistic view). At the last epoch, you should read that a LeNet5 built in a few steps achieves an accuracy of 0.989, meaning that out every 100 handwritten numbers that it tries to recognize, the network should guess about 99 correctly.

Detecting Edges and Shapes from Images

Convolutions process images automatically and perform better than a densely connected layer because they learn image patterns at a local level and can retrace them in any other part of the image (a characteristic called *translation invariance*). On the other hand, traditional dense neural layers can determine the overall characteristics of an image in a rigid way without the benefit of translation invariance. It's like the difference between learning a book by memorizing the text in meaningful chunks or memorizing it word by word. The student (the convolutions) who learned chunk by chunk can better abstract the book content and is ready to apply that knowledge to similar cases. The student (the dense layer) who learned it word by word struggles to extract something useful.

CNNs are not magic, nor are they a black box. You can understand them through image processing and leverage their functionality to extend their capabilities to new problems. This feature helps solve a series of computer vision problems that data scientists deemed too hard to crack using older strategies.

Visualizing convolutions

A CNN uses different layers to perform specific tasks in a hierarchical way. Yann LeCun (see the "Beginning the CNN Tour with Character Recognition" section, early in this chapter) noticed how LeNet first processed edges and contours, and then motifs, and then categories, and finally objects. Recent studies further unveil how convolutions really work:

>> **Initial layers:** Discover the image edges

>> **Middle layers:** Detect complex shapes (created by edges)

>> **Final layers:** Uncover distinctive image features characteristic of the image type that you want the network to classify (for instance, the nose of a dog or the ears of a cat)

This hierarchy of patterns discovered by convolutions also explains why deep convolutional networks perform better than shallow ones: the more stacked convolutions there are, the better the network can learn more and more complex and useful patterns for successful image recognition. Figure 10-7 provides an idea of how things work. The image of a dog is processed by convolutions, and the first layer grasps patterns. The second layer accepts these patterns and assembles them into a cat. If the patterns processed by the first layer seem too general to be of any use, the patterns unveiled by the second layer recreate more characteristic dog features that provide an advantage to the neural network in recognizing dogs.

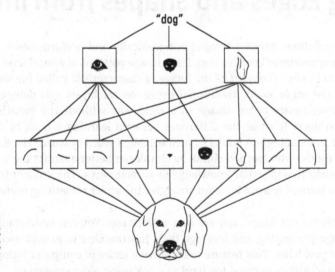

FIGURE 10-7:
Processing a dog image using convolutions.

The difficulty in determining how a convolution works is in understanding how the kernel (matrix of numbers) creates the convolutions and how they work on image patches. When you have many convolutions working one after the other, determining the result through direct analysis is difficult. However, a technique designed for understanding such networks builds images that activate the most convolutions. When an image strongly activates a certain layer, you have an idea of what that layer perceives the most.

TIP

Analyzing convolutions helps you understand how things work, both to avoid bias in prediction and to devise new ways to process images. For instance, you may discover that your CNN is distinguishing dogs from cats by activating on the background of the image because the images you used for the training represents dogs outdoors and cats indoors.

A 2017 paper called "Feature Visualization," by Chris Olah, Alexander Mordvintsev, and Ludwig Schubert from the Google Research and Google Brain Team explains this process in detail (https://distill.pub/2017/feature-visualization/). You can even inspect the images yourself by clicking and pointing at the layers of GoogleLeNet, a CNN built by Google at https://distill.pub/2017/feature-visualization/appendix/. The images from the Feature Visualization may remind you of *deepdream* images, if you had occasion to see some when they were a hit on the web (read the original deepdream paper and glance at some images at https://ai.googleblog.com/2015/06/inceptionism-going-deeper-into-neural.html). It's the same technique, but instead of looking for images that activate a layer the most, you pick a convolutional layer and let it transform an image.

You can also copy the style of works from a great artist of the past, such as Picasso or van Gogh, using a similar technique based on using convolutions to transform an existing image, a process called *artistic style transfer.* The resulting picture is modern, but the style isn't. You can get some interesting examples of artistic style transfer from the original paper, "A Neural Algorithm of Artistic Style," by Leon Gatys, Alexander Ecker, and Matthias Bethge: https://arxiv.org/pdf/1508.06576.pdf.

In Figure 10-8, the original image is transformed in style by applying the drawing and color characteristics found in the Japanese Ukiyo-e "The Great Wave off Kanagawa," a woodblock print by the Japanese artist Katsushika Hokusai, who lived from 1760 to 1849.

FIGURE 10-8:
The content of an image is transformed by style transfer.

Original image

Style image

Resulting image

Unveiling successful architectures

In recent years, data scientists have achieved great progress thanks to deeper investigation of how CNNs work. Other methods have also added to the progress in how CNNs work. Image competitions have played a major role by challenging researchers to improve their networks, which has made large quantities of images available.

The architecture update process started during the last AI winter. Fei-Fei Li, a computer science professor at the University of Illinois at Urbana Champaign (and now chief scientist at Google Cloud as well as professor at Stanford) decided to provide more real-world datasets to better test algorithms for neural networks. She started amassing an incredible number of images representing a large number of object classes. She and her team performed such a huge task by using Amazon's Mechanical Turk, a service that you use to ask people to do microtasks for you (such as classifying an image) for a small fee.

The resulting dataset, completed in 2009, was called ImageNet and initially contained 3.2 million labeled images (it now contains more than 10 million images) arranged into 5,247 hierarchically organized categories. If interested, you can explore the dataset at http://www.image-net.org/ or read the original paper at http://www.image-net.org/papers/imagenet_cvpr09.pdf.

ImageNet soon appeared at a 2010 competition in which neural networks, using convolutions (hence the revival and further development of the technology developed by Yann LeCun in the 1990s), proved their capability in correctly classifying images arranged into 1,000 classes. In seven years of competition (the challenge closed in 2017), the winning algorithms improved the accuracy of predicting images from 71.8 percent to 97.3 percent, which surpasses human capabilities (humans make mistakes in classifying objects). Here are some notable CNN architectures that were devised for the competition:

>> **AlexNet (2012):** Created by Alex Krizhevsky from the University of Toronto. It used CNNs with an 11-x-11-pixel filter, won the competition, and introduced the use of GPUs for training neural networks, together with the ReLU activation to control overfitting.

>> **VGGNet (2014):** This appeared in two versions, 16 and 19. It was created by the Visual Geometry Group at Oxford University and defined a new 3-x-3 standard in filter size for CNNs.

>> **ResNet (2015):** Created by Microsoft. This CNN not only extended the idea of different versions of the network (50, 101, 152) but also introduced *skip layers,* a way to connect deeper layers with shallower ones to prevent the vanishing gradient problem (see Chapters 8 and 9 for more about this problem) and allow much deeper networks that are more capable of recognizing patterns in images.

You can take advantage of all the innovations introduced by the ImageNet competition and even use each of the neural networks. This accessibility allows you to replicate the network performance seen in the competitions and successfully extend them to myriad other problems.

Discussing transfer learning

Networks that distinguish objects and correctly classify them require a lot of images, a long processing time, and vast computational capacity to learn what to do. Adapting a network's capability to new image types that weren't part of the initial training means transferring existing knowledge to the new problem. This process of adapting a network's capability is called *transfer learning,* and the network you are adapting is often referred to as a *pretrained* network. You can't apply transfer learning to other machine learning algorithms; only deep learning has the capability of transferring what it learned on one problem to another.

Transfer learning is something new to most machine learning algorithms and opens a possible market for transferring knowledge from one application to another, and from one company to another. Google is already doing that; it is sharing its immense data repository by making public the networks it built on TF Hub (https://www.tensorflow.org/hub).

For instance, you can transfer a network that's capable of distinguishing between dogs and cats to perform a job that involves spotting dishes of macaroni and cheese. From a technical point of view, you achieve this task in different ways, depending on how similar the new image problem is to the previous one and how many new images you have for training. (A small image dataset amounts to a few thousands of images, sometimes even less.)

If your new image problem is similar to the old one, your network may know all the convolutions necessary (edge, shape, and high-level feature layers) to decipher similar images and classify them. In this case, you don't need to put too many images into training, add much computational power, or adapt your pretrained network too deeply. This type of transfer is the most common application of transfer learning, and you usually apply it by leveraging a network trained during the ImageNet competition (because those networks were trained on so many images that you probably have all the convolutions needed to transfer the knowledge to other tasks).

TIP

Say that the task you want to extend involves not only spotting dogs in images but also in determining the dog's breed. You use the majority of the layers of an ImageNet network such as VGG16 as they are, without further adjustment. In transfer learning, you freeze the values of the pretrained coefficients of the convolutions so that they are not affected by any further training and the network won't overfit to the data you have, if it is too little.

With the new images, you then train the output layers set on the new problem (a process known as fine-tuning). In a short time and with just a few examples, the network will apply what it learned in distinguishing dogs and cats to breeds of dogs. It will perform even better than a neural network trained only to recognize breeds of dogs because in fine-tuning, it is leveraging what the network has learned before from millions of images.

REMEMBER

A neural network will identify only objects that it has been trained to identify. Consequently, if you train a CNN to recognize major breeds of dogs such as a Labrador Retriever or a Husky, the CNN won't recognize mixes of those two breeds, such as a Labsky. Instead, the CNN will output the closest match based on the internal weights it develops during training.

If the task you have to transfer to the existing neural network is different from the task it was trained to do, which is spotting dishes of macaroni and cheese starting from a network used to identify dogs and cats, you have some options:

>> If you have little data, you can freeze the first and middle layers of the pretrained network and discard the final layers because they contain high-level features that probably aren't useful for your problem. Instead of the final convolutions, you then add a response layer suitable to your problem. The fine-tuning will work out the best coefficients for the response layer, given the pretrained convolutional layers available.

» If you have lots of data, you add the suitable response layer to the pretrained network, but you don't freeze the convolutional layers. You use the pretrained weights as a starting point and let the network fit your problem in the best way because you can train on lots of data.

The Keras package offers a few pretrained models that you can use for transfer learning. You can read about all the available models and their architectures at https://keras.io/applications/. The model descriptions also talk about some of the award winning networks mentioned earlier in the chapter: VGG16, VGG19, and ResNet50. Chapter 12 demonstrates how to use these networks in practice and how to transfer the coefficients learned from the ImageNet competition to other problems.

» Creating image captions and translating languages using deep learning

» Discovering the long short-term memory (LSTM) technology

» Knowing about possible alternatives to LSTM

Chapter **11**

Introducing Recurrent Neural Networks

This chapter explores how deep learning can deal with information that flows. Reality is not simply changeable, but is changeable in a progressive way that is made predictable by observing the past. If a picture is a static snapshot of a moment in time, a video, consisting of a sequence of related images, is flowing information, and a film can tell you much more than a single photo or a series of photos can. Likewise for short and long textual data (from tweets to entire documents or books) and for all numeric series that represent something occurring along a timeline (for instance, a series the about sales of a product or the quality of the air by day in a city).

This chapter explains a series of new layers, the recurrent networks, and all their improvements, such as the LSTM and GRU layers. These technologies are behind the most astonishing deep learning applications that you can experiment with today. You commonly see them used on your mobile phone or at home. For example, you use this kind of application when chatting with smart speakers such as Siri, Google Home, or Alexa. Another application is translating your conversation into another language using Google Translate.

Behind each of these technologies are a distinctive neural architecture and application-specific data used for training — some public and some proprietary. Even with these differences in data source and technique, the layers that make everything possible are precisely the same layers that you import from Tensor-Flow and Keras (Chapter 4 tells you about these two deep learning frameworks) and use when coding your applications.

Introducing Recurrent Networks

Neural networks provide a transformation of your input into a desired output. Even in deep learning, the process is the same, although the transformation is more complex. In contrast to a simpler neural network made up of few layers, deep learning relies on more layers to perform complex transformations. The output from a data source connects to the input layer of the neural network, and the input layer starts processing the data. The hidden layers map the patterns and relate them to a specific output, which could be a value or a probability. This process works perfectly for any kind of input, and it works especially well for images, as described in Chapter 10.

After each layer processes its data, it outputs the transformed data to the next layer. That next layer processes the data with complete independence from the previous layers. The use of this strategy implies that if you are feeding a video to your neural network, the network will process each image singularly, one after the other, and the result won't change at all even if you shuffled the order of the provided images. When running a network in such a fashion, using the architectures described in previous chapters of this book, you won't get any advantage from the order of the information processing.

However, experience also teaches that to understand a process, you sometimes have to observe events in sequence. When you use the experience gained from a previous step to explore a new step, you can reduce the learning curve and lessen the time and effort needed to understand each step.

Modeling sequences using memory

The kind of neural architectures seen so far don't allow you to process a sequence of elements simultaneously using a single input. For instance, when you have a series of monthly product sales, you accommodate the sales figures using twelve inputs, one for each month, and let the neural network analyze them at one time. It follows that when you have longer sequences, you need to accommodate them using a larger number of inputs, and your network becomes quite huge because each input should connect with every other input. You end up having a network characterized by a large number of connections (which translates into many weights), too.

Recurrent Neural Networks (RNNs) are an alternative to the solutions found in previous chapters, such as the perceptron in Chapter 7 and CNNs in Chapter 10. They first appeared in the 1980s, and various researchers have worked to improve them until they recently gained popularity thanks to the developments in deep learning and computational power. The idea behind RNNs is simple, they examine each element of the sequence once and retain memory of it so they can reuse it when examining the next element in the sequence. It's akin to how the human mind works when reading text: a person reads letter by letter the text but understands words by remembering each letter in the word. In a similar fashion, an RNN can associate a word to a result by remembering the sequence of letters it receives. An extension of this technique makes it possible ask an RNN to determine whether a phrase is positive or negative—a widely used analysis called *sentiment analysis*. The network connects a positive or negative answer to certain word sequences it has seen in training examples.

You represent an RNN graphically as a neural unit (also known as a *cell*) that connects an input to an output but also connects to itself, as shown in Figure 11-1. This self-connection represents the concept of *recursion*, which is a function applied to itself until it achieves a particular output. One of the most commonly used examples of recursion is computing a factorial, as described at https://www. geeksforgeeks.org/recursion/. The figure shows a specific RNN example using a letter sequence to make the word *jazz*. The right side of the figure depicts a representation of the RNN unit behavior receiving *jazz* as an input, but there is actually only the one unit, as shown on the left.

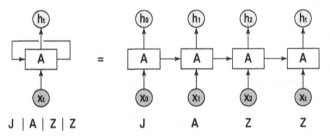

FIGURE 11-1:
A folded and unfolded RNN cell processing a sequence input.

Figure 11-1 shows a recursive cell on the left and expands it as an unfolded series of units that receives the single letters of the word *jazz* on the right. It starts with *j*, followed by the other letters. As this process occurs, the RNN emits an output and modifies its internal parameters. By modifying its internal parameters, the unit learns from the data it receives and from the memory of the previous data. The sum of this learning is the state of the RNN cell.

REMEMBER

When discussing neural networks in previous chapters, this book talks solely about weights. With RNNs, you also need to know the term *state*. The weights help process the input into an output in an RNN, but the *state* contains the traces of the information the RNN has seen so far, so the state affects the functioning of the RNN. The state is a kind of short-term memory that resets after a sequence completes. As an RNN cell gets pieces of a sequence, it does the following:

1. Processes them, changing the state with each input.

2. Emits an output.

3. After seeing the last output, the RNN learns the best weights for mapping the input into the correct output using backpropagation.

Recognizing and translating speech

The capability to recognize and translate between languages becomes more important each day as economies everywhere become increasingly globalized. Language translation is an area in which AI has a definite advantage over humans — so much so that articles like https://www.digitalistmag.com/digital-economy/2018/07/06/artificial-intelligence-is-changing-translation-industry-but-will-it-work-06178661 and https://www.forbes.com/sites/bernardmarr/2018/08/24/will-machine-learning-ai-make-human-translators-an-endangered-species/#535ec9703902 are beginning to question how long the human translator will remain viable.

Of course, you must make the translation process viable using deep learning. From a neural architecture perspective, you have a couple of choices:

>> Keep all the outputs provided by the RNN cell

>> Keep the last RNN cell output

The last output is the output of the entire RNN because it's produced after completing the sequence examination. However, you can use the previous outputs if you need to predict another sequence or you intend to stack more RNN cells after the current one, such as when working with Convolutional Neural Networks (CNNs). Staking RNNs vertically enables the network to learn complex sequence patterns and become more effective in producing predictions.

You can also stack RNNs horizontally in the same layer. Allowing multiple RNNs to learn from a sequence can help it get more from the data. Using multiple RNNs is similar to CNNs, in which each single layer uses depths of convolutions to learn details and patterns from the image. In the multiple RNNs case, a layer can grasp different nuances of the sequence they are examining.

Designing grids of RNNs, both horizontally and vertically, improves predictive performances. However, deciding how to use the output determines what a deep learning architecture powered by RNNs can achieve. The key is the number of elements used as inputs and the sequence length expected as output. As the deep learning network synchronizes the RNN outputs, you get your desired outcome.

You have a few possibilities when using multiple RNNs, as depicted in Figure 11-2:

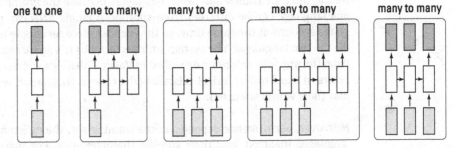

FIGURE 11-2:
Different RNNs input/output configurations.

>> **One to one:** When you have one input and expect one output. The examples in this book so far use this approach. They take one case, made up of a certain number of informative variables, and provide an estimate, such as a number or probability.

>> **One to many:** Here you have one input and you expect a sequence of outputs as a result. Automatic captioning neural networks use this approach: You input a single image and produce a phrase describing image content.

>> **Many to one:** The classic example for RNNs. For example, you input a textual sequence and expect a single result as output. You see this approach used for producing a sentiment analysis estimate or another classification of the text.

>> **Many to many:** You provide a sequence as input and expect a resulting sequence as output. This is the core architecture for many of the most impressive deep learning-powered AI applications. This approach is used for machine translation (such as a network that can automatically translate a phrase from English to German), chatbots (a neural network that can answer your questions and argue with you), and sequence labeling (classifying each of the images in a video).

Machine translation is the capability of a machine to translate, correctly and meaningfully, one human language into another one. This capability is something that scientists have striven to achieve for long time, especially for military purposes. You can read the fascinating story of all the attempts to perform machine translation by U.S. and Russian scientists in the article at http://vas3k.com/blog/machine_translation/ by Vasily Zubarev. The real breakthrough happened only after Google launched its Google Neural Machine Translation (GNMT), which you can read more about on the Google AI blog: https://ai.googleblog.com/2016/09/a-neural-network-for-machine.html. GNMT relies on a series of RNNs (using the many-to-many paradigm) to read the word sequence in the language you want to translate from (called the encoder layer) and return the results to another RNN layer (the decoder layer) that transforms it into translated output.

Neural machine translation needs two layers because the grammar and syntax of one language can be different from another. A single RNN can't grasp two language systems at the same time, so the encoder-decoder couple is needed to handle the two languages. The system isn't perfect, but it's an incredible leap forward from the previous solutions described in Vasily Zubarev's article, greatly reducing errors in word order, lexical mistakes (the chosen translation word), and grammar (how words are used).

Moreover, performance depends on the training set, the differences between the languages involved, and their specific characteristics. For instance, because of how sentence structure is built in Japanese, the Japanese government is now investing in a real-time voice translator to help during the Tokyo Olympic Games in 2020 and to boost tourism by developing an advanced neural network solution (see https://www.japantimes.co.jp/news/2015/03/31/reference/translation-tech-gets-olympic-push/ for details).

REMEMBER

RNNs are the reason your voice assistant can answer you or your automatic translator can give you a foreign language translation. Because an RNN is simply a recurring operation of multiplication and summation, deep learning networks can't really understand any meaning; they simply process words and phrases based on what they learned during training.

Placing the correct caption on pictures

Another possible application of RNNs using the many-to-many approach is *caption generation*, which involves providing an image to a neural network and receiving a text description that explains what's happening in the image. In contrast to chatbots and machine translators, whose output is consumed by humans, caption generation works with robotics. It does more than simply generate image or video descriptions. Caption generation can help people with impaired vision perceive their environment using devices like the Horus wearable (https://horus.tech/horus/?l=en_us) or build a bridge between images and knowledge bases (which are text based) for robots — allowing them to understand their surroundings better. You start from specially devised datasets such as the Pascal Sentence Dataset (see it at http://vision.cs.uiuc.edu/pascal-sentences/); the Flickr 30K (http://shannon.cs.illinois.edu/DenotationGraph/), which consists of Flickr images annotated by crowd sourcing; or the MS Coco dataset (http://cocodataset.org). In all these datasets, each image includes one or more phrases explaining the image content. For example, in the MS Coco dataset sample number 5947 (http://cocodataset.org/#explore?id=5947) you see four flying airplanes that you could correctly caption as:

>> Four airplanes in the sky overhead on an overcast day

>> Four single-engine planes in the air on a cloudy day

>> A group of four planes flying in formation

>> A group of airplanes flying through the sky

>> A fleet of planes flying through the sky

A well-trained neural network should be able to produce analogous phrases, if presented with a similar photo. Google first published a paper on the solution for this problem, named the *Show and Tell network* or *Neural Image Caption* (NIC), in 2014, and then updated it one year later (see the article at https://arxiv.org/pdf/1411.4555.pdf).

Google has since open sourced the NIC and offered it as part of the TensorFlow framework. As a neural network, it consists of a pretrained CNN (such as Google LeNet, the 2014 winner of the ImageNet competition; see the "Describing the LeNet architecture" section of Chapter 10 for details) that processes images similarly to transfer learning. An image is turned into a sequence of values representing the high-level image features detected by the CNN. During training, the embedded image passes to a layer of RNNs that memorize the image characteristics in their internal state. The CNN compares the results produced by the RNNs to all the possible descriptions provided for the training image and an error is computed. The error then backpropagates to the RNN's part of the network to adjust the RNN's weights and help it learn how to caption images correctly. After repeating this process many times using different images, the network is ready to see new images and provide its description of these new images.

Explaining Long Short-Term Memory

The use of short-term memory in RNNs may seem to be able to solve every possible deep learning problem. However, RNNs don't come entirely without flaws. The problem with RNNs arises from their key characteristic, which is the recursion of the same information over time. The same information, passing many times through the same cells, can become progressively dampened and then disappear if the cell weights are too small. This is the so-called *vanishing gradient problem*, when a backpropagated error-correcting signal disappears when passed through a neural network. Because of the vanishing gradient problem, you can't stack too many layers of RNNs or updating them becomes difficult.

REMEMBER

RNNs experience problems that are even more difficult. In backpropagation, the gradient (a correction) deals with the error correction that the networks produce when predicting. The layers before the prediction distribute the gradient to the input layers, and they provide the correct weight update. Layers reached by a small gradient update effectively stop learning.

In fact, the internally backpropagated signals of RNNs tend to disappear after a few recursions, so the sequences that the neural network updates and learns better are the most recent ones. The network forgets early signals and can't relate previously seen signals to more recent input. An RNN, therefore, can easily become too shortsighted, and you can't successfully apply it to problems that require a longer memory.

REMEMBER

Backpropagation in an RNN layer operates both through the layer toward other layers and internally, inside each RNN cell, adjusting its memory. Unfortunately, no matter how strong the signal is, after a while the gradient dampens and vanishes.

Short memory and the vanishing gradient make it hard for RNNs to learn longer sequences. Applications like image captioning or machine translation need a keen memory on all the parts of the sequence. Consequently, most applications require an alternative, and basic RNNs have been replaced by different recurrent cells.

Defining memory differences

Two scientists studied the vanishing gradient problem in RNNs and published a milestone paper in 1997 that proposed a solution for RNNs. Sepp Hochreiter, a computer scientist who made many contributions to the fields of machine learning, deep learning, and bioinformatics, and Jürgen Schmidhuber, a pioneer in the field of artificial intelligence, published "Long Short-Term Memory" in the MIT Press Journal *Neural Computation*.(http://www.bioinf.at/publications/older/2604.pdf). The article introduced a new recurrent cell concept that now serves as the foundation of all the incredible deep learning applications using sequences. Originally refused because it was too innovative (ahead of its time), the new cell concept proposed by the article, named LSTM (short for *long short-term memory*) is used today to perform more than 4 billion neural operations per day, according to Schmidhuber's personal home page (http://people.idsia.ch/~juergen/). LTSM is considered the standard for machine translation and chatbots.

REMEMBER

Google, Apple, Facebook, Microsoft, and Amazon have all developed products around the LSTM technology devised by Hochreiter and Schmidhuber. Products such as smart voice assistants and machine translators would work differently if LSTM were not invented.

The core idea behind LSTM is for the RNN to discriminate the state between short and long term. The state is the memory of the cell, and LSTM separates into different channels:

>> **Short term:** Input data directly mixes with data arriving from the sequence

>> **Long term:** Picks up from short-term memory only the elements that need to be retained for a long time

Moreover, the channel for long-term memory has fewer parameters to tune. Long-term memory uses some additions and multiplications with the elements arriving from the short-term memory and nothing more, making it an almost direct information highway. (The vanishing gradient can't stop the flow of information.)

Walking through the LSTM architecture

LSTMs are arranged around *gates*, which are internal mechanisms that use summation, multiplication, and an activation function to regulate the flow of information inside the LSTM cell. By regulating the flow, a gate can maintain, enhance, or discard the information that has arrived from a sequence in both short- and long-term memory. This flow is reminiscent of an electric circuit. Figure 11-3 shows how an LSTM is structured internally.

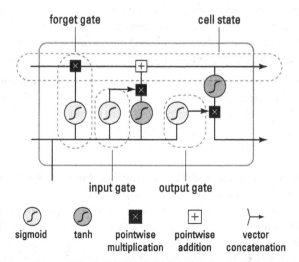

FIGURE 11-3:
The internal structure of an LSTM, with the two memory flows and gates.

The different roots and gates may seem a bit complicated at first, but the following sequence of steps helps you understand them:

1. The short-term memory arriving from a previous state (or from random values) meets the newly inputted part of the sequence and they mix together, creating a first derivation.

2. The short-term memory signal, carrying both the exiting signal and the newly inputted signal, tries to reach the long-term memory by passing through the *forget gate*, which is used to forget certain data. (Technically, you see branching where the signal is duplicated.)

3. The forget gate decides what short-term information it should discard before passing it to the long-term memory. A sigmoid activation cancels the signals that aren't useful and enhances what instead seems important to keep and remember.

4. Information passing through the forget gate arrives at the long-term memory channel carrying the information from the previous states.

5. The values of the long-term memory and the output from the forget gate are multiplied together.

6. The short-term memory that didn't pass through the forget gate is duplicated again and takes another branch; that is, one part proceeds to the output gate and the other one faces the input gate.

7. At the input gate, the short-term memory data passes separately through a sigmoid function and a tanh function. The outputs of these two functions are then first multiplied together, and then added to the long-term memory. The effect on long-term memory depends on the sigmoid, which acts in order to forget or remember if the signal is deemed important.

8. After the addition with the outputs from the input gate, the long-term memory doesn't change. Being made of selected inputs from short-term memory, the long-term memory carries information longer in the sequence and doesn't react to a temporal gap between.

9. Long-term memory provides information directly to the next state. It's also sent to the output gate, where the short-term memory also converges. This last gate normalizes the data from long-term memory using tanh activation and filters the short-term memory using the sigmoid function. The two results are multiplied by one another and then sent to the next state.

TIP

LSTMs use both sigmoid and tanh activations for their gates. The principle to remember is that a tanh function normalizes its input between −1 and 1, and a sigmoid function reduces it between 0 and 1. Therefore, whereas a tanh activation function keeps the input between a workable range of values, a sigmoid can switch the input off because it pushes weaker signals toward zero, extinguishing them. In other words, the sigmoid function helps remembering (enhancing the signal) and forgetting (dampening the signal).

Discovering interesting variants

LSTM has some variants, all called with additional numbers or letters in the name, such as LSTM4, LSTM4a, LSTM5, LSTM5a, and LSMT6, to show that they have a modified architecture although the core concepts of the solution remain. A popular and relevant modification that you find in these variants is the use of *peephole connections,* which are simply data pipelines that allow all or some of the gate layers to look at the long-term memory (in RNN terms, the cell's state). By allowing peeping at long-term memory, the RNN can base decisions for the short term on previously seen patterns that were consolidated in the run. On Keras, you can find the regular LSTM implementation using the `keras.layers.LSTM` command (`keras.layers.CuDNNLST` is the GPU version), which suffices for most applications. If you need to test the peephole variants, you can explore the TensorFlow implementation (see `https://www.tensorflow.org/api_docs/python/tf/nn/rnn_cell/LSTMCell`) that offers more options at the architecture level of the LSTM cell.

Another variant is more radical. The Gated Recurrent Units (also known as GRUs) first appeared in the paper called "Learning Phrase Representations using RNN Encoder-Decoder for Statistical Machine Translation" at `https://arxiv.org/pdf/1406.1078.pdf`. GRUs act as a simplification of the LSTM architecture. In fact, they operate using information gates whose parameters are learnable in the same fashion as LSTM. Overall, the flow of information in a GRU cell takes a linear route because GRU uses only a working memory (equivalent to the long-term memory in LSTM terms). This working memory is refreshed by an *update gate* using the present information provided to the network. The updated information is then summed again with the original working memory in a gate combining the two, which is called a *reset gate* because it selects the working memory information to effectively retain a memory of the data being released to the next sequence step. You can see a simple schema of the flow in Figure 11-4.

Contrary to the LSTM, GRUs use a reset gate that stops the information that should be forgotten. GRUs also use an update gate that maintains the useful signals. GRUs have a unique memory, with no distinction between a long and short one.

You can use both GRUs and LSTM layers in your networks without changing the code too much. Import the layer using `keras.layers.GRU` (or `keras.layers.CuDNNGRU` for the GPU-only version that relies on the NVIDIA CuDNN library; see

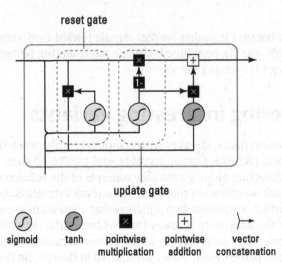

reset gate

update gate

FIGURE 11-4:
The internal
structure of a
GRU, with a single
memory flow a
two gates.

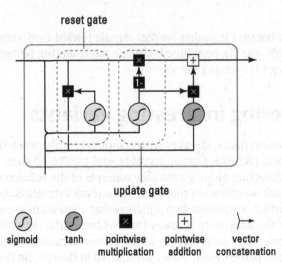 sigmoid   tanh   pointwise   pointwise   vector
                                      multiplication   addition   concatenation

`https://developer.nvidia.com/cudnn` for details) and interact with it as an
LSTM layer. You specify the parameter `units` by defining the number of GRU units
needed in one layer. Switching from LSTM to GRU provides these advantages as
well as some trade-offs:

>> GRUs treat the signals as LSTMs do and potentially avoid the vanishing
gradient problem, but they don't distinguish between long and short memory
because they rely on a single working memory — a cell state processed
repeatedly through a GRU cell.

>> GRUs are less complex than LSTMs, but they are also less capable of remem-
bering past signals, thus LSTMs have an advantage when dealing with longer
sequences.

>> GRUs train faster than LSTMs (they have fewer parameters to adjust).

>> GRUs perform better than LSTMs when you have less training data, because
they are less likely to overfit the information they receive.

Getting the necessary attention

When reading about LSTM and GRU layers applied to language problems, frequently you find the *attention mechanism* mentioned as the most effective way to
solve complex problems, such as

>> Asking a neural network answer questions

>> Classifying phrases

>> Translating a text from one language into another

The attention mechanism is considered the state-of-the-art solution for solving these complex problems and, in spite of being absent from presently available layers in the TensorFlow and Keras packages, finding a working open source implementation of it or even programming one yourself isn't difficult.

TIP

You can start to create your own attention mechanism by looking at the open source implementation developed by Philippe Rémy, a research engineer, at `https://github.com/philipperemy/keras-attention-mechanism`.

First exposed in the paper "Neural machine translation by jointly learning to align and translate," by Dzmitry Bahdanau, Kyunghyun Cho, and Yoshua Bengio in 2014 (`https://arxiv.org/abs/1409.0473v7`), attention layers that implement an attention mechanism are vectors of weights expressing the importance of an element in a set processed by a deep neural network. Often the set of elements includes a sequence processed by RNNs, but it could also be an image. In fact, an attention layer can solve two kinds of problems:

>> When processing long sequences of words, related words might appear far apart in the sequence. For instance, pronouns are typically difficult for RNNs to handle because they can't relate the pronoun to elements passed previously in the sequence. An attention layer can highlight key elements in a phrase before the RNN starts processing the sequence.

>> When processing large images, many objects appearing in the picture can distract the neural network from learning how to classify target objects correctly. An example is when building a network to recognize landmarks in holiday photos. An attention layer can detect what portion of the photo the neural network should process and suggest that the RNN ignore irrelevant elements such as a person, dog, or car present in the picture.

REMEMBER

In a neural network, the attention layer is usually placed following a recurrent layer such as an LSTM or a GRU. In 2017, researchers from Google created a stand-alone attention mechanism that can work without relying on previous recurrent layers and that performs much better than previous solutions. They called such architecture a *Transformer*.

3
Interacting with Deep Learning

IN THIS PART . . .

Learn to classify images.

Work with CNNs.

Discover language processing fundamentals.

Generate visual art and music.

Delve into deep Reinforcement Learning.

Chapter **12**

Performing Image Classification

nderstanding how convolutional layers work, as shown in Chapter 10, is just a starting point. Theory can only explain how things work, but it can't adequately describe the success of deep neural network solutions in the image-recognition field. The great part of this technology's success, especially in AI applications, comes from the availability of suitable data to train and test image networks, their application to different problems thanks to transfer learning, and further sophistication of the technology that allows it to answer complex questions about image content.

In this chapter, you delve into the topic of object classification and detection challenges to discover their contribution in the foundation of the present deep learning renaissance. Competitions, such as those based on the ImageNet dataset, not only provide the right data to train reusable networks for different purposes (thanks to transfer learning, as previously discussed in Chapter 10) but also push researchers to find smarter new solutions for increasing the capability of neural network to understand images. Local response normalization and inception modules are technological solutions too complex to discuss in this book, but you should be aware that they're revolutionary. All were introduced by neural networks that won the ImageNet competition: AlexNet (in 2012), GoogleLeNet (in 2014), and ResNet (in 2015).

Thanks to the German Traffic Sign Benchmark dataset, provided by the Institute für NeuroInformatik at Ruhr-Universität Bochum in Germany, the chapter closes with an example of how to use an image dataset. Using the dataset, you build your own CNN for recognizing traffic signs using image augmentation and weighting for balancing the frequency of different classes in the examples.

REMEMBER

You don't have to type the source code for this chapter manually. In fact, using the downloadable source is a lot easier. The source code for this chapter appears in the DL4D_12_German_Traffic_Sign_Benchmark.ipynb source code file (see the Introduction for details on how to find that source file).

Using Image Classification Challenges

The CNN layers for image recognition were first conceived by Yann LeCun and a team of researchers. AT&T actually implemented LeNet5 (the neural network for handwritten numbers described in Chapter 10) into ATM check readers. However, the invention didn't prevent another AI winter that started in 1990s, with many researchers and investors losing faith again that computers could achieve any progress toward having a meaningful conversation with humans, translating from different languages, understanding images, and reasoning in the manner of human beings.

Actually, expert systems had already undermined public confidence. *Expert systems* are a set of automatic rules set by humans to allow computers to perform certain operations. Nevertheless, the new AI winter prevented neural networks from being developed in favor of different kinds of machine learning algorithms. At the time, computers lacked computational power and had certain limits, such as the vanishing gradient problem. (Chapter 9 discusses the vanishing gradient and other limitations that prevented deep neural architectures.) The data also lacked complexity at the time, and consequently a complex and revolutionary CNN like LeNet5, which already worked with the technology and limitations of the time, had little opportunity to show its true power.

Only a handful of researchers, such as Geoffrey Hinton, Yann LeCun, Jürgen Schmidhuber, and Yoshua Bengio, kept developing neural network technologies striving to get a breakthrough that would have ended the AI winter. Meanwhile, 2006 saw an effort by Fei-Fei Li, a computer science professor at the University of Illinois Urbana-Champaign (now an associate professor at Stanford, as well as the director of the Stanford Artificial Intelligence Lab and the Stanford Vision Lab) to provide more real-world datasets to better test algorithms. She started amassing an incredible number of images, representing a large number of object classes. You can read about this effort in the "Unveiling successful architectures" section of Chapter 10. The proposed classes range through different types of objects, both natural (for instance, 120 dog breeds) and human made (such as means of transportation). You can explore all of them at http://image-net.org/challenges/LSVRC/2014/browse-synsets. By using this huge image dataset for training, researchers noticed that their algorithms started working better (nothing like ImageNet existed at that time) and then they started testing new ideas and improved neural network architectures.

Delving into ImageNet and MS COCO

The impact and importance of the ImageNet competition (also known as ImageNet Large Scale Visual Recognition Challenge, or ILSVRC; http://image-net.org/challenges/LSVRC/) on the development of deep learning solutions for image recognition can be summarized in three key points:

>> **Helping establish a deep neural network renaissance:** The AlexNet CNN architecture (developed by Alex Krizhevsky Ilya Sutskever, and Geoffrey Hinton) won the 2012 ILSVRC challenge by a large margin over other solutions.

>> **Pushing various teams of researchers to develop more sophisticated solutions:** ILSVRC advanced the performance of CNNs. VGG16, VGG19, ResNet50, Inception V3, Xception, and NASNet are all neural networks tested on ImageNet images that you can find in the Keras package (https://keras.io/applications/). Each architecture represents an improvement over the previous architectures and introduces key deep learning innovations.

>> **Making transfer learning possible:** The ImageNet competition helped make the set of weights that made them work available. The 1.2 million ImageNet training images, distributed over 1,000 separate classes, helped create convolutional networks whose upper layers can actually generalize to problems other than ImageNet.

Recently, a few researchers started suspecting that the more recent neural architectures are overfitting the ImageNet dataset. After all, the same test set has been used for many years to select the best networks, as researchers Benjamin Recht, Rebecca Roelofs, Ludwig Schmidt, and Vaishaal Shankar speculate at https://arxiv.org/pdf/1806.00451.pdf.

REMEMBER

Other researchers from the Google Brain team (Simon Kornblith, Jonathon Shlens, and Quoc V.Le) have discovered a correlation between the accuracy obtained on ImageNet and the performance obtained by transfer learning of the same network on other datasets. They published their findings in the paper "Do Better ImageNet Models Transfer Better?" (https://arxiv.org/pdf/1805.08974.pdf). Interestingly, they also pointed out that if a network is overtuned on ImageNet, it could experience problems generalizing. It is therefore a good practice to test transfer learning based on the most recent and best performing network found on ImageNet, but not to stop there. You may find that some less performing networks are actually better for your problem.

Other objections about using ImageNet is that common pictures in everyday scenes contain more objects and that these objects may not be clearly visible when partially obstructed by other objects or because they mix with the background. If you want to use an ImageNet pretrained network in an everyday context, such as when creating an application or a robot, the performance may disappoint you. Consequently, since the ImageNet competition stopped (claiming that improving performance by continuing to work on the dataset wouldn't be possible), researchers have increasingly focused on using alternative public datasets to challenge one's own CNNs and improve the state-of-the-art in image recognition. Here are the alternatives so far:

>> **PASCAL VOC (Visual Object Classes)** http://host.robots.ox.ac.uk/pascal/VOC/: Developed by the University of Oxford, this dataset sets a neural network training standard for labeling multiple objects in the same picture, the PASCAL VOC xml standard. The competition associated with this dataset was halted in 2012.

>> **SUN** https://groups.csail.mit.edu/vision/SUN/: Created by the Massachusetts Institute of technology (MIT), this dataset provides benchmarks to help you determine your CNN performance. No competition is associated with it.

>> **MS COCO** http://cocodataset.org/: Prepared by Microsoft Corporation, this dataset offers a series of active competitions.

In particular, the Microsoft Common Objects in the Context dataset (hence the name MS COCO) offers fewer training images for your model than you find in ImageNet, but each image contains multiple objects. In addition, all objects appear in realistic positions (not staged) and settings (often in the open air and in public settings such as roads and streets). To distinguish the objects, the dataset provides both contours in pixel coordinates and labeling in the PASCAL VOC XML standard, having each object defined not just by a class but also by its coordinates in the images (a picture rectangle that shows where to find it). This rectangle is called a *bounding box*, defined in a simple way using four pixels, in contrast to the many pixels necessary for defining an object by its contours.

The ImageNet dataset has recently started offering, in at least one million images, multiple objects to detect and their bounding boxes.

REMEMBER

Learning the magic of data augmentation

Even if you have access to large amounts of data for your deep learning model, such as the ImageNet and MS COCO datasets, that may be not enough because of the multitude of parameters found in most complex neural architectures. In fact, even if you use techniques such as dropout (as explained in the "Adding regularization by dropout" section of Chapter 9), overfitting is still possible. *Overfitting* occurs when the network memorizes the input data and learns no generally useful data patterns. Apart from dropout, other techniques that could help a network fight overfitting are LASSO, Ridge, and ElasticNet. However, nothing is as effective for enhancing your neural network's predictive capabilities as adding more examples to your training schedule.

REMEMBER

Originally, LASSO, Ridge, and ElasticNet were ways to constrain the weights of a linear regression model, which is a statistical algorithm for computing regression estimates. In a neural network, they work in a similar way by forcing the total sum of the weights in a network to be the lowest possible without harming the correctness of predictions. LASSO strives to put many weights down to zero, thus achieving a selection of the best weights. By contrast, Ridge instead tends to dampen all the weights, avoiding higher weights that can generate overfitting. Finally, ElasticNet is a mix of the LASSO and Ridge approaches, amounting to a trade-off between the selection and dampening strategies.

Image augmentation provides a solution to the problem of a lack of examples to feed a neural network to artificially create new images from existing ones. *Image augmentation* consists of different image-processing operations that are carried out separately or conjointly to produce an image different from the initial one. The result helps the neural network learn its recognition task better.

For instance, if you have training images that are too bright or too blurry, image processing modifies the existing images into darker and sharper versions. These new versions exemplify the characteristics that the neural network must focus on, rather than provide examples that focus on image quality. In addition, turning, cutting, or bending the image, as shown in Figure 12-1, could help because, again, they force the network to learn useful image features, no matter how the object appears.

The most common image augmentation procedures, as shown in Figure 12-1, are

>> **Flip:** Flipping your image on its axis tests the algorithm's capability to find it regardless of perspective. The overall sense of your image should hold even when flipped. Some algorithms can't find objects when upside down or even mirrored, especially if the original contains words or other specific signs.

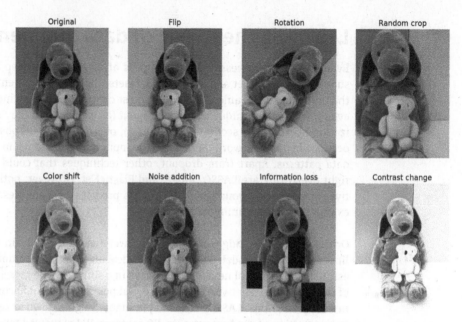

FIGURE 12-1:
Some common
image
augmentations.

>> **Rotation:** Rotating your image allows algorithm testing at certain angles; simulating different perspectives or imprecisely calibrated visuals.

>> **Random crop:** Cropping your image forces the algorithm to focus on an image component. Cutting an area and expanding it to the same size of a standard image enables you to test for recognition of partially hidden image features.

>> **Color shift:** Changing the nuances of image colors generalizes your example because the colors can change or be recorded differently in the real world.

>> **Noise addition:** Adding random noise tests the algorithm's capability to detect an object even when object quality is less than perfect.

>> **Information loss:** Randomly removing parts of an image simulates visual obstruction. It also helps the neural network rely on general image features, not on particulars (which could be randomly eliminated).

>> **Contrast change:** Changing the luminosity makes the neural network less sensible to the light conditions (for instance, to daylight or to artificial light).

You don't need to specialize in image processing to leverage this powerful image-augmentation technique. Keras offers a way to easily incorporate augmentation into any training using the ImageDataGenerator function (https://faroit.github.io/keras-docs/1.2.2/preprocessing/image/).

The `ImageDataGenerator`'s main purpose is to generate batches of inputs to feed your neural network. This means that you can get your data as chunks from a NumPy array using the `.flow` method. In addition, you don't need to have all the training data in memory because the `.flow_from_directory` method can get it for you directly from disk. As `ImageDataGenerator` pulls the batches of images, it can transform them using rescaling (images are made of integers, ranging from 0 to 255, but neural networks work best with floats ranging from zero to one) or by applying some transformations, such as:

>> **Standardization:** Getting all your data on the same scale by setting the mean to zero and the standard deviation to one (as the statistical standardization), based on the mean and standard deviation of the entire dataset (*feature-wise*) or separately for each image (*sample-wise*).

>> **ZCA whitening:** Removing any redundant information from the image while maintaining the original image resemblance.

>> **Random rotation, random shifts, and random flips:** Orienting, shifting, and flipping the image so that objects appear in a different pose than the original.

>> **Reordering dimensions:** Matching the dimensions of data between images. For instance, converting BGR images (a color image format previously popular among camera manufacturers) into standard RGB.

When you use `ImageDataGenerator` to process batches of images, you're not bound by the size of computer memory on your system, but rather by your storage size (for instance, the size of your hard disk) and its speed of transfer. You could even get the data you need on the fly from the Internet, if your connection is fast enough.

TIP

You can get even more powerful image augmentations using a package such as albumentations (`https://github.com/albu/albumentations`). Alexander Buslaev, Alex Parinov, Vladimir I. Iglovikov, and Evegene Khvedchenya created it based on their experience with many image-detection challenges. The package offers an incredible array of possible image processing tools based on the task to accomplish and the kind of neural network you use.

Distinguishing Traffic Signs

After discussing the theoretical grounds and characteristics of CNNs, you can try building one. TensorFlow and Keras can construct an image classifier for a specific delimited problem. Specific problems don't imply learning a large variety of image features to accomplish the task successfully. Therefore, you can easily solve them using simple architectures, such as LeNet5 (the CNN that revolutionized neural image recognition, discussed in Chapter 10) or something similar. This example performs an interesting, realistic task using the German Traffic Sign Recognition Benchmark (GTSRB) found at this Institute für NeuroInformatik at Ruhr-Universität Bochum page: `http://benchmark.ini.rub.de/?section=gtsrb`.

Reading traffic signs is a challenging task because of differences in visual appearance in real-world settings. The GTSRB provides a benchmark to evaluate different machine learning algorithms applied to the task. You can read about the construction of this database in the paper by J. Stallkampand others called "Man vs. computer: Benchmarking machine learning algorithms for traffic sign recognition" at `https://www.ini.rub.de/upload/file/1470692859_c57fac98ca9d02ac701c/stallkampetal_gtsrb_nn_si2012.pdf`.

The GTSRB dataset offers more than 50,000 images arranged in 42 classes (traffic signs), which allows you to create a multiclass classification problem. In a multiclass classification problem, you state the probability of the image's being part of a class and take the highest probability as the correct answer. For instance, an "Attention: Construction Site" sign will cause the classification algorithm to generate high probabilities for all attention signs. (The highest probability should match its class.) Blurriness, image resolution, different lighting, and perspective conditions make the task challenging for a computer (as well as sometimes for a human), as you can see from some of the examples extracted from the dataset in Figure 12-2.

FIGURE 12-2: Some examples from the German Traffic Sign Recognition Benchmark.

Preparing image data

The example begins by configuring the model, setting the optimizer, preprocessing the images, and creating the convolutions, the pooling, and the dense layers, as shown in the following code. (See Chapter 4 for how to work with TensorFlow and Keras.)

```
import numpy as np
import zipfile
import pprint
from skimage.transform import resize
from skimage.io import imread
import matplotlib.pyplot as plt
% matplotlib inline

import warnings
warnings.filterwarnings("ignore")

from keras.models import Sequential
from keras.optimizers import Adam
from keras.preprocessing.image import ImageDataGenerator
from keras.utils import to_categorical
from keras.layers import Conv2D, MaxPooling2D
from keras.layers import (Flatten, Dense, Dropout)
```

TIP

The dataset comprises more than 50,000 images, and the associated neural network can achieve a near-human level of accuracy in recognizing traffic signs. Such an application will require a large amount of computer calculations, and running this code locally could take a long time on your computer, depending on the kind of computer you have. Likewise, Colab can take longer depending on the resources that Google makes available to you, including whether you actually have access to a GPU, as mentioned in Chapter 4. Timing this initial application on your setup will help you know whether your local machine or Colab is the fastest environment in which to run larger datasets. However, the best environment is the one that produces the most consistent and reliable results. You may not have a solid Internet connection to use, making Colab a poorer choice.

At this point, the example retrieves the GTSRB dataset from its location on the Internet (the INI Benchmark website, at the Ruhr-Universität Bochum specified before). The following code snippet downloads it to the same directory as the Python code. Note that the download process can take a little time to complete, so now might be a good time to refill your teacup.

```
import urllib.request
url = "http://benchmark.ini.rub.de/Dataset/\
GTSRB_Final_Training_Images.zip"
filename = "./GTSRB_Final_Training_Images.zip"
urllib.request.urlretrieve(url, filename)
```

After retrieving the dataset as a .zip file from the Internet, the code sets an image size. (All images are resized to square images, so the size represents the sides in pixels.) The code also sets the portion of data to keep for testing purposes, which means excluding certain images from training to have a more reliable measure of how the neural network works.

A loop through the files stored in the downloaded .zip file retrieves individual images, resizes them, stores the class labels, and appends the images to two separate lists: one for the training and one for testing purposes. The sorting uses a hash function, which translates the image name into a number and, based on that number, decides where to append the image.

```python
IMG_SIZE = 32
TEST_SIZE = 0.2
X, Xt, y, yt = list(), list(), list(), list()

archive = zipfile.ZipFile(
                './GTSRB_Final_Training_Images.zip', 'r')
file_paths = [file for file in archive.namelist()
                if '.ppm' in file]

for filename in file_paths:
    img = imread(archive.open(filename))
    img = resize(img,
                output_shape=(IMG_SIZE, IMG_SIZE),
                mode='reflect')
    img_class = int(filename.split('/')[-2])

    if (hash(filename) % 1000) / 1000 > TEST_SIZE:
        X.append(img)
        y.append(img_class)
    else:
        Xt.append(img)
        yt.append(img_class)

archive.close()
```

After the job is completed, the code reports the consistency of the train and test examples.

```python
test_ratio = len(Xt) / len(file_paths)
print("Train size:{} test size:{} ({:0.3f})".format(len(X),
                len(Xt),
                test_ratio))
```

The train size is more than 30,000 images, and the test almost is 8,000 (20 percent of the total):

```
Train size:31344 test size:7865 (0.201)
```

Your results may vary a little from those shown. For example, another run of the example produced a train size of 31,415 and a test size of 7,794. Neural networks can learn multiclass problems better when the classes are numerically similar or they tend to concentrate their attention on learning just the more populated classes. The following code checks the distribution of classes:

```
classes, dist = np.unique(y+yt, return_counts=True)
NUM_CLASSES = len(classes)
print ("No classes:{}".format(NUM_CLASSES))

plt.bar(classes, dist, align='center', alpha=0.5)
plt.show()
```

Figure 12-3 shows that the classes aren't balanced. Some traffic signs appear more frequently than others do (for instance, while driving, stop signs are encountered more frequently than a deer crossing sign).

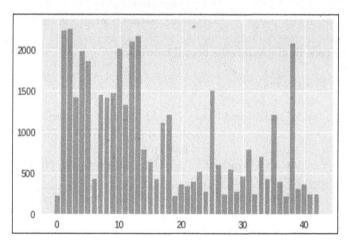

FIGURE 12-3: Distribution of classes.

As a solution, the code computes a *weight*, which is a ratio based on frequencies of classes that the neural network uses to increase the signal it receives from rarer examples and to dump the more frequent ones:

```
class_weight = {c:dist[c]/np.sum(dist) for c in classes}
```

Running a classification task

After setting the weights, the code defines the image generator, the part of the code that retrieves the images in batches (samples of a predefined size) for training and validation, normalizes their values, and applies augmentation to fight overfitting by slightly shifting and rotating them. Notice that the following code applies augmentation only on the training image generator, not the validation generator, because it's necessary to test the original images only.

```
batch_size = 256
tgen=ImageDataGenerator(rescale=1./255,
                        rotation_range=5,
                        width_shift_range=0.10,
                        height_shift_range=0.10)

train_gen = tgen.flow(np.array(X),
                      to_categorical(y),
                      batch_size=batch_size)

vgen=ImageDataGenerator(rescale=1./255)

val_gen = vgen.flow(np.array(Xt),
                    to_categorical(yt),
                    batch_size=batch_size)
```

The code finally builds the neural network:

```
def small_cnn():
    model = Sequential()
    model.add(Conv2D(32, (5, 5), padding='same',
                     input_shape=(IMG_SIZE, IMG_SIZE, 3),
                     activation='relu'))
    model.add(Conv2D(64, (5, 5), activation='relu'))
    model.add(Flatten())
    model.add(Dense(768, activation='relu'))
    model.add(Dropout(0.4))
    model.add(Dense(NUM_CLASSES, activation='softmax'))
    return model

model = small_cnn()
model.compile(loss='categorical_crossentropy',
              optimizer=Adam(),
              metrics=['accuracy'])
```

The neural network consists of two convolutions, one with 32 channels, the other with 64, both working with a kernel of size (5,5). The convolutions are followed by a dense layer of 768 nodes. Dropout (dropping 40 percent of the nodes) regularizes this last layer and softmax activates it (thus the sum of the output probabilities of all classes will sum to 100 percent).

CONSIDERING THE COST OF REALISTIC OUTPUT

As mentioned a few times in this book already, deep learning training can take a considerable amount of time to complete. Whenever you see a fit function in the code, such as model.fit_generator, you're likely asking the system to perform training. The example code will always strive to provide you with realistic output — that is, what a scientist in the real world would consider acceptable.

Unfortunately, realistic output may cost you too much in the way of time. Not everyone has access to the latest high-technology system, and not everyone will get a GPU on Colab. The example in this chapter consumes a great deal of time to train in some cases. For example, in testing the code on Colab, it required a little over 16 hours to complete when Colab didn't provide a GPU. The same example might run in as little as an hour if Colab does provide a GPU. (Chapter 4 tells you more about the GPU issue.) Likewise, using a CPU-only system, a 16-core Xeon system required 4 hours and 23 minutes to complete training, but an Intel i7 processor with 8 cores required a little over 9 hours to do the same thing.

One way around this issue is to change the number of epochs used to train your model. The epochs=100 setting used for the example in this chapter provides an output accuracy of a little over 99 percent. However, if time is a factor, you may want to use a lower epochs setting when running this example to reduce the time you wait for the example to complete.

Another alternative for avoiding the problem is using GPU support on your local machine. However, to use this alternative, you must have a display adapter with the right kind of chip. Because the setup is complex and you're not likely to have the right GPU, this book takes the CPU-only route. However, you can certainly install the correct support by using Chapter 4 as a starting point and then adding CUDA support. The article at https://towardsdatascience.com/tensorflow-gpu-installation-made-easy-use-conda-instead-of-pip-52e5249374bc provides additional details.

On the optimization side, the loss to minimize is the categorical crossentropy. The code measures success on *accuracy*, which is the percentage of correct answers provided by the algorithm. (The traffic sign class with the highest predicted probability is the answer.)

```
history = model.fit_generator(train_gen,
                   steps_per_epoch=len(X) // batch_size,
                   validation_data=val_gen,
                   validation_steps=len(Xt) // batch_size,
                   class_weight=class_weight,
                   epochs=100,
                   verbose=2)
```

Using the `fit_generator` on the model, the batches of images start being randomly extracted, normalized, and augmented for the training phase. After pulling out all the training images, the code sees an *epoch* (a training iteration using a full pass on the dataset) and computes a validation score on the validation images. After reading 100 epochs, the training and the model are completed.

TIP

If you don't use any augmentation, you can train your model in just about 30 epochs and reach a performance of your model that is almost comparable to a driver's skill in recognizing the different kinds of traffic signs (which is about 98.8 percent accuracy). The more aggressive the augmentation you use, the more epochs necessary for the model to reach its top potential, although accuracy performances will be higher, too. At this point, the code plots a graph depicting how the training and validation accuracy behaved during training:

```
print("Best validation accuracy: {:0.3f}"
      .format(np.max(history.history['val_acc'])))

plt.plot(history.history['acc'])
plt.plot(history.history['val_acc'])
plt.ylabel('accuracy'); plt.xlabel('epochs')
plt.legend(['train', 'test'], loc='lower right')
plt.show()
```

The code will report to you the best validation accuracy recorded and plot the accuracy curves achieved on train and validation data during the increasing epochs of learning, as shown in Figure 12-4. Notice how the training and validation accuracies are nearly similar at the end of training, although the validation is always better than the training. That's easily explained because the validation images are actually "easier" to guess than the training images because no augmentation is applied to them.

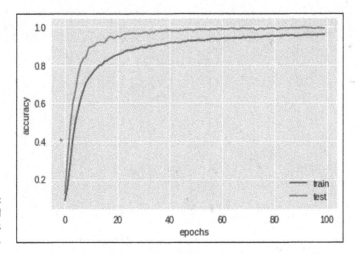

FIGURE 12-4:
Training and
validation errors
compared.

Given the code can initialize the neural network in different ways, you may see different best results at the end of the training optimization. However, by the end of the 100 epochs set in the code, the validation accuracy should exceed 99 percent (sample runs achieved up to 99.5 percent on Colab).

REMEMBER

A difference exists between the performance you obtain on the train data (which is often less) and on your validation subset, because train data is more complex and variable than validation data, given the image augmentations that the code sets up.

TECHNICAL STUFF

You should consider this result to be quite an excellent one based on the state-of-the-art benchmarks that you can read about in the paper called "HALOI, Mrinal. Traffic sign classification using deep inception based convolutional networks (https://arxiv.org/pdf/1511.02992.pdf). The paper hints at what can be easily achieved in terms of image recognition on limited problems using clean data and readily available tools such as TensorFlow and Keras.

Chapter **13**

Learning Advanced CNNs

D eep learning solutions for image recognition have become so impressive in their human-level performance that you see them used in developing or already marketed applications, such as self-driving cars and video-surveillance appliances. The video-surveillance appliances already perform tasks, such as automatic satellite image monitoring, facial detection, and people localization and counting. Yet you can't imagine a complex application when your network labels an image with only a single prediction. Even a simple dog or cat detector may not prove useful when the photos you analyze contain multiple dogs and cats. The real world is messy and complex. You can't expect, except in limited and controlled cases, laboratory style images that consist of single, clearly depicted objects.

The need to handle complex images paved the way for variants of Convolutional Neural Networks (CNNs). Such variants offer sophistication that's still being developed and refined, such as multiple-object detection and localization. Multiple-object detection can deal with many different objects at a time. Localization can tell you where they are in the picture and segmentation can find their exact contours. These new capabilities require complex neural architectures and image processing more advanced than the basic CNNs discussed in previous chapters. This chapter illustrates the fundamentals of how these solutions work, names key approaches and architectures, and finally tests one of the best performing object detection implementations.

The chapter closes by unveiling an expected weakness in an otherwise unbelievable technology. Someone could maliciously trick CNNs to report misleading detections or ignore seen objects using appropriate image-manipulation techniques. This puzzling discovery opens a new research front that shows that deep learning performance must also consider security for private and public use.

Distinguishing Classification Tasks

CNNs are the building blocks of deep learning–based image recognition, yet they answer only a basic classification need: Given a picture, they can determine whether its content can be associated with a specific image class learned through previous examples. Therefore, when you train a deep neural network to recognize dogs and cats, you can feed it a photo and obtain output that tells you whether the photo contains a dog or cat. If the last network layer is a softmax layer, the network outputs the probability of the photo containing a dog or a cat (the two classes you trained it to recognize) and the output sums to 100 percent. When the last layer is a sigmoid-activated layer, you obtain scores that you can interpret as probabilities of content belonging to each class, independently. The scores won't necessarily sum to 100 percent. In both cases, the classification may fail when the following occurs:

>> The main object isn't what you trained the network to recognize, such as presenting the example neural network with a photo of a raccoon. In this case, the network will output an incorrect answer of dog or cat.

>> The main object is partially obstructed. For instance, your cat is playing hide and seek in the photo you show the network, and the network can't spot it.

>> The photo contains many different objects to detect, perhaps including animals other than cats and dogs. In this case, the output from the network will suggest a single class rather than include all the objects.

Figure 13-1 shows image 47780 (http://cocodataset.org/#explore?id=47780) taken from the MS Coco dataset (released as part of the open source Creative Commons Attribution 4.0 License). The series of three outputs shows how a CNN has detected, localized, and segmented the objects appearing in the image (a kitten and a dog standing on a field of grass). A plain CNN can't reproduce the examples in Figure 13-1 because its architecture will output the entire image as being of a certain class. To overcome this limitation, researchers extend the basic CNNs capabilities to make them capable of the following:

FIGURE 13-1:
Detection, localization and segmentation example from the Coco dataset.

Multiple detection   Localization by   Semantic Segmentation
                            bounding boxes

>> **Detection:** Determining when an object is present in an image. Detection is different from classification because it involves just a portion of the image, implying that the network can detect multiple objects of the same and of different types. The capability to spot objects in partial images is called *instance spotting*.

>> **Localization:** Defining exactly where a detected object appears in an image. You can have different types of localizations. Depending on granularity, they distinguish the part of the image that contains the detected object.

>> **Segmentation:** Classification of objects at the pixel level. Segmentation takes localization to the extreme. This kind of neural model assigns each pixel of the image to a class or even an entity. For instance, the network marks all the pixels in a picture relative to dogs and distinguishes each one using a different label (called *instance segmentation*).

Performing localization

Localization is perhaps the easiest extension that you can get from a regular CNN. It requires that you train a regressor model alongside your deep learning classification model. A *regressor* is a model that guesses numbers. Defining object location in an image is possible using corner pixel coordinates, which means that you can train a neural network to output key measures that make it easy to determine where the classified object appears in the picture using a bounding box. Usually a bounding box uses the x and y coordinates of the lower-left corner, together with the width and the height of the area that encloses the object.

Classifying multiple objects

A CNN can detect (predicting a class) and localize (by providing coordinates) only a single object in an image. If you have multiple objects in an image, you may still use a CNN and locate each object present in the picture by means of two old image-processing solutions:

>> **Sliding window:** Analyzes only a portion (called a *region of interest*) of the image at a time. When the region of interest is small enough, it likely contains only a single object. The small region of interest allows the CNN to correctly classify the object. This technique is called *sliding window* because the software uses an image window to limit visibility to a particular area (the way a window in a home does) and slowly moves this window around the image. The technique is effective but could detect the same image multiple times, or you may find that some objects go undetected based on the window size that you decide to use to analyze the images.

>> **Image pyramids:** Solves the problem of using a window of fixed size because it generates increasingly smaller resolutions of the image. Therefore, you can apply a small sliding window. In this way, you transform the objects in the image, and one of the reductions may fit exactly into the sliding window used.

These techniques are computationally intensive. To apply them, you have to resize the image multiple times and then split it into chunks. You then process each chunk using your classification CNN. The number of operations for these activities is so large that rendering the output in real time is impossible.

The sliding window and image pyramid have inspired deep learning researchers to discover a couple of conceptually similar approaches that are less computationally intensive. The first approach is *one-stage detection*. It works by dividing the images into grids, and the neural network makes a prediction for every grid cell, predicting the class of the object inside. The prediction is quite rough, depending on the grid resolution (the higher the resolution, the more complex and slower the deep learning network). One-stage detection is very fast, having almost the same speed as a simple CNN for classification. The results have to be processed to gather the cells representing the same object together, and that may lead to further inaccuracies. Neural architectures based on this approach are Single-Shot Detector (SSD), You Only Look Once (YOLO), and RetinaNet. One-stage detectors are very fast, but not so precise.

The second approach is *two-stage detection*. This approach uses a second neural network to refine the predictions of the first one. The first stage is the proposal network, which outputs its predictions on a grid. The second stage fine-tunes these proposals and outputs a final detection and localization of the objects. R-CNN, Fast R-CNN, and Faster R-CNN are all two-stage detection models that are much slower than their one-stage equivalents, but more precise in their predictions.

Annotating multiple objects in images

To train deep learning models to detect multiple objects, you need to provide more information than in simple classification. For each object, you provide both a classification and coordinates within the image using the annotation process, which contrasts with the labeling used in simple image classification.

Labeling images in a dataset is a daunting task even in simple classification. Given a picture, the network must provide a correct classification for the training and test phases. In labeling, the network decides on the right label for each picture, and not everyone will perceive the depicted image in the same way. The people who created the ImageNet dataset used the classification provided by multiple users from the Amazon Mechanical Turk crowdsourcing platform (ImageNet used the Amazon service so much that in 2012, it turned out to be Amazon's most important academic customer.)

In a similar way, you rely on the work of multiple people when annotating an image using bounding boxes. Annotation requires that you not only label each object in a picture but also must determine the best box with which to enclose each object. These two tasks make the annotation even more complex than labeling and more prone to producing erroneous results. Performing annotation correctly requires the work of more people who can provide a consensus on the accuracy of the annotation.

TIP

Some open source software can help in annotation for image detection (as well as for image segmentation, discussed in the following section). Two tools are particularly effective:

>> LabelImg, created by TzuTa Lin (https://github.com/tzutalin/labelImg) with a tutorial at https://www.youtube.com/watch?v=p0nR2YsCY_U).

>> LabelMe (https://github.com/wkentaro/labelme) is a powerful tool for image segmentation that provides an online service.

>> FastAnnotationTool, based on the computer vision library OpenCV (https://github.com/christopher5106/FastAnnotationTool). The package is less well maintained but still viable.

Segmenting images

Semantic segmentation predicts a class for each pixel in the image, which is a different perspective from either labeling or annotation. Some people also call this task *dense prediction* because it makes a prediction for every pixel in an image.

The task doesn't specifically distinguish different objects in the prediction. For instance, a semantic segmentation can show all the pixels that are of the class cat, but it won't provide any information about what the cat (or cats) are doing in the picture. You can easily get all the objects in a segmented image by *post-processing*, because after performing the prediction, you can get the object pixel areas and distinguish between different instances of them, if multiple separated areas exist under the same class prediction.

Different deep learning architectures can achieve image segmentation. Fully Convolutional Networks (FCNs) and U-NETs are among the most effective. FCNs are built for the first part (called the *encoder*), which is the same as CNNs. After the initial series of convolutional layers, FCNs end with another series of CNNs that operate in a reverse fashion as the encoder (making them a *decoder*). The decoder is constructed to recreate the original input image size and output as pixels the classification of each pixel in the image. In such a fashion, the FCN achieves the semantic segmentation of the image. FCN are too computationally intensive for most real-time applications. In addition, they require large training sets to learn their tasks well; otherwise, their segmentation results are often coarse.

Finding the encoder part of the FCN pretrained on ImageNet, which accelerates training and improves learning performance, is common.

U-NETs are an evolution of FCN devised by Olaf Ronneberger, Philipp Fischer, and Thomas Brox in 2015 for medical purposes (see `https://lmb.informatik.uni-freiburg.de/people/ronneber/u-net/`). U-NETs present advantages compared to FCNs. The encoding (also called *contraction*) and the decoding parts (also referred to as *expansion*) are perfectly symmetric. In addition, U-NETs use shortcut connections between the encoder and the decoder layers. These shortcuts allow the details of objects to pass easily from the encoding to the decoding parts of the U-NET, and the resulting segmentation is precise and fine-grained.

Building a segmentation model from scratch can be a daunting task, but you don't need to do that. You can use some pretrained U-NET architectures and immediately start using this kind of neural network by leveraging the segmentation *model zoo* (a term used to describe the collection of pretrained models offered by many frameworks; see `https://modelzoo.co/` for details) offered by segmentation models, a package offered by Pavel Yakubovskiy. You can find installation instructions, the source code, and plenty of usage examples at `https://github.com/qubvel/segmentation_models`. The commands from the package seamlessly integrate with Keras.

Perceiving Objects in Their Surroundings

Integrating vision capabilities into the sensing system of a self-driving car could enhance how confidently and safely it drives. A segmentation algorithm could help the car distinguish lanes from sidewalks, as well as from other obstacles the car should notice. The car could even feature a complete end-to-end system, such as NVIDIA's, that controls steering, acceleration, and braking in a reactive manner based on its visual inputs. (NVIDIA is a major player in deep learning, and the book mentions it in Chapters 4, 9, and 11 as well. You can learn more about the NVIDIA self-driving car efforts at https://www.nvidia.com/en-us/self-driving-cars/.) A visual system could spot certain objects on the road relevant to driving, such as traffic signs and traffic lights. It could visually track the trajectories of other cars. In all cases, a deep learning network could provide the solution.

The "Distinguishing Classification Tasks" section discusses how object detection improves upon single-object classification offered by CNNs. That section also clarifies the architectures and current models of the two main approaches: one-stage detection (or one-shot detection) and two-stage detection (also known as region proposal). This section tells how a one-stage detection system works and provides help for an autonomous vehicle.

Programming such a detection system from scratch would be a daunting task, one requiring an entire book of its own. Fortunately, you can employ open source projects on GitHub such as Keras-RetinaNet (https://github.com/fizyr/keras-retinanet). Keras-RetinaNet is the Keras implementation of the RetinaNet model proposed by Tsung-Yi Lin, Priya Goyal, Ross Girshick, Kaiming He, and Piotr Dollár in the paper "Focal Loss for Dense Object Detection" published in August 2017 at https://arxiv.org/abs/1708.02002.

TIP

Isaac Newton stated, "If I have seen further, it is by standing on the shoulders of Giants." Likewise, you can achieve more in deep learning when you make use of existing neural architectures and pretrained networks. For instance, you can find many models on GitHub (www.github.com) such as the TensorFlow model zoo (https://github.com/tensorflow/models).

Discovering how RetinaNet works

The RetinaNet is a sophisticated and interesting object-detection model that strives to be as fast as other one-stage detection models while also achieving the accuracy of bounding box predictions of two-stage detection systems like Faster R-CNN (the top-performing model). Thanks to its architecture, RetinaNet achieves its goals, using techniques similar to the U-NET architecture discussed for semantic segmentation. RetinaNet is part of a group of models called Feature Pyramid Networks (FPN).

RetinaNet owes its performance to its authors, Tsung-Yi Lin, Priya Goyal, Ross Girshick, Kaiming He, and Piotr Dollár, who noted that one-stage detection models don't always detect objects precisely because they are affected by the overwhelming presence of distracting elements in the images used for training. Their paper, "Focal Loss for Dense Object Detection (https://arxiv.org/pdf/1708.02002.pdf), provides details of the techniques RetinaNet uses. The problem is that the images present few objects of interest to detect. In fact, one-stage detection networks are trained to guess the class of each cell in an image divided by a fixed grid, where the majority of cells are empty of objects of interest.

REMEMBER

In semantic segmentation, the targets of the classification are single pixels. In one-stage detection, the targets are sets of contiguous pixels, performing a similar task to semantic segmentation but at a different granularity level.

Here's what happens when you have such a predominance of null examples in images and are using a training approach that examines all available cells as examples. The network will be more likely to predict that nothing is in a processed image cell than to provide a correctly predicted class. Neural networks always take the most efficient route to learn, and in this case it's easier to predict the background than anything else. In this situation, which goes under the name of *unbalanced learning*, many objects are undetected by the neural network using a single-shot object detection approach.

In machine learning, when you want to predict two numerically different classes (one is the majority class, and the other one is the minority class), you have an unbalanced classification problem. Most algorithms don't perform properly when the classes are unbalanced because they tend to prefer the majority class. A few solutions are available for this problem:

>> **Sampling:** Selecting some examples and discarding others.

>> **Downsample:** Reducing the effect of the majority class by choosing to use only a part of it, which balances the majority and minority predictions. In many cases, this is the easiest approach.

>> **Upsample:** Increasing the effect of the minority class by replicating its examples many times until the minority class has the same number of examples as the majority class.

The creators of RetinaNet take a different route, as they note in their paper *Focal Loss for Dense Object Detection* mentioned earlier in this section. They discount the majority class examples that are easier to classify and concentrate on the cells that are difficult to classify. The result is that the network cost function focuses more on adapting its weights to recognize background objects. This is the *focal loss* solution and represents a smart way to make one-stage detection perform more correctly, yet speedily, which is a real-time application requirement, such as for obstacle or object detection in self-driving cars, or processing large quantities of images in video surveillance.

Using the Keras-RetinaNet code

Released under the open source Apache License 2.0, Keras-RetinaNet is a project sponsored by the Dutch robotic company Fitz and made possible by many contributors (the top contributors are Hans Gaiser and Maarten de Vries). It's an implementation of the RetinaNet neural network written in Python using Keras (https://github.com/fizyr/keras-retinanet/). You find Keras-RetinaNet used successfully used by many projects — the most notable and impressive of which is the winning model for the NATO Innovation Challenge, a competition whose task was to detect cars in aerial images. (You can read the narrative from the winning team in this blog post: https://medium.com/data-from-the-trenches/object-detection-with-deep-learning-on-aerial-imagery-2465078db8a9.)

Object detection network code is too complex to explain in a few pages, plus you can use an existing network to set up deep learning solutions, so this section demonstrates how to download and use Keras-RetinaNet on your computer. Before you try this process, ensure that you have configured your computer as described in Chapter 4, and consider the trade-offs involved in using various execution options described in the "Considering the cost of realistic output" sidebar in Chapter 12.

As a first step, you upload the necessary packages and start downloading the zipped version of the GitHub repository. This example uses the 0.5.0 version of Keras-RetinaNet, which was the most recent version available at the time of writing.

```
import os
import zipfile
import urllib.request
import warnings
warnings.filterwarnings("ignore")
url = "https://github.com/fizyr/\
keras-retinanet/archive/0.5.0.zip"
urllib.request.urlretrieve(url, './'+url.split('/')[-1])
```

After downloading the zipped code, the example code automatically extracts it using these commands:

```
zip_ref = zipfile.ZipFile('./0.5.0.zip', 'r')
for name in zip_ref.namelist():
  zip_ref.extract(name, './')
zip_ref.close()
```

The execution creates a new directory called keras-retinanet-0.5.0, which contains the code for setting up the neural network. The code then executes the compilation and installation of the package using the pip command:

```
os.chdir('./keras-retinanet-0.5.0')
!python setup.py build_ext --inplace
!pip install .
```

All these commands have just retrieved the code that builds the architecture of the network. The example now needs the pretrained weights and relies on weights trained on the MS Coco dataset using the ResNet50 CNN, the neural network that Microsoft used to win the 2015 ImageNet competition.

```
os.chdir('../')
url = "https://github.com/fizyr/\
        keras-retinanet/releases/download/0.5.0/\
        resnet50_coco_best_v2.1.0.h5"
urllib.request.urlretrieve(url, './'+url.split('/')[-1])
```

Downloading all the weights takes a while, so now it would be a good time to refill your coffee. After this step completes, the example is ready to import all the necessary commands and to initialize the RetinaNet model using the pretrained weights retrieved from the Internet. This step also sets a dictionary to convert the numeric network results into understandable classes. The selection of classes is useful for the detector on a self-driving car or any other solution that has to understand images taken from a road or an intersection.

```
import os
import numpy as np
from collections import defaultdict
import keras
from keras_retinanet import models
from keras_retinanet.utils.image import (read_image_bgr,
        preprocess_image, resize_image)
from keras_retinanet.utils.visualization import (draw_box,
        draw_caption)
from keras_retinanet.utils.colors import label_color
```

```
import matplotlib.pyplot as plt
%matplotlib inline

model_path = os.path.join('.',
          'resnet50_coco_best_v2.1.0.h5')

model = models.load_model(model_path,
          backbone_name='resnet50')

labels_to_names = defaultdict(lambda: 'object',
          {0: 'person', 1: 'bicycle', 2: 'car',
          3: 'motorcycle', 4: 'airplane', 5: 'bus',
          6: 'train', 7: 'truck', 8: 'boat',
          9: 'traffic light', 10: 'fire hydrant',
          11: 'stop sign', 12: 'parking meter',
          25: 'umbrella'})
```

To make the example useful, you need a sample image to test the RetinaNet model. The example relies on a free image from Wikimedia representing an intersection with people expecting to cross the road, some stopped vehicles, traffic lights, and traffic signs.

```
url = "https://upload.wikimedia.org/wikipedia/commons/\
thumb/f/f8/Woman_with_blue_parasol_at_intersection.png/\
640px-Woman_with_blue_parasol_at_intersection.png"
urllib.request.urlretrieve(url, './'+url.split('/')[-1])
```

After completing the image download, it's time to test the neural network. In the code snippet that follows this explanation, the code reads the image from disk and then switches the blue with red image channels (because the image is uploaded in BGR format, but RetinaNet works with RGB images). Finally, the code preprocesses and resizes the image. All these steps complete using the provided functions and require no special settings.

The model will output the detected bounding boxes, the level of confidence (a probability score that the network truly detected something), and a code label that will convert into text using the previously defined dictionary of labels. The loop filters the boxes printed on the image by the example. The code uses a confidence threshold of 0.5, implying that the example will keep any detection whose confidence is at least at 50 percent. Using a lower confidence threshold results in more detections, especially of those objects that appear small in the image, but also increases wrong detections (for instance, some shadows may start being detected as objects).

Depending on your objectives using RetinaNet, you may decide that using a lower confidence threshold is fine. You'll notice that as you lower the confidence, the proportion of the resulting exact guesses (those with near 100 percent confidence) will diminish. Such a proportion is called the *precision* of the detection, and by deciding what precision you can tolerate, you can set the best confidence for your purposes.

```python
image = read_image_bgr('640px-Woman_with_blue_parasol_at_
    intersection.png')
draw = image.copy()
draw[:,:,0], draw[:,:,2] = image[:,:,2], image[:,:,0]

image = preprocess_image(image)
image, scale = resize_image(image)

boxes, scores, labels = model.predict_on_batch(np.expand_
    dims(image, axis=0))
boxes /= scale

for box, score, label in zip(boxes[0], scores[0], labels[0]):
    if score > 0.5:
        color = label_color(label)
        b = box.astype(int)
        draw_box(draw, b, color=color)
        caption = "{} {:.3f}".format(labels_to_names[label],
    score)
        draw_caption(draw, b, caption.upper())

plt.figure(figsize=(12, 6))
plt.axis('off')
plt.imshow(draw)
plt.show()
```

It may take a while the first time you run the code, but after some computations, you should obtain the output reproduced in Figure 13-2.

The network can successfully detect various objects, some extremely small (such as a person in the background), some partially shown (such as the nose of a car on the right of the image). Each detected object is delimited by its bounding box, which creates a large range of possible applications.

FIGURE 13-2:
Object detection
resulting from
Keras-RetinaNet.

For instance, you could use the network to detect that an umbrella — or some object — is being used by a person. When processing the results, you can relate the fact that two bounding boxes are overlapping, with one being an umbrella and the other one being a person, and that the first box is positioned on top of the second in order to infer that a person is holding an umbrella. This is called *visual relationship detection*. In the same way, by the overall setting of detected objects and their relative positions, you can train a second deep learning network to infer an overall description of the scene.

Overcoming Adversarial Attacks on Deep Learning Applications

As deep learning finds many applications in self-driving cars, such as detecting and interpreting traffic signs and lights; detecting the road and its lanes; detecting crossing pedestrians and other vehicles; controlling the car by steering and braking in an end-to-end approach to automatic driving; and so on, questions may arise about the safety of a self-driving car. driving isn't the only common activity that's undergoing a revolution. because of deep learning applications. Recently introduced applications that are accessible by the public include facial recognition for security access. (You can read about this use in ATMs in China at https://www.telegraph.co.uk/news/worldnews/asia/china/11643314/ China-unveils-worlds-first-facial-recognition-ATM.html.) Another example of a deep learning application is in speech recognition used for Voice

Controllable Systems (VCSs), as provided by a plethora of companies such as Apple, Amazon, Microsoft, and Google in a wide variety of applications that include Siri, Alexa, and Google Home.

Some of these deep learning applications may cause economic damage or even be life threatening when they fail to provide the correct answer. Therefore, you may be surprised to discover that hackers can intentionally trick deep neural networks and guide them into failing predictions by using particular techniques called adversarial examples.

An *adversarial example* is a handcrafted piece of data that is processed by a neural network as training or test inputs. A hacker modifies the data to force the algorithm to fail in its task. Each adversarial example bears modifications that are indeed slight, subtle, and deliberately made imperceptible to humans. The modifications, while ineffective on humans, are still quite effective in reducing the effectiveness and usefulness of a neural network. Often, such malicious examples aim at leading a neural network to fail in a predictable way to create some illegal advantage for the hacker. Here are just a few malicious uses of adversarial examples (the list is far from exhaustive):

>> Misleading a self-driving car into a accident

>> Obtaining money from an insurance fraud by having fake claim photos trusted as true ones by automatic systems

>> Tricking a facial recognition system to recognize the wrong face and grant access to money in a bank account or personal data on a mobile device

REMEMBER

Chapter 16 discusses generative adversarial networks (GANs) and adversarial training, which have a completely different purpose than adversarial examples. These techniques are a way to train a deep neural network to generate new examples of any kind from it.

Tricking pixels

First made known by the paper "Intriguing Properties of Neural Networks" (go to https://arxiv.org/pdf/1312.6199.pdf), adversarial examples have attracted much attention in recent years, and successful (and shocking) discoveries in the field have led many researchers to devise faster and more effective ways of creating such examples than the original paper pointed out.

DISCOVERING THAT A MUFFIN IS NOT A CHIHUAHUA

Sometimes deep learning image classification fails to provide the right answer because the target image is inherently ambiguous or rendered to puzzle observers. For instance, some images are so misleading that they can even mystify a human examiner for a while, such as the Internet memes Chihuahua versus Muffin (see https://imgur.com/QWQiBYU) or Labradoodle versus Fried Chicken (see https://imgur.com/5EnWOJU). A neural network can misunderstand confusing images if its architecture isn't adequate to the task and its training hasn't been exhaustive in terms of seen examples. The AI technology columnist Mariya Yao has compared different computer vision APIs at https://medium.freecodecamp.org/chihuahua-or-muffin-my-search-for-the-best-computer-vision-api-cbda4d6b425d) and found that even full-fledged vision products can be tricked by ambiguous pictures.

Recently, other studies have challenged deep neural networks by proposing unexpected perspectives of known objects. In the paper called "Strike (with) a Pose: Neural Networks Are Easily Fooled by Strange Poses of Familiar Objects at https://arxiv.org/pdf/1811.11553.pdf, researchers found that simple ambiguity can trick state-of-the-art image classifiers and object detectors trained on large-scale image datasets. Often, objects are learned by neural networks from pictures taken in *canonical poses* (which means in common and usual situations). When faced with an object in an unusual pose or outside its usual environment, some neural networks can't categorize the resulting object. For instance, you expect a school bus to be running on the road, but if you rotate and twist it in the air and then land it in the middle of the road, a neural network can easily see it as a garbage truck, a punching bag, or even a snowplow. You may argue that the misclassification occurs because of learning bias (teaching a neural network using only images in canonical poses). Yet that implies that at present, you shouldn't rely such technology under all circumstances, especially, as the authors of the paper pointed out, in self-driving car applications because objects may suddenly appear on the road in new poses or circumstances.

REMEMBER

Adversarial examples are still confined to deep learning research laboratories. For this reason, you find many scientific papers quoted in these paragraphs when referring to various kinds of examples. However, you should never discount adversarial examples as being some kind of academic diversion because their potential for damage is high.

At the foundations of all these approaches the idea that mixing some numeric information, called a perturbation, with the image can lead a neural network to behave differently from expectations, although in a controlled way. When you create an adversarial example, you add some specially devised noise (looking as what appears to be random numbers) to an existing image, and that's enough to trick most CNNs (because often the same trick works with different architectures when trained by the same data). Generally, you can discover such perturbations by having access to the model (its architecture and weights). You then exploit its backpropagation algorithm to systematically discover the best set of numeric information to add to an image so that you can mutate one predicted class into another one.

TIP

You can create the perturbation effect by changing a single pixel in an image. Researchers have obtained perfectly working adversarial examples using this approach, as discovered by researchers from Kyushu University and described in their paper "One Pixel Attack for Fooling Deep Neural Networks" (https://arxiv.org/pdf/1710.08864.pdf).

Hacking with stickers and other artifacts

Most adversarial examples are laboratory experiments on vision robustness, and those examples can demonstrate all their capabilities because they are produced by directly modifying data inputs and tested images during the training phase. However, many applications based on deep learning operate in the real world, and the use of laboratory techniques don't prevent malicious attacks. Such attacks don't need access to the underlying neural model to be effective. Some examples may take the form of a sticker or an inaudible sound that the neural network doesn't know how to handle.

A paper called "Adversarial Examples in the Physical World" (found at https://arxiv.org/pdf/1607.02533.pdf) demonstrates that various attacks are also possible in a nonlaboratory setting. All you need is to print the adversarial examples and show them to the camera feeding the neural network (for instance, by using the camera in a mobile phone). This approach demonstrates that the efficacy of an adversarial example is not strictly due to the numerical input fed into a neural network. It's the ensemble of shapes, colors, and contrast present in the image that achieves the trick, and you don't need any direct access to the neural model to find out what ensemble works best. You can see how a network could mistake the image of a washing machine for a safe or a loudspeaker directly from this video made by the authors who tricked the TensorFlow camera demo, an application for mobile devices that performs on-the-fly image classification: https://www.youtube.com/watch?v=zQ_uMenoBCk.

Other researchers from Carnegie Mellon University have found a way to trick face detection into believing a person is a celebrity by fabricating eyeglass frames that can affect how a deep neural network recognizes instances. As automated security systems become widespread, the ability to trick the system by using simple add-ons like eyeglasses could turn into a serious security threat. A paper called "Accessorize to a Crime: Real and Stealthy Attacks on State-of-the-Art Face Recognition" (https://www.cs.cmu.edu/~sbhagava/papers/face-rec-ccs16.pdf) describes how accessories could allow both dodging personal recognition and impersonation.

Finally, another disturbing real-world use of an adversarial example appears in the paper "Robust Physical-World Attacks on Deep Learning Visual Classification" (https://arxiv.org/pdf/1707.08945.pdf). Plain black-and-white stickers placed on a stop sign can affect how a self-driving car understands the signal, misunderstanding it for another road indication. When you use more colorful (but also more noticeable) stickers, such as the ones described in the paper "Adversarial Patch" (https://arxiv.org/pdf/1712.09665.pdf), you can guide the predictions of a neural network in a particular direction by having it ignore anything but the sticker and its misleading information. As explained in the paper, a neural network could predict a banana to be anything else just by placing a proper deceitful sticker nearby.

At this point, you may wonder whether any defense against adversarial examples is possible, or if sooner or later they will destroy the public confidence in deep learning applications, especially in the self-driving car field. By intensely studying how to mislead a neural network, researchers are also finding how to protect it against any misuse. First, neural networks can approximate any function. If the neural networks are complex enough, they can also determine by themselves how to rule out adversarial examples when taught by other examples. Second, novel techniques such as constraining the values in a neural network or reducing the neural network size after training it (a technique called *distillation,* used previously to make a network viable on devices with little memory) have been successfully tested against many different kinds of adversarial attacks.

Chapter **14**

Working on Language Processing

Acomputer can't understand language; it only processes language for specific applications. In addition, a computer can't process language unless it's highly formal and precise, such as a programming language. Rigid syntax rules and grammar enables a computer to turn a program written by a developer in a computer language like Python into the machine language that determines what tasks the computer will perform. Human language is not at all similar to a computer's language. Human language often lacks a precise structure and is full of errors, contradictions, and ambiguities, yet it works well for humans, with some effort on the part of the hearer, to serve human society and the progress of knowledge.

Programming a computer to process human language is therefore a daunting task, which is only recently possible using Natural Language Processing (NLP), deep learning Recurrent Neural Networks (RNNs), and word embeddings. *Word embeddings* is the name of the language-modeling and feature-learning technique in NLP that maps vocabulary to real number vectors using products like Word-2vec, GloVe, and fastText. You also see it used in pretrained networks such as Google's open-sourced BERT. In this chapter, you start with the basics needed to understand NLP and see how it can serve you in building better deep learning models for language problems. The chapter then explains word embeddings, how pretrained networks will revolutionize deep learning, and how computers can communicate through chatbots. The chapter closes with an example of a deep learning model applied sentiment analysis that discovers opinions in text.

REMEMBER

You don't have to type the source code for this chapter manually. In fact, it's a lot easier if you use the downloadable source. The source code for this chapter appears in the `DL4D_14_Processing_Language.ipynb` and `DL4D_14_Movie_Sentiment.ipynb` source code files (see the Introduction for details on how to find those source files).

Processing Language

As a simplification, you can view language as a sequence of words made of letters (as well as punctuation marks, symbols, emoticons, and so on). Deep learning processes language best by using layers of RNNs, such as LSTM or GRU (see Chapter 11). However, knowing to use RNNs doesn't tell you how to use sequences as inputs; you need to determine the kind of sequences. In fact, deep learning networks accept only numeric input values. Computers encode letter sequences that you understand into numbers according to a protocol, such as Unicode Transformation Format-8 bit (UTF-8). UTF-8 is the most widely used encoding. (You can read the primer about encodings at `https://www.alexreisner.com/code/character-encoding`.)

REMEMBER

Deep learning can also process textual data using Convolutional Neural Networks (CNNs) instead of RNNs by representing sequences as matrices (similar to image processing). Keras supports CNN layers, such as the `Conv1D` (`https://keras.io/layers/convolutional/`), which can operate on ordered features in time — that is, sequences of words or other signals. The 1D convolution output is usually followed by a `MaxPooling1D` layer that summarizes the outputs. CNNs applied to sequences find a limit in their insensitivity to the global order of the sequence. (They tend to spot local patterns.) For this reason, they're best used in sequence processing in combination with RNNs, not as their replacement.

Natural Language Processing (NLP) consists of a series of procedures that improve the processing of words and phrases for statistical analysis, machine learning algorithms, and deep learning. NLP owes its roots to computational linguistics that powered AI rule-based systems, such as expert systems, which made decisions based on a computer translation of human knowledge, experience, and way of thinking. NLP digested textual information, which is unstructured, into more structured data so that expert systems could easily manipulate and evaluate it. Deep learning has taken the upper hand today, and expert systems are limited to specific applications in which interpretability and control of decision processes are paramount (for instance, in medical applications and driving behavior decision systems on some self-driving cars). Yet, the NLP pipeline is still quite relevant for many deep learning applications.

Defining understanding as tokenization

In an NLP pipeline, the first step is to obtain raw text. Usually you store it in memory or access it from disk. When the data is too large to fit in memory, you maintain a pointer to it on disk (such as the directory name and the filename). In the following example, you use three documents (represented by string variables) stored in a list (the document container is the *corpus* in computational linguistics):

```
import numpy as np

texts = ["My dog gets along with cats",
         "That cat is vicious",
         "My dog is happy when it is lunch"]
```

After obtaining the text, you process it. As you process each phrase, you extract the relevant features from the text (you usually create a *bag-of-words* matrix) and pass everything to a learning model, such as a deep learning algorithm. During text processing, you can use different transformations to manipulate the text (with tokenization being the only mandatory transformation):

>> **Normalization:** Remove capitalization.

>> **Cleaning:** Remove nontextual elements such as punctuation and numbers.

>> **Tokenization:** Split a sentence into individual words.

>> **Stop word removal:** Remove common, uninformative words that don't add meaning to the sentence, such as the articles *the* and *a*. Removing negations such as *not* could be detrimental if you want to guess the sentiment.

>> **Stemming:** Reduce a word to its stem (which is the word form before adding inflectional affixes, as you can read here: https://www.thoughtco.com/ stem-word-forms-1692141). An algorithm, called a stemmer, can do this based on a series of rules.

>> **Lemmatization:** Transform a word into its dictionary form (the lemma). It's an alternative to stemming, but it's more complex because you don't use an algorithm. Instead, you use a dictionary to convert every word into its lemma.

>> **Pos-tagging:** Tag every word in a phrase with its grammatical role in the sentence (such as tagging a word as a verb or as a noun).

>> **N-grams:** Associate every word with a certain number (the *n* in n-gram), of following words and treat them as a unique set. Usually, *bi-grams* (a series of two adjacent elements or tokens) and *tri-grams* (a series of three adjacent elements or tokens) work the best for analysis purposes.

To achieve these transformations, you may need a specialized Python package such as NLTK (http://www.nltk.org/api/nltk.html) or Scikit-learn (see the tutorial at https://scikit-learn.org/stable/tutorial/text_analytics/working_with_text_data.html). When working with deep learning and a large number of examples, you need only basic transformations: normalization, cleaning, and tokenization. The deep learning layers can determine what information to extract and process. When working with few examples, you do need to provide as much NLP processing as possible to help the deep learning network determine what to do in spite of the little guidance provided by the few examples.

TIP

Keras offers a function, keras.preprocessing.text.Tokenizer, that normalizes (using the lower parameter set to True), cleans (the filters parameter contains a string of the characters to remove, usually these: '!"#$%&()*+,-./:;<=>?@[\]^_`{|}~ ') and tokenizes.

Putting all the documents into a bag

After processing the text, you have to extract the relevant features, which means transforming the remaining text into numeric information for the neural network to process. This is commonly done using the bag-of-words approach, which is obtained by frequency encoding or binary encoding the text. This process equates to transforming each word into a matrix column as wide as the number of words you need to represent. The following example shows how to achieve this process and what it implies. The example uses the texts list instantiated earlier in the chapter. As a first step, you prepare a basic normalization and tokenization using a few Python commands to determine the word vocabulary size for processing:

```
unique_words = set(word.lower() for phrase in texts for
                   word in phrase.split(" "))
print(f"There are {len(unique_words)} unique words")
```

The code reports 14 words. You now proceed to load the Tokenizer function from Keras and set it to process the text by providing the expected vocabulary size:

```
from keras.preprocessing.text import Tokenizer
vocabulary_size = len(unique_words) + 1
tokenizer = Tokenizer(num_words=vocabulary_size)
```

TIP

Using a `vocabulary_size` that's too small may exclude important words from the learning process. One that's too large may uselessly consume computer memory. You need to provide `Tokenizer` with a correct estimate of the number of distinct words contained in the list of texts. You also always add 1 to the `vocabulary_size` to provide an extra word for the start of a phrase (a term that helps the deep learning network). At this point, `Tokenizer` maps the words present in the texts to indexes, which are numeric values representing the words in text:

```
tokenizer.fit_on_texts(texts)
print(tokenizer.index_word)
```

The resulting indexes are as follows:

```
{1: 'is', 2: 'my', 3: 'dog', 4: 'gets', 5: 'along',
 6: 'with', 7: 'cats', 8: 'that', 9: 'cat', 10: 'vicious',
 11: 'happy', 12: 'when', 13: 'it', 14: 'lunch'}
```

The indexes represent the column number that houses the word information:

```
print(tokenizer.texts_to_matrix(texts))
```

Here's the resulting matrix:

```
[[0. 0. 1. 1. 1. 1. 1. 1. 0. 0. 0. 0. 0. 0. 0.]
 [0. 1. 0. 0. 0. 0. 0. 0. 1. 1. 1. 0. 0. 0. 0.]
 [0. 1. 1. 1. 0. 0. 0. 0. 0. 0. 0. 1. 1. 1. 1.]]
```

The matrix consists of 15 columns (14 words plus the start of phrase pointer) and three rows, representing the three processed texts. This is the text matrix to process using a shallow neural network (RNNs require a different format, as discussed later), which is always sized as `vocabulary_size` by the number of texts.

The numbers inside the matrix represent the number of times a word appears in the phrase. This isn't the only representation possible, though. Here are the others:

» **Frequency encoding:** Counts the number of word appearances in the phrase.

» **one-hot encoding or binary encoding:** Notes the presence of a word in a phrase, no matter how many times it appear.

» **Term Frequency-Inverse Document Frequency (TF-IDF) score:** Encodes a measure relative to how many times a word appears in a document relative to the overall number of words in the matrix. (Words with higher scores are more distinctive; words with lower scores are less informative.)

You can use the TF-IDF transformation from Keras directly. The `Tokenizer` offers a method, `texts_to_matrix`, that by default encodes your text and transforms it into a matrix in which the columns are your words, the rows are your texts, and the values are the word frequency within a text. If you apply the transformation by specifying `mode='tfidf'`, the transformation uses TF-IDF instead of word frequencies to fill the matrix values:

```
print(np.round(tokenizer.texts_to_matrix(texts,
                                mode='tfidf'), 1))
```

Note that by using a matrix representation, no matter whether you use binary, frequency, or the more sophisticated TF-IDF, you have lost any sense of word ordering that exists in the phrase. During processing, the words scatter in different columns, and the neural network can't guess the word order in a phrase. This lack of order is why you call it a bag-of-words approach. The bag-of-words approach is used in many machine learning algorithms, often with results ranging from good to fair, and you can apply it to a neural network using dense architecture layers. Transformations of words encoded into `n_grams` (discussed in the previous paragraph as an NLP processing transformation) provide some more information, but again, you can't relate the words.

RNNs keep track of sequences, so they still use one-hot encoding, but they don't encode the entire phrase, rather, they individually encode each token (which could be a word, a character, or even a bunch of characters). For this reason, they expect a sequence of indexes representing the phrase:

```
print(tokenizer.texts_to_sequences(texts))
```

As each phrase passes to a neural network input as a sequence of index numbers, the number is turned into a one-hot encoded vector. The one-hot encoded vectors are then fed into the RNN's layers one at a time, making them easy to learn. For instance, here's the transformation of the first phrase in the matrix:

```
[[0. 0. 1. 0. 0. 0. 0. 0. 0. 0. 0. 0. 0. 0. 0. 0.]
 [0. 0. 0. 1. 0. 0. 0. 0. 0. 0. 0. 0. 0. 0. 0. 0.]
 [0. 0. 0. 0. 1. 0. 0. 0. 0. 0. 0. 0. 0. 0. 0. 0.]
 [0. 0. 0. 0. 0. 1. 0. 0. 0. 0. 0. 0. 0. 0. 0. 0.]
 [0. 0. 0. 0. 0. 0. 1. 0. 0. 0. 0. 0. 0. 0. 0. 0.]
 [0. 0. 0. 0. 0. 0. 0. 1. 0. 0. 0. 0. 0. 0. 0. 0.]]
```

In this representation, you get a distinct matrix for each piece of text. Each matrix represents the individual texts as distinct words using columns, but now the rows represent the word appearance order. (The first row is the first word, the second row is the second word, and so on.)

Memorizing Sequences that Matter

Working with TF-IDF and n-grams (either of letters or words) enables you to create language models using few examples. Encoding phrases as sequences of single word one-hot encodings helps you effectively use RNNs. However, a better way to process textual data with greater speed (a way that creates powerful deep learning models) is by using embeddings.

Embeddings have a long history. The concept of embeddings appeared in statistical multivariate analysis under the name of multivariate correspondence analysis. Since the 1970s, Jean-Paul Benzécri, a French statistician and linguist, along with many other French researchers from the French School of Data Analysis discovered how to map a limited set of words into low-dimensional spaces (usually 2-D representations, such as a topographic map). This process turns words into meaningful numbers and projections, a discovery that brought about many applications in linguistics and in the social sciences and paved the way for the recent advancements in language processing using deep learning.

Understanding semantics by word embeddings

Neural networks are incredibly fast at processing data and finding the right weights to achieve the best predictions, and so are all the deep learning layers discussed so far: from CNNs to RNNs. These neural networks have effectiveness limits based on the data they have to process, such as normalizing data to allow a neural network to work properly or forcing its range of input values between 0 to +1 or −1 to +1 to reduce trouble when updating network weights.

REMEMBER

Normalization is done internally to the network by using activation functions like tanh, which squeezes values to appear in the range from −1 to +1 (https://tex.stackexchange.com/questions/176101/plotting-the-graph-of-hyperbolic-tangent), or by using specialized layers like BatchNormalization (https://keras.io/layers/normalization/), which apply a statistical transformation on values transferred from one layer to another.

Another kind of problematic data that a neural network finds difficult to handle is sparse data. You have sparse data when your data mostly consists of zero values, which is exactly what happens when you process textual data using frequency or binary encoding, even if you don't use TF-IDF. When working with sparse data, not only will the neural network have difficulties finding a good solution (as technically explained in these Quora answers: https://www.quora.com/Why-are-deep-neural-networks-so-bad-with-sparse-data), but you'll also need to have a huge number of weights for the input layer because sparse matrices are usually quite wide (they have many columns).

Sparse data problems motivated the use of *word embeddings*, which is a way to transform a sparse matrix into a dense one. Word embeddings can reduce the number of columns in the matrix from hundreds of thousands to a few hundred. Also, they allow no zero values inside the matrix. The word embedding process isn't done randomly but is devised so that words get similar values when they have the same meaning or are found within the same topics. In other words, it's a complex mapping; each embedding column is a specialty map (or a scale, if you prefer) and the similar or related words gather near each other.

TIP

Word embeddings aren't the only advanced technique that you can use to make deep learning solutions shine with unstructured text. Recently, a series of pre-trained networks appeared that make it even easier to model language problems. For instance, one of the most promising is the Google Bidirectional Encoder Representations from Transformers (BERT). Here's a link to the Google AI blog post describing the technique: https://ai.googleblog.com/2018/11/open-sourcing-bert-state-of-art-pre.html.

As another example, you can have an embedding that transforms the name of different foods into columns of numeric values, which is a matrix of embedded words. On that matrix, the words that show fruits can have a similar score on a particular column. On the same column, vegetables can get different values, but not too far from those of fruit. Finally, the names of meat dishes can be far away in value from fruits and vegetables. An embedding performs this work by converting words into values in a matrix. The values are similar when the words are synonymous or refer to a similar concept. (This is called *semantic similarity*, with *semantic* referring to the meaning of words.)

REMEMBER

Because the same semantic meaning can occur across languages, you can use carefully built embeddings to help you translate from one language to another: A word in one language will have the same embedded scores as the same word in another language. Researchers at Facebook AI Research (FAIR) lab have found a way to synchronize different embeddings and leverage them to provide multilingual applications based on deep learning (go to https://code.fb.com/ml-applications/under-the-hood-multilingual-embeddings/ for details).

An important aspect to keep in mind when working with word embeddings is that they are a product of data and thus reflect the content of the data used to create them. Because word embeddings require large amounts of text examples for proper generation, the content of texts fed into the embeddings during the training is often retrieved automatically from the web and not fully scrutinized. The use of unverified input may lead to word embedding biases. For instance, you may be surprised to discover that the word embeddings create improper associations between words. You should be aware of such a risk and test your application carefully because the consequence is adding the same unfair biases to the deep learning applications you create.

For now, the most popular word embeddings commonly used for deep learning applications are

>> **Word2vec:** Created by a team of researchers led by Tomáš Mikolov at Google (you can read the original paper about this patented method here: https:// arxiv.org/pdf/1301.3781.pdf). It relies on two shallow neural network layers that attempt to learn to predict a word by knowing the words that precede and follow it. Word2vec comes in two versions: one based on something like a bag of words model (called continuous bag-of-words, or CBOW), which is less sensitive to word order; and another based on n-grams (called continuous skip-gram), which is more sensitive to the order. Word2vec learns to predict a word given its context using *distributional hypothesis,* which means that similar words appear in similar contexts of words. By learning what words should appear in different contexts, Word2vec internalizes the contexts. Both versions are suitable for most applications, but the skip-gram version is actually better at representing infrequent words.

>> **GloVe (Global Vectors):** Developed as an open source project at Stanford University (https://nlp.stanford.edu/projects/glove/), the GloVe approach is similar to statistical linguist methods. It takes word-word co-occurrence statistics from a corpus and reduces the resulting sparse matrix to a dense one using *matrix factorization,* which is an algebraic method widely used in multivariate statistics.

>> **fastText:** Created by Facebook's AI Research (FAIR) lab, fastText (https:// fasttext.cc/) is a word embedding, available in multiple languages that works with word subsequences instead of single words. It breaks a word down into many chunks of letters and embeds them. This technique has interesting implications because fastText offers a better representation of rare words (which are often composed of subsequences that aren't rare) and determines how to project misspelled words. The capability to handle misspellings and errors allows an effective use of the embedding with text coming from social networks, e-mails, and other sources people don't usually use a spell checker with.

EXPLAINING WHY (KING – MAN) + WOMAN = QUEEN

Word embeddings translate a word into a series of numbers representing its position in the embedding itself. This series of numbers is the *word vector*. It's usually made up of about 300 vectors (the number of vectors Google used in their model trained on the Google news dataset), and neural networks use it to process textual information better and more effectively. In fact, words with similar meaning or that are used in similar contexts have similar word vectors; therefore, neural networks can easily spot words with similar meaning. In addition, neural networks can work with analogies by manipulating vectors, which means that you can obtain amazing results such as

- king – man + woman = queen

- paris – france + poland = warsaw

It may seem like magic but it's simple mathematics. You can see how things work by looking at the following figure, which represents two Word2vec vectors.

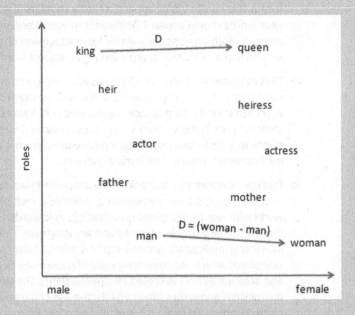

Each vector in Word2vec represents a different semantic; it could be food type, quality of a person, nationality, or gender. There are many semantics and they aren't predefined; the embedding training created them automatically based on the presented examples. The figure shows two vectors from Word2vec: one representing the quality of a person;

another representing the gender of a person. The first vector defines roles, starting with king and queen with higher scores, passing through actor and actress, and finally ending with man and woman having lower scores. If you add this vector to the gender vector, you see that the male and female variants separate by different scores on that vector. Now, when you subtract man and add woman to king, you are simply moving away from the coordinates of king and shifting along the gender vector until you reach the position of queen. This simple trick of coordinates, which doesn't imply any understanding of words by Word2vec, is possible because all the vectors of a word embedding are synchronized, representing the meaning of a language, and you can meaningfully shift from one coordinate to another as you were shifting concepts in reasoning.

Using AI for Sentiment Analysis

Sentiment analysis computationally derives from a written text using the writer's attitude (whether positive, negative, or neutral), toward the text topic. This kind of analysis proves useful for people working in marketing and communication because it helps them understand what customers and consumers think of a product or service and thus, act appropriately (for instance, trying to recover unsatisfied customers or deciding to use a different sales strategy). Everyone performs sentiment analysis. For example, when reading text, people naturally try to determine the sentiment that moved the person who wrote it. However, when the number of texts to read and understand is too huge and the text constantly accumulates, as in social media and customer e-mails, automating the task is important.

The upcoming example is a test run of RNNs using Keras and TensorFlow that builds a sentiment analysis algorithm capable of classifying the attitudes expressed in a film review. The data is a sample of the IMDb dataset that contains 50,000 reviews (split in half between train and test sets) of movies accompanied by a label expressing the sentiment of the review (0=negative, 1=positive). IMDb (https://www.imdb.com/) is a large online database containing information about films, TV series, and video games. Originally maintained by a fan base, it's now run by an Amazon subsidiary. On IMDb, people find the information they need about their favorite show as well as post their comments or write a review for other visitors to read.

Keras offers a downloadable wrapper for IMDb data. You prepare, shuffle, and arrange this data into a train and a test set. This dataset appears among other useful datasets at https://keras.io/datasets/. In particular, the IMDb textual data offered by Keras is cleansed of punctuation, normalized into lowercase, and transformed into numeric values. Each word is coded into a number representing its ranking in frequency. Most frequent words have low numbers; less frequent words have higher numbers.

As a starter point, the code imports the imdb function from Keras and uses it to retrieve the data from the Internet (about a 17.5MB download). The parameters that the example uses encompass just the top 10,000 words, and Keras should shuffle the data using a specific random seed. (Knowing the seed makes it possible to reproduce the shuffle as needed.) The function returns two train and test sets, both made of text sequences and the sentiment outcome.

```
from keras.datasets import imdb

top_words = 10000
((x_train, y_train),
 (x_test, y_test)) = imdb.load_data(num_words=top_words,
                                    seed=21)
```

After the previous code completes, you can check the number of examples using the following code:

```
print("Training examples: %i" % len(x_train))
print("Test examples: %i" % len(x_test))
```

After inquiring about the number of cases available for use in the training and test phase of the neural network, the code outputs an answer of 25,000 examples for each phase. (This dataset is a relatively small one for a language problem; clearly the dataset is mainly for demonstration purposes.) In addition, the code determines whether the dataset is balanced, which means it has an almost equal number of positive and negative sentiment examples.

```
import numpy as np
print(np.unique(y_train, return_counts=True))
```

The result, array([12500, 12500]), confirms that the dataset is split evenly between positive and negative outcomes. Such a balance between the response classes is exclusively because of the demonstrative nature of the dataset. In the real world, you seldom find balanced datasets. The next step creates some Python dictionaries that can convert between the code used in the dataset and the real words. In fact, the dataset used in this example is preprocessed and provides sequences of numbers representing the words, not the words themselves. (LSTM and GRU algorithms that you find in Keras expect sequences of numbers as numbers.)

```
word_to_id = {w:i+3 for w,i in imdb.get_word_index().items()}
id_to_word = {0:'<PAD>', 1:'<START>', 2:'<UNK>'}
id_to_word.update({i+3:w for w,i in imdb.get_word_index().
   items()})
```

```
def convert_to_text(sequence):
    return ' '.join([id_to_word[s] for s in sequence if s>=3])

print(convert_to_text(x_train[8]))
```

The previous code snippet defines two conversion dictionaries (from words to numeric codes and vice versa) and a function that translates the dataset examples into readable text. As an example, the code prints the ninth example: "this movie was like a bad train wreck as horrible as it was . . .". From this excerpt, you can easily anticipate that the sentiment for this movie isn't positive. Words such as *bad, wreck,* and *horrible* convey a strong negative feeling, and that makes guessing the correct sentiment easy.

TIP

In this example, you receive the numeric sequences and turn them back into words, but the opposite is common. Usually, you get phrases made up of words and turn them into sequences of integers to feed to a layer of RNNs. Keras offers a specialized function, Tokenizer (see https://keras.io/preprocessing/text/# tokenizer), which can do that for you. It uses the methods fit_on_text, to learn how to map words to integers from training data, and texts_to_matrix, to transform text into a sequence.

However, in other phrases, you may not find such revealing words. The feeling is expressed in a more subtle or indirect way, and understanding the sentiment early in the text may not be possible because revealing phrases and words may appear much later in the discourse. For this reason, you also need to decide how much of the phrase you want to analyze. Conventionally, you take an initial part of the text and use it as representative of the entire review. Sometimes you just need a few initial words — for instance the first 50 words — to get the sense; sometimes you need more. Especially long texts don't reveal their orientation early. It is therefore up to you to understand the type of text you are working with and decide how many words to analyze using deep learning. This example considers only the first 200 words, which should suffice.

TIP

You have noticed that the code starts giving code to words beginning with the number 3, thus leaving codes from 0 to 2. Lower numbers are used for special tags, such as signaling the start of the phrase, filling empty spaces to have the sequence fixed at a certain length, and marking the words that are excluded because they're not frequent enough. This example picks up only the most frequent 10,000 words. Using tags to point out start, end, and notable situations is a trick that works with RNNs, especially for machine translation.

```
from keras.preprocessing.sequence import pad_sequences

max_pad = 200
x_train = pad_sequences(x_train,
                        maxlen=max_pad)

x_test = pad_sequences(x_test,
                       maxlen=max_pad)

print(x_train[0])
```

By using the pad_sequences function from Keras with max_pad set to 200, the code takes the first two hundred words of each review. In case the review contains fewer than two hundred words, as many zero values as necessary precede the sequence to reach the required number of sequence elements. Cutting the sequences to a certain length and filling the voids with zero values is called *input padding*, an important processing activity when using RNNs like deep learning algorithms. Now the code designs the architecture:

```
from keras.models import Sequential
from keras.layers import Bidirectional, Dense, Dropout
from keras.layers import GlobalMaxPool1D, LSTM
from keras.layers.embeddings import Embedding

embedding_vector_length = 32
model = Sequential()
model.add(Embedding(top_words,
                    embedding_vector_length,
                    input_length=max_pad))

model.add(Bidirectional(LSTM(64, return_sequences=True)))
model.add(GlobalMaxPool1D())
model.add(Dense(16, activation="relu"))
model.add(Dense(1, activation="sigmoid"))

model.compile(loss='binary_crossentropy',
              optimizer='adam',
              metrics=['accuracy'])

print(model.summary())
```

The previous code snippet defines the shape of the deep learning model, where it uses a few specialized layers for natural language processing from Keras. The example also has required a summary of the model (model.summary() command) to determine what is happening with architecture by using different neural layers.

You have the Embedding layer, which transforms the numeric sequences into a dense word embedding. That type of word embedding is more suitable for being learned by a layer of RNNs, as discussed in the previous paragraph in this chapter. Keras provides an Embedding layer, which, apart from necessarily having to be the first layer of the network, can accomplish two tasks:

>> Applying pretrained word embedding (such as Word2vec or GloVe) to the sequence input. You just need to pass the matrix containing the embedding to its parameter weights.

>> Creating a word embedding from scratch, based on the inputs it receives.

In this second case, Embedding just needs to know:

>> input_dim: The size of the vocabulary expected from data

>> output_dim: The size of the embedding space that will be produced (the so-called dimensions)

>> input_length: The sequence size to expect

After you determine the parameters, Embedding will find the better weights to transform the sequences into a dense matrix during training. The dense matrix size is given by the length of sequences and the dimensionality of the embedding.

REMEMBER

If you use The Embedding layer provided by Keras, you have to remember that the function provides only a weight matrix of the size of the vocabulary by the dimension of the desired embedding. It maps the words to the columns of the matrix and then tunes the matrix weights to the provided examples. This solution, although practical for nonstandard language problems, is not analogous to the word embeddings discussed previously, which are trained in a different way and on millions of examples.

The example uses Bidirectional wrapping — an LSTM layer of 64 cells. Bidirectional transforms a normal LSTM layer by doubling it: On the first side, it applies the normal sequence of inputs you provide; on the second, it passes the reverse of the sequence. You use this approach because sometimes you use words in a different order, and building a bidirectional layer will catch any word pattern, no matter the order. The Keras implementation is indeed straightforward: You just apply it as a function on the layer you want to render bidirectionally.

The bidirectional LSTM is set to return sequences (return_sequences=True); that is, for each cell, it returns the result provided after seeing each element of the sequence. The results, for each sequence, is an output matrix of 200 x 128, where 200 is the number of sequence elements and 128 is the number of LSTM cells used in the layer. This technique prevents the RNN from taking the last result of each LSTM cell. Hints about the sentiment of the text could actually appear anywhere in the embedded words sequence.

In short, it's important not to take the last result of each cell, but rather the best result of it. The code therefore relies on the following layer, GlobalMaxPool1D, to check each sequence of results provided by each LSTM cell and retain only the maximum result. That should ensure that the example picks the strongest signal from each LSTM cell, which is hopefully specialized by its training to pick some meaningful signals.

After the neural signals are filtered, the example has a layer of 128 outputs, one for each LSTM cell. The code reduces and mixes the signals using a successive dense layer of 16 neurons with ReLU activation (thus making only positive signals pass through; see the "Choosing the right activation function" section of Chapter 8 for details). The architecture ends with a final node using sigmoid activation, which will squeeze the results into the 0–1 range and make them look like probabilities. Having defined the architecture, you can now train the network. Three epochs (passing the data three times through the network to have it learn the patterns) will suffice. The code uses batches of 256 reviews each time, which allows the network to see enough variety of words and sentiments each time before updating its weights using backpropagation. Finally, the code focuses on the results provided by the validation data (which isn't part of the training data). Getting a good result from the validation data means the neural net is processing the input correctly. The code reports on validation data just after each epoch finishes.

```
history = model.fit(x_train, y_train,
                    validation_data=(x_test, y_test),
                    epochs=3, batch_size=256)
```

Getting the results takes a while, but if you are using a GPU, it will complete in the time you take to drink a cup of coffee. At this point, you can evaluate the results, again using the validation data. (The results shouldn't have any surprises or differences from what the code reported during training.)

```
loss, metric = model.evaluate(x_test, y_test, verbose=0)
print("Test accuracy: %0.3f" % metric)
```

The final accuracy, which is the percentage of correct answers from the deep neural network, will be a value of around 85—86 percent. The result will change slightly each time you run the experiment because of randomization when building your neural network. That's perfectly normal given the small size of the data you are working with. If you start with the right lucky weights, the learning will be easier in such a short training session.

In the end, your network is a sentiment analyzer that can guess the sentiment expressed in a movie review correctly about 85 percent of the time. Given even more training data and more sophisticated neural architectures, you can get results that are even more impressive. In marketing, a similar tool is used to automate many processes that require reading text and taking action. Again, you could couple a network like this with a neural network that listens to a voice and turns it into text. (This is another application of RNNs, now powering Alexa, Siri, Google Voice, and many other personal assistants.) The transition allows the application to understand the sentiment even in vocal expressions, such as a phone call from a customer.

Chapter **15**

Generating Music and Visual Art

You can find considerable discussions online about whether computers can be creative by employing deep learning. The dialogue goes to the very essence of what it means to be creative. Philosophers and others have discussed the topic endlessly throughout human history without arriving at a conclusion as to what, precisely, creativity means. Consequently, a single chapter in a book written in just a few months won't solve the problem for you.

However, to provide a basis for the discussions in this chapter, this book defines *creativity* as the ability to define new ideas, patterns, relationships, and so on. The emphasis is on new: the originality, progressiveness, and imagination that humans provide. It doesn't include copying someone else's style and calling it one's own. Of course, this definition will almost certainly raise the ire of some while garnering the accepting nods of others, but to make the discussion work at all, you need a definition. Mind you, this definition doesn't exclude creativity by nonhumans. For example, some people can make a case for creative apes (see http://www.bbc.com/future/story/20140723-are-we-the-only-creative-species for more details).

This chapter does help you understand how creativity and computers can come together in a fascinating collaboration. First, you must consider that computers rely on math to do everything, and art and music are no exception. A computer can transfer existing art or music patterns to a neural network and use the result to generate something that looks new but actually relies on the existing pattern. However, along with this revelation, a second consideration is that a human designed the algorithm used to perform the statistical analysis of the pattern and subsequently output the new art. In other words, the computer didn't perform this task on its own; it relied on a human to provide the means to accomplish the task. Moreover, a human will decide on which style to mimic and define what sort of output might prove aesthetically pleasing. In short, the computer ends up being a tool in the hands of an exceptionally smart human to automate the process of creating what could be deemed as new, but really isn't.

As part of the process of defining how some can see a computer as creative, the chapter also defines how computers mimic an established style. You can see for yourself that deep learning relies on math to perform a task generally not associated with math at all. An artist or musician doesn't rely on calculations to create something new, but could rely on calculations to see how others performed their task. When an artist or musician employs math to study another style, the process is called learning, not creating. Of course, this entire book is about how deep learning performs learning tasks, and even that process differs greatly from how humans learn.

Learning to Imitate Art and Life

You have likely seen interesting visions of AI art, such as those mentioned in the articleathttps://news.artnet.com/art-world/ai-art-comes-to-market-is-it-worth-the-hype-1352011. The art undeniably has aesthetic appeal. In fact, the article mentions that Christie's, one of the most famous auction houses in the world, originally expected to sell the piece of art for $7,000 to $10,000 but it actually sold for $432,000, according to the *Guardian* (https://www.theguardian.com/artanddesign/shortcuts/2018/oct/26/call-that-art-can-a-computer-be-a-painter) and the *New York Times* (https://www.nytimes.com/2018/10/25/arts/design/ai-art-sold-christies.html). So not only is type of art appealing, it can also generate a lot of money. However, in every unbiased story you read, the question remains as to whether the AI art actually is art at all. The following sections help you understand that computer generation doesn't correlate to creative—it translates to amazing algorithms employing the latest in statistics.

Transferring an artistic style

One of the differentiators of art is the artistic style. Even when someone takes a photograph and displays it as art (http://www.wallartprints.com.au/blog/artistic-photography/), the method in which the photograph is taken, processed, and optionally touched up all define a particular style. In many cases, depending on the skill of the artist, you can't even tell that you're looking at a photograph because of its artistic elements (https://www.pinterest.com/lorimcneeartist/artistic-photography/?lp=true).

Some artists become so famous for their particular style that others take time to study it in depth to improve their own technique. For example, Vincent van Gogh's unique style is often mimicked (https://www.artble.com/artists/vincent_van_gogh/more_information/style_and_technique). Van Gogh's style — his use of colors, methods, media, subject matter, and a wealth of other considerations — requires intense study for humans to replicate. Humans improvise, so the adjective suffix *esque* often appears as a descriptor of a person's style. A critic might say that a particular artist uses a van Goghesque methodology.

REMEMBER

To create art, the computer relies on a particular artistic style to modify the appearance of a source picture. In contrast to a human, a computer can perfectly replicate a particular style given enough consistent examples. Of course, you could create a sort of mixed style by using examples from various periods in the artist's life. The point is that the computer isn't creating a new style, nor is it improvising. The source image isn't new, either. You see a perfectly copied style and a perfectly copied source image when working with a computer, and you transfer the style to the source image to create something that looks a little like both.

The process used to transfer the style to the source picture and produce an output is complex and generates a lot of discussion. For example, considering where source code ends and elements such as training begin is important. The article at https://www.theverge.com/2018/10/23/18013190/ai-art-portrait-auction-christies-belamy-obvious-robbie-barrat-gans discusses one such situation that involves the use of existing code but different training from the original implementation, which has people wondering over issues such as attribution when art is generated by computer. Mind you, all the discussion focuses on the humans who create the code and perform the training of the computer; the computer itself doesn't figure in to the discussion because the computer is simply crunching numbers.

OTHER SORTS OF GENERATED ART

Keep in mind that this book discusses a particular kind of computer art — the sort generated by a deep learning network. You can find all sorts of other computer generated art that doesn't necessarily rely on deep learning. One of the earlier examples of generated art is the fractal (http://www.arthistory.net/fractal-art/), created by using an equation. The first of these fractals is the Mandelbrot set (http://mathworld.wolfram.com/MandelbrotSet.html) created in 1980 by Benoit B. Mandelbrot, a Polish mathematician. Some fractals today are quite beautiful (https://www.creativebloq.com/computer-arts/5-eye-popping-examples-fractal-art-71412376) and even incorporate some real world elements. Even so, the creativity belongs not to the computer, which is simply crunching numbers, but to the mathematician or artist who designs the algorithm used to generate the fractal.

A next step in generated art is Computer Generated Imagery (CGI). You have likely seen some amazing examples of CGI art in movies, but it appears just about everywhere today (https://www.vice.com/en_us/topic/cgi-art). Some people restrict CGI to 3-D art and some restrict it to 3-D dynamic art of the sort used for video games and movies. No matter what restrictions you place on CGI art, the process is essentially the same. An artist decides on a series of transformations to create effects on the computer screen, such as water that looks wet and fog that looks misty (https://www.widewalls.ch/cgi-artworks/). CGI also sees use in building models based on designs, such as architectural drawings (https://archicgi.com/3d-modeling-things-youve-got-know/ and https://oceancgi.com/). These models help you visualize what the finished product will look like long before the first spade of earth is turned. However, in the end what you see is the creativity of an artist, architect, mathematician, or other individual in telling the computer to perform various kinds of calculations to transform design into something that looks real. The computer understands nothing in all this.

Reducing the problem to statistics

Computers can't actually see anything. Someone takes a digital image of a real-world object or creates a fanciful drawing like the one in Figure 15-1, and each pixel in that image appears as tuples of numbers representing the red, blue, and green values of each pixel, as shown in Figure 15-2. These numbers, in turn, are what the computer interacts with using an algorithm. The computer doesn't understand that the numbers form a tuple — that's a human convention. All it knows is that the algorithm defines the operations that must take place on the series of numbers. In short, the art becomes a matter of manipulating numbers using a variety of methods, including statistics.

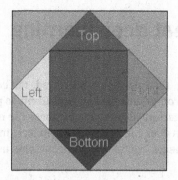

FIGURE 15-1:
A human might see a fanciful drawing.

FIGURE 15-2:
The computer sees a series of numbers.

Deep learning relies on a number of algorithms to manipulate the pixels in a source drawing in a variety of ways to reflect the particular style you want to use. In fact, you can find a dizzying array of such algorithms because everyone appears to have a different idea of how to force a computer to create particular kinds of art. The point is that all these methods rely on algorithms that act on a series of numbers to perform the task; the computer never takes brush in hand to actually create something new. Two methods appear to drive the current strategies, though:

>> **Convolutional Neural Networks (CNNs):** See Chapter 10 for an overview; also see the "Defining a new piece based on a single artist" section, later in this chapter, for the artistic perspective

>> **Generative Adversarial Networks (GANs):** See Chapter 16 for an overview; also check out the "Visualizing how neural networks dream" section, later in this chapter, again for the artistic perspective

Understanding that deep learning doesn't create

For art created by deep learning, the images are borrowed, the computer doesn't understand them at all, and the computer relies on algorithms to perform the task of modifying the images. Deep learning doesn't even choose the method of learning about the images — a human does that. In short, deep learning is an interesting method of manipulating images created by someone else using a style that another person also created.

REMEMBER

Whether deep learning can create something isn't the real question to ask. The question that matters is whether humans can appreciate the result of the deep learning output. Despite its inability to understand or create, deep learning can deliver some amazing results. Consequently, creativity is best left to humans, but deep learning can give everyone an expressive tool, even people who aren't artistic. For example, you could use deep learning to create a van Gogh version of a loved one to hang on your wall. The fact that you participated in the process and that you have something that looks professionally drawn is the point to consider — not whether the computer is creative.

Mimicking an Artist

Deep learning helps you mimic a particular artist. You can mimic any artist you want because the computer doesn't understand anything about style or drawing. The deep learning algorithm will faithfully reproduce a style based on the inputs you provide. Consequently, mimicking is a flexible way to produce a particular output, as described in the following sections.

Defining a new piece based on a single artist

Convolutional Neural Networks (CNNs) appear in a number of uses for deep learning applications. For example, they're used for self-driving cars and facial recognition systems. Chapter 10 provides some additional examples of how CNNs do their job, but the point is that a CNN can perform recognition tasks well given enough training.

Interestingly, CNNs work particularly well in recognizing art style. So you can combine two pieces of art into a single piece. However, those two pieces supply two different kinds of input for the CNN:

>> **Content:** The image that defines the desired output. For example, if you provide a content image of a cat, the output will look like a cat. It won't be the same cat you started with, but the content defines the desired output with regard to what a human will see.

>> **Style:** The image that defines the desired modification. For example, if you provide an example of a van Gogh painting, the output will reflect this style.

TIP

In general, you see CNNs that rely on a single content image and a single style image. Using just the two images like this lets you see how content and style work together to produce a particular output. The example at `https://medium.com/mlreview/making-ai-art-with-style-transfer-using-keras-8bb5fa44b216` provides a method for combining two images in this manner.

Of course, you need to decide how to combine the images. In fact, this is where the statistics of deep learning come into play. To perform this task, you use a *neural style transfer,* as outlined in the paper "A Neural Algorithm of Artistic Style" by Leon A. Gatys, Alexander S. Ecker, and Matthias Bethge (`https://arxiv.org/pdf/1508.06576.pdf` or `https://www.robots.ox.ac.uk/~vgg/rg/papers/1508.06576v2.pdf`).

The algorithm works with these kinds of images: a *content image,* which depicts the object you want to represent; a *style image,* which provides the art style you want to mimic; and an *input image,* which is the image to transform. The input image is usually a random image or the same image as the content image. Transferring the style implies preserving the content (that is, if you start with a photo of a dog, the result will still depict a dog). However, the transformed input image is nearer to the style image in presentation. The algorithm you use will define two loss measures:

>> **Content loss:** Determines the amount of the original image that the CNN uses to provide output. A greater loss here means that the output will better reflect the style you provide. However, you can reach a point at which the loss is so great that you can no longer to see the content.

>> **Style loss:** Determines the manner in which the style is applied to the content. A higher level of loss means that the content retains more of its original style. The style loss must be low enough for you to end up with a new piece of art that reflects the desired style.

Having just two images doesn't allow for extensive training, so you use a pre-trained deep learning network, such as VGG-19 (the 2014 winner of the ImageNet challenge created by the Visual Geometry Group, VGG, at Oxford University). The pretrained deep learning network already knows how to process an image into image features of different complexity. The algorithm for neural style transfer picks the CNN of a VGG-19, excluding the final fully connected layers. In this way, you have the network that acts as a processing filter for images. When you send in an image, VGG-19 transforms it into a neural network representation, which could be completely different from the original. However, when you use only the top layers of the network as image filters, the network transforms the resulting image but doesn't completely change it.

Taking advantage of such transformative neural network properties, the neural transfer style doesn't use all the convolutions in the VGG-19. Instead, it monitors them using the two loss measures to assure that, in spite of the transformations applied to the image, the network maintains the content and applies the style. In this way, when you pass the input image through VGG-19 several times, its weights adjust to accomplish the double task of content preservation and style learning. After a few iterations, which actually require a lot of computations and weight updates, the network transforms your input image into the anticipated image and art style.

TIP

You often see the output of a CNN referred to as a *pastiche*. It's a fancy word that generally means an artistic piece composed of elements borrowed from motifs or techniques of other artists. Given the nature of deep learning art, the term is appropriate.

Combining styles to create new art

If you really want to get fancy, you can create a pastiche based on multiple style images. For example, you could train the CNN using multiple Monet works so that the pastiche looks more like a Monet piece in general. Of course, you could just as easily combine the styles of multiple impressionist painters to create what appears to be a unique piece of art that reflects the impressionist style in general. The actual method for performing this task varies, but the article at `https:// ai.googleblog.com/2016/10/supercharging-style-transfer.html` offers ideas for accomplishing the task.

Visualizing how neural networks dream

Using a CNN is essentially a manual process with regard to choosing the loss functions. The success or failure of a CNN depends on the human setting the various values. A GAN takes a different approach. It relies on two interactive deep networks to automatically adjust the values to provide better output. You can see these two deep networks having these names:

>> **Generator:** Creates an image based on the inputs you provide. The image needs to retain the original content, but with the appropriate level of style to produce a pastiche that is hard to distinguish from an original.

>> **Discriminator:** Determines whether the generator output is real enough to pass as an original. If not, the discriminator provides feedback telling the generator what is wrong with the pastiche.

To make this setup work, you actually train two models: one for the generator and another for the discriminator. The two act in concert, with the generator creating new samples and the discriminator telling the generator what is wrong with each sample. The process goes back and forth between generator and discriminator until the pastiche achieves a specific level of perfection. In Chapter 16, you can find an even more detailed explanation about how GANs work.

TIP

This approach is advantageous because it provides a greater level of automation and a higher probability of good results than using a CNN. The disadvantage is that this approach also requires considerable time to implement, and the processing requirements are much greater. Consequently, using the CNN approach is often better to achieve a result that's good enough. You can see an example of the GAN approach at https://towardsdatascience.com/gan-by-example-using-keras-on-tensorflow-backend-1a6d515a60d0.

Using a network to compose music

This chapter focuses mainly on visual art because you can easily judge the subtle changes that occur to it. However, the same techniques also work with music. You can use CNNs and GANs to create music based on a specific style. Computers can't see visual art, nor can they hear music. The musical tones become numbers that the computer manipulates just as it manipulates the numbers associated with pixels. The computer doesn't see any difference at all.

However, deep learning does detect a difference. Yes, you use the same algorithms for music as for visual art, but the settings you use are different, and the training is unique as well. In addition, some sources say that training for music is a lot harder than for art (see https://motherboard.vice.com/en_us/article/qvq54v/why-is-ai-generated-music-still-so-bad for details). Of course, part of the difficulty stems from the differences among the humans listening to the music. As a group, humans seem to have a hard time defining aesthetically pleasing music, and even people who like a particular style or particular artists rarely like everything those artists produce.

In some respects, the tools used to compose music using AI are more formalized and mature than those used for visual art. This doesn't mean that the music composition tools always produce great results, but it does mean that you can easily buy a package to perform music composition tasks. Here are the two most popular offerings today:

>> **Amper:** https://www.ampermusic.com/

>> **Jukedeck:** https://www.jukedeck.com/

REMEMBER

AI music composition is different from visual art generation because the music tools have been around for a longer time, according to the article at https://www.theverge.com/2018/8/31/17777008/artificial-intelligence-taryn-southern-amper-music. The late songwriter and performer David Bowie used an older application called Verbasizer (https://motherboard.vice.com/en_us/article/xygxpn/the-verbasizer-was-david-bowies-1995-lyric-writing-mac-app) in 1995 to aid in his work. The key idea here is that this tool aided in, rather than produced, work. The human being is the creative talent; the AI serves as a creative tool to produce better music. Consequently, music takes on a collaborative feel, rather than giving the AI center stage.

Chapter **16**

Building Generative Adversarial Networks

Deep learning has turned into a hot technology, and new research produces ever more impressive discoveries all the time. Discoveries always appear at an even faster rate during the Neural Information Processing Systems (NeurIPS) conference (`https://neurips.cc/`), which serves as the stage for everything related to deep learning. The conference is held every year at a different location around the world (most recently, before this book's publication, in Montréal, Canada).

The conference always makes new technologies available for people to see, but a few fields have received all the attention. Among the impressive variety of applications and new technologies related to deep learning recently introduced at the conference, here are the ones to pay the most attention to: Natural Language Processing (especially for pretrained embeddings like BERT discussed in Chapter 14); Reinforcement Learning (the topic of the next chapter); and Generative Adversarial Networks (GANs). GANs are a thinking-outside--the box idea. Yann LeCun, now Director of Facebook AI, defines it as "the most interesting idea in the last ten years in machine learning".

This chapter describes what GANs are and demonstrates how they're capable of generating new data, especially images, from preexisting ones. The chapter completes the overview of GANs by building a network using Keras and TensorFlow.

After you see a GAN in action, the chapter goes on to discuss the most interesting developments and achievements of GANs.

REMEMBER

Save yourself the time and mistakes of typing the code manually. You can find the downloadable source for this chapter in the DL4D_16_MNIST_GAN.ipynb file. (The Introduction tells you where to download the source code for this book.)

Making Networks Compete

In 2014, at the Department d'informatique et de recherche opérationnelle at the University of Montreal, Ian Goodfellow and other researchers (among whom is Yoshua Bengio, one of Canada's most noted scientists working on artificial neural networks and deep learning) published the first paper on GANs. You can read the work at https://arxiv.org/pdf/1406.2661v1.pdf or https://papers.nips. cc/paper/5423-generative-adversarial-nets.pdf. In the following months, the paper attracted attention and was deemed innovative for its proposed mix of deep learning and game theory. The idea became widespread because of its accessibility in terms of neural network architecture: You can train a working GAN using standard a computer. (The technique works better if you can invest a lot of computational power.)

Contrary to other deep learning neural networks that classify images or sequences, the specialty of GANs is their capability to generate new data by deriving inspiration from training data. This capability becomes particularly impressive when dealing with image data, because well-trained GANs can generate new pieces of art that people sell at auctions (such as the artwork sold at Christie's for nearly half a million dollars, mentioned in Chapter 15: https://www.dezeen. com/2018/10/29/christies-ai-artwork-obvious-portrait-edmond- de-belamy-design/). This feat is even more incredible because previous results obtained using other mathematical and statistical techniques were far from credible or usable.

Finding the key in the competition

The GAN name contains the term adversarial in it because the key idea behind GANs is the competition between two networks, which play as adversaries against each other. Ian Goodfellow, the principal author of the original paper on GANs, used a simple metaphor to describe how everything works. Goodfellow described the process as an endless challenge between a forger and a detective: the forger has to create a fake piece of art by copying some real art masterpiece, so he starts painting something. After the forger completes the fake painting, a detective examines it and decides whether the forger created a real piece of art or simply a fake. If the detective sees a fake, the forger receives notice that something is wrong with the work (but not where the fault lies). When the forger shows that the art is real despite the negative feedback of the detective, the detective receives notice of the mistake and changes the detection technique to avoid failure during the next attempt. As the forger continues attempts to fool the detective, both the forger and the detective grow in expertise of their respective duties. Given time, the art produced by the forger becomes extremely high in quality and is almost undistinguishable from the real thing except by someone with an expert eye.

Figure 16-1 illustrates the story of GANs as a simple schema, in which inputs and neural architectures interact together in closed loop of reciprocal feedbacks. The generator network plays the part of the forger and a discriminator network plays the detective. GANs use the term *discriminator* because of the similarity in purpose to electronic circuits that accept or reject signals based on their characteristics. The discriminator in a GAN accepts (wrongly) or refuses (correctly) the work created by the generator. The interesting aspect of this architecture is that the generator never sees a single training example. Only the discriminator accesses such data in its training. The generator receives random inputs (noise) to provide a random starting point each time, which forces it to produce a different result.

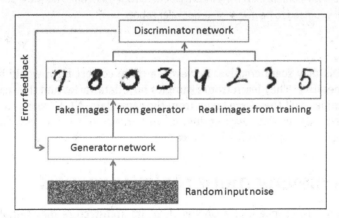

FIGURE 16-1:
How a GAN
operates.

The generator may seem take all the glory (after all it, generates the data product). However, the real powerhouse of the architecture is the discriminator. The discriminator computes errors that are backpropagated to its own network to learn how best to distinguish between real and fake data. The errors also propagate to the generator, which optimizes itself to cause the discriminator to fail during the next round.

REMEMBER

GANs may seem creative. However, a more correct term would be that they are generative: They learn from examples how data varies and they can generate new samples as if they were taken from the same data. A GAN learns to mimic a previously existing data distribution; it can't create something new. As stated in other chapters, deep learning isn't creative.

Achieving more realistic results

Even if the concept of a GAN is clear, its architecture may initially appear to be complicated. Creating a basic GAN example has become quite accessible using Keras with TensorFlow, and learning by doing is a good way to explain details of the technology that would otherwise remain theoretical. The process has a few tricky parts, but in the end, everything is exactly as described in the previous paragraphs using the Ian Goodfellow metaphor.

In the following pages, you build a simple GAN that learns how to recreate handwritten numbers from zero to nine after learning them from the MNIST dataset. The MNIST dataset is a set of digitized, normalized, 28-x-28-pixel, handwritten samples (written by both high school students and employees of the American

Census Bureau) that are often used for training image systems. You can find the dataset on Yann LeCun's website at http://yann.lecun.com/exdb/mnist/.

The example starts by importing the necessary functions and classes. You don't need anything fancy for the task, and you have already dealt with or even already tested everything the code imports:

```
import numpy as np
from keras.datasets import mnist
from keras.models import Sequential, Model
from keras.layers import Input, Dense, Dropout
from keras.layers import BatchNormalization
from keras.layers.advanced_activations import LeakyReLU
from keras.optimizers import Adam
import matplotlib.pyplot as plt
%matplotlib inline
```

Note that the code downloads the MNIST dataset using the Keras mnist function. The distinct 28-x-28-pixel image arrays and expresses pixel values from 0 to 255. The code processes them to make them useful for a deep learning network using these steps:

1. Make them a vector, that is, a list of values, by reshaping the data.

2. Convert their values to the floating-point type using the 32-bit precision suitable for GPUs because the 64 bit version is only applicable to CPU processing.

3. Rescale their values in the range 0–1.

TIP

Normalization is the process of transforming image data before deep learning processing. You can use different kinds of normalization, such as rescaling the range from 0 to 1 to −1 to 1, or applying statistical normalization by subtracting the mean and dividing by the standard deviation. Usually, rescaling all values in the range from 0 to 1 is a good working solution.

```
def normalize(X):
    X = X.reshape(len(X), 784)
    X = X.astype('float32')/255
    return X

(X_train, Y_train), (X_test, Y_test) = mnist.load_data()
X_train = normalize(X_train)
```

Having prepared the dataset for the neural network to learn, you can start preparing the GAN architecture. You begin by defining a few parameters, such as the type of data input provided to the GAN to generate its images. A good choice for this project is to use a list of random numbers. Imagine these random numbers as instructions provided to the GAN to decide what to represent. You have little control of what the GAN does with the numbers, but on other models, you can effectively use the inputs and obtain a desired output.

You also set the optimizer (the Adam optimizer in this case) and define the first part of the architecture, the generator. The generator takes the random input and passes it through a series of four dense layers. The only notable aspect of this process is that, except for the last layer, LeakyReLU powers all the layers, which is an activation that dampens negative inputs. BatchNormalization controls the distribution of outputs by applying statistical normalization to them. Using this approach avoids the situation that occurs when an extreme number pops up during training.

Notably, the last layer is different; it uses a sigmoid activation to generate outputs from zero to one. This last layer releases the image produced by the GAN, making it the generator part of the architecture. Because it produces 784 outputs whose values range from 0 to 1, the outputs could be easily reshaped and rescaled into 28-x-28-pixel arrays with values ranging from 0 to 255 (that is a MNIST image).

```
input_dim = 100
np.random.seed(42)
optimizer = Adam(lr=0.0002, beta_1=0.5)

gen = Sequential()
gen.add(Dense(256, input_dim=input_dim))
gen.add(LeakyReLU(alpha=0.2))
gen.add(BatchNormalization())
gen.add(Dense(512))
gen.add(LeakyReLU(alpha=0.2))
gen.add(BatchNormalization())
gen.add(Dense(1024))
gen.add(LeakyReLU(alpha=0.2))
gen.add(BatchNormalization())
gen.add(Dense(784, activation='sigmoid'))
gen.compile(loss='binary_crossentropy',
            optimizer=optimizer)
```

The second part of the architecture, the discriminator, is similar in construction to the generator. It has four dense layers again, and all but the last one is powered by LeakyReLU activation functions. The discriminator doesn't use BatchNormalization, but it has Dropout to avoid overfitting because this part performs a supervised classification task. In fact, the output is a single node that outputs a probability value from 0 to 1. The purpose of this part of the neural network is to differentiate the fake images produced by the generator part from the real images.

```
dsc = Sequential()
dsc.add(Dense(1024, input_dim=784))
dsc.add(LeakyReLU(alpha=0.2))
dsc.add(Dropout(0.3))
dsc.add(Dense(512))
dsc.add(LeakyReLU(alpha=0.2))
dsc.add(Dropout(0.3))
dsc.add(Dense(256))
dsc.add(LeakyReLU(alpha=0.2))
dsc.add(Dropout(0.3))
dsc.add(Dense(1, activation='sigmoid'))
dsc.compile(loss='binary_crossentropy',
            optimizer=optimizer)
```

At this point, you have the tricky part done, you've put the first and second half of the network together and ensured that they work together. Using the Keras functional API (see `https://keras.io/getting-started/functional-api-guide/` for details), you set architectures that are more complex than the sequential architectures used earlier in this section. In sum, the generator part processes the input and outputs the result to the discriminator part. The discriminator acts like a mathematical function applied to other functions — that is, it's a function discriminator (function generator [input]). In this way, you also control the network optimization because you can freeze part of it using the `make_trainable` function `def make_trainable(dnn, flag)`. (In fact, you do train the generator and discriminator toward maximizing different objectives.)

```
    dnn.trainable = flag
    for l in dnn.layers:
        l.trainable = flag

make_trainable(dsc, False)
inputs = Input(shape=(input_dim, ))
hidden = gen(inputs)
output = dsc(hidden)
gan = Model(inputs, output)
gan.compile(loss='binary_crossentropy',
            optimizer=optimizer)
```

Now you can test the setup. You prepare two useful, handy functions for generating the input noise and plotting the results of the generator:

```python
def create_noise(n, z):
    return np.random.normal(0, 1, size=(n, z))

def plot_sample(n, z):
    samples = gen.predict(create_noise(n, z))
    plt.figure(figsize=(15,3))
    for i in range(n):
        plt.subplot(1, n, (i+1))
        plt.imshow(samples[i].reshape(28, 28),
                   cmap='gray_r')
        plt.axis('off')
    plt.show()
```

The actual test begins by configuring the code for 100 epochs of training and setting the training batch to 128 images. The code starts iterating through the number of epochs and batches necessary to pass all the training images to the GAN. As with other examples in the book, this one takes a while to run. If you can gain access to a GPU, you're better off running it on Google Colab or on a computer with a GPU card. When you can obtain access to a GPU, plan on waiting for half an hour for it to run on Google Colab. (Your own local GPU setup may do better.) The sample example could well exceed several hours to complete on a CPU system.

```python
epochs = 100
batch_size = 128
batch_no = int(len(X_train) / batch_size)
gen_errors, dsc_errors = (list(), list())


for i in range(0, epochs):
    for j in range(batch_no):

        # Drawing a random sample of the training set
        rand_sample = np.random.randint(0, len(X_train),
            size=batch_size)
        image_batch = X_train[rand_sample]

        # Creating noisy inputs for the generator
        input_noise = create_noise(batch_size, input_dim)

        # Generating fake images from the noisy input
        generated_images = gen.predict(input_noise)
        X = np.concatenate((image_batch,
            generated_images))
```

```
# Creating somehow noisy labels
y = np.concatenate([[0.9]*batch_size,
   [0.0]*batch_size])

# Training discriminator to distinguish fakes from
# real ones
make_trainable(dsc, True)
dsc_loss = dsc.train_on_batch(X, y)
make_trainable(dsc, False)

# Trainining generating fakes
input_noise = create_noise(batch_size, input_dim)
fakes = np.ones(batch_size)
for _ in range(4):
  gen_loss = gan.train_on_batch(input_noise,
    fakes)

# Recording the losses
gen_errors.append(gen_loss)
dsc_errors.append(dsc_loss)

# Showing intermediate results
if i % 10 == 0:
  print("Epoch %i" % i)
  plot_sample(10, input_dim)
```

As the code completes running through the many calculations, it can revise the steps that it takes:

1. Generate a bunch of fake images by calling the generator function alone. Because this is a simple prediction, with no learning involved, the output images from the generator will appear completely random at the beginning.

2. Concatenate the fake images with a batch of real images.

3. Feed the images to the discriminator to determine whether the discriminator can separate the fake images from the real ones. This is a training activity, and the discriminator learns to separate the state-of-the-art images from the generator from the true source images.

4. Freeze the discriminator after it finishes learning so that the code can run it together with the generator, but this time only the generator will learn. During this step, the code feeds a few random inputs through the generator to transform into images and then pass the fakes to the discriminator to determine whether the discriminator can be fooled into believing that they are real images.

When the discriminator can determine that these images are the product of the generator, the code will use the discriminator score as an error for the generator to learn from (the success of the discriminator is a failure for the generator).

TIP

The code contains a couple of tricks to ensure that the GAN always produces good results:

» When training the discriminator, you provide some uncertainty to the labels of the true, thereby making the discriminator less severe.

» Every time you train the discriminator, you also train the generator four times. That's because learning to generate images is actually a longer process, and using this approach accelerates the process.

These are the two most effective tricks, but you can read about even more of them at this page maintained by Soumith Chintala at `https://github.com/soumith/ganhacks`. Clearly, deep learning is still more of an art (an explainable one) than a science. Plotting some of the results as shown in the following code reveals that the GAN has learned how to generate almost credible handwritten numbers, though they are not perfect. Looking at Figure 16-2, you can see what a GAN can achieve in such a short learning time.

```
# Plotting the final result
plot_sample(10, input_dim)
```

FIGURE 16-2: Some results from the trained GAN after 100 epochs.

You can also observe the errors that the two networks composing the GAN produced during the training. Use the following code (Figure 16-3 shows the output):

```
# Plotting the errors
plt.figure(figsize=(15, 5))
plt.plot(dsc_errors, label='discriminitive loss')
plt.plot(gen_errors, label='generative loss')
plt.legend()
plt.show()
```

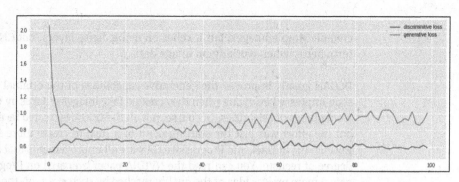

FIGURE 16-3:
The training
errors of a GAN's
generator and
discriminator
network.

Figure 16-3 shows that errors are on a different scale because the discriminator error is always lower than the generator error. In addition, the discriminator error tends to decrease because seeing more examples helps the discriminator separate fake images from the real ones, even if the generator improves its ability. As for the generator, the errors are at first strongly reduced but then tend to build up again because the discriminator gains experience in detection. If you run more epochs, you will see the generator error taking on a sinusoidal shape as it regularly increases its error rate for a while (as the generator becomes more skillful) and then decreases again (after finding out some new trick to fool the discriminator). It's an endless struggle between the two parts of the GAN network — a struggle that always produces more realistic images as the training continues.

Considering a Growing Field

After starting with a plain-vanilla implementation, similar to the one just completed, researchers have grown the GAN idea into a large number of variants that achieve tasks more complex than simply creating new images. The list of GANs and their applications grows every day, and keeping up is difficult. Avinash Hindupur has built a "GAN Zoo" by tracking all the variants, a task that's becoming more difficult daily. (You can see the most recent updates at https://github.com/hindupuravinash/the-gan-zoo.) Zheng Liu favors a historical approach instead, and you can see the GAN timeline he maintains at https://github.com/dongb5/GAN-timeline. No matter how you approach GANs, seeing how each new idea sprouts from previous ones is a useful exercise.

Inventing realistic pictures of celebrities

The chief application of GANs is to create images. The first GAN network that evolved from the original paper by Goodfellow and others is the DCGAN, which was based on convolutional layers. The example in this chapter does produce credible simple images, but it relies on using dense layers, not CNNs, which perform better when working on image data.

DCGAN greatly improved the generative capabilities of the original GANs, and they soon impressed everyone when they created fake images of faces by taking examples from photos of celebrities. Of course, not all the DCGAN-created faces were realistic, but the effort was just the starting point of a rush to create more realistic images. EBGAN-PT, BEGAN, and Progressive GAN are all improvements that achieve a higher degree of realism. You can read the NVIDIA paper prepared on Progressive GANs to gain a more precise idea of the quality reached by such state-of-the-art techniques: https://research.nvidia.com/publication/2017-10_Progressive-Growing-of.

Another great enhancement to GANs is the conditional GAN (CGAN). Although having a network produce realistic images of all the kinds is interesting, it's of little use when you can't control the type of output you receive in some way. CGANs manipulate the input and the network to suggest to the GAN what it should produce. Now, for instance, you have networks that produce images of faces of persons that don't exist, based on your preferences of how hair, eyes, and other details appear, as shown by this demonstrative video by NVIDIA: https://www.youtube.com/watch?v=kSLJriaOumA.

Enhancing details and image translation

Producing images of higher quality and possibly controlling the output generated has opened the way to more applications. This chapter doesn't have room to discuss them all, but the following list offers an overview of what you can find:

» **Cycle GAN:** Applied to neural transfer style (as discussed in Chapter 10). For example, you can turn a horse into a zebra or a Monet painting into one that appears to come from van Gough. By exploring the project at https://github.com/junyanz/CycleGAN, you can see how it works and consider the kind of transformations it can apply to images.

» **Super Resolution GAN (SRGAN):** Transforms images by making blurred, low-resolution images into clear, high-resolution ones. The application of this technique to photography and cinema is interesting because it improves low-quality images at nearly no cost. You can find the paper describing the technique and the results here: https://arxiv.org/pdf/1609.04802.pdf.

» **Pose Guided Person Image Generation:** Controls the pose of the person depicted in the created image. The paper at https://arxiv.org/pdf/1705.09368.pdf describes practical uses in the fashion industry to generate more poses of a model, but you might be surprised to know that the same approach can create videos of one person dancing exactly the same as another one: https://www.youtube.com/watch?v=PCBTZh41Ris

>> **Pix2Pix:** Translates sketches and maps into real images and vice versa. You can use this application to transform architectural sketches into a picture of a real building or to convert a satellite photo into a drawn map. The paper at https://arxiv.org/pdf/1611.07004.pdf discusses more of the possibilities offered the Pix2Pix network.

>> **Image repairing:** Repairs or modifies an existing image by determining what's missing, cancelled, or obscured: https://github.com/pathak22/context-encoder.

>> **Face Aging:** Determines how a face will age. You can read about it at https://arxiv.org/pdf/1702.01983.pdf.

>> **Midi Net:** Creates music in your favorite style, as described at https://arxiv.org/pdf/1703.10847.pdf.

Chapter **17**

Playing with Deep Reinforcement Learning

part from the example of GANs, you may be tempted to identify deep learning with supervised learning predictions. However, you also use deep learning for unsupervised learning and reinforcement learning (RL). Unsupervised learning supports a number of established techniques, such as autoencoders and self-organizing maps (SOMs), which this book doesn't cover. Unsupervised techniques can help you to segment your data into homogeneous groups or to detect anomalies in your variables.

RL techniques are even more popular than unsupervised learning techniques among practitioners. Recently the object of intense research, RL achieves smarter solutions for problems such as parking a car, learning to drive in as little as twenty minutes (as this paper illustrates: https://arxiv.org/abs/1807.00412), controlling an industrial robot, and more. (This article by Yuxi Li provides a complete list of applications: https://medium.com/@yuxili/rl-applications-73ef685c07eb.) This chapter tells you about some of these techniques, including one called AlphaGo, which was featured on the news after becoming the first algorithm to beat a human professional player at Go (an ancient Chinese board game) in an even game.

You also get some practical experience by working with some examples, which introduce you to OpenAI Gym (https://gym.openai.com/), a complete toolkit for experimenting with deep learning, and to keras-rl (https://github.com/keras-rl/keras-rl), a ready-to-use implementation of the state-of-the-art RL algorithms, such as Google's Deep Q-Network (DQN). DQN is the algorithm used to play vintage Atari 2600 games at expert human level and win. DQN is just one of the possible applications of this technique, which Google DeepMind has patented). After showing you how to build a working deep learning example network capable of successfully playing a simple game, the chapter explores how AlphaGo works and why its victory is such a milestone for deep learning and AI in general.

REMEMBER

Save yourself the time and mistakes of typing the code manually. You can find the downloadable source for this chapter in the DL4D_17_Reinforcement_Learning.ipynb file. (The Introduction tells you where to download the source code for this book.)

Playing a Game with Neural Networks

As a toddler, you may have enjoyed discovering the world around you and taking risks to test your abilities under the vigilant eye of your parents. Only later did you replace knowledge built on direct experience with knowledge received from others. Just as a supervised machine learning algorithm resembles a student learning about the world from someone else's past experiences described in books (in this metaphor, experiences are the data), an RL algorithm is more like a toddler — a clean whiteboard that accumulates knowledge by trying something and testing whether that knowledge provides a reward or a penalty.

RL provides a compact way of learning without gathering large masses of data, but it also involves complex interaction with the external world. Because RL begins without any data, interacting with the external world and receiving feedback defines the method used to obtain the data it requires. You could use this approach for a robot, moving in the physical world, or for a bot, wandering in the digital one. In particular, RL seems alluring for problems that aren't easy to crack using static (provided) data alone. Examples of such problems are teaching a computer to play a game by itself or working out the best possible outcome in uncertain situations, such as online advertising optimization. Advertising is one of the best examples because the application has to deliver the right campaigns to the right audience, but previous experience is lacking (for static or existing data) because all the campaigns are new.

Introducing reinforcement learning

In RL, you have an *agent* (which could be a robot in the real world or a bot in the digital one) interacting with an environment that could include a virtual or other sort of world with its own rules. The agent can receive information from the environment (called the *state*) and can act on it, sometimes changing it. More important, the agent can receive an input from the environment, a positive or negative one, based on its sequence of actions or inactions. The input is a *reward* even when negative. The purpose of RL is to have the agent learn how to behave to maximize the total sum of rewards received during its experience inside the environment.

You can determine the relationship between the agent and the environment from Figure 17-1. Note the time subscripts. If you consider the present instant in time as t, the previous instant is t−1. At time t−1, the agent acts and then receives both a state and a reward from the environment. Based on the sets of values relative to the action at time t, state at time t−1, and reward at time t, an RL algorithm can learn the action to obtain a certain environmental state.

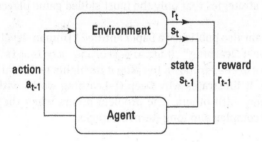

FIGURE 17-1:
A schema of how an agent and an environment relate in RL.

Ian Goodfellow, the AI research scientist behind the creation of GANs, believes that better integration between RL and deep learning is among the top priorities for further deep learning advances. Better integration leads to smarter robots (see https://www.forbes.com/sites/quora/2017/07/21/whats-next-for-deep-learning/#36131b871002 for details). Integration is now a hot topic, but until recently, RL typically had stronger bonds to statistics and algorithms than neural networks. Some people attempted to make the two operate together at an earlier time. In the early 1990s, Gerald Tesauro, at IBM Research Center, devised a way for a computer to learn to play Backgammon (one of the oldest board games known: http://www.bkgm.com/rules.html) and defeat a world (human) champion. He successfully used a neural network to power an RL algorithm by crafting a computer program that he called TD-Gammon. TD-Gammon raised widespread interest on the application of neural networks to RL problems, so many people tried after Tesauro to show some other possible use for the technique, but they all failed, and the idea died.

Later, some researchers noticed that Backgammon is a game based partly on chance. Other games (such as chess or Go) and real-world problems that didn't respond well to a combination of deep learning and RL aren't dependent on luck. The lack of a luck component only partially explains the problem with getting deep learning to work well with some games (for instance, poker is a game of chance but it has been beyond reach of RL and deep learning for a while). In spite of this insight (that is, deep learning works better with uncertainty), scientists still couldn't find a solution that allows neural networks to support RL on new problems until a few years later, when the Google deep learning research team proved the contrary.

At Google DeepMind, they took a well-known RL technique called Q-learning and made it work with deep learning rather than the classical computation algorithm. The new variant, named Deep Q-Learning, uses both convolutions and regular dense layers to obtain problem input and process it. This solution not only put deep learning and RL together again but also resulted in superhuman capabilities for playing some Atari 2600 games (see `https://www.youtube.com/watch?v=V1eYniJ0Rnk`). The algorithm learned to play in a relatively short time and found clever strategies that only the most skilled game players use.

TIP

The DeepMind team also published a paper entitled "Human-level control through deep reinforcement learning" (`https://storage.googleapis.com/deepmind-media/dqn/DQNNaturePaper.pdf`). In spite of its highly technical topic, the paper is quite readable. It illustrates why Deep Q-Learning works with certain games and performs badly with others. The problem occurs when the neural network needs to develop complex and long-term strategies.

Simulating game environments

Even if you don't work with preconstituted datasets when working with RL (meaning that you don't have to gather and label data), you have to consider interactions between the algorithm and the external world, which is a different challenge. For instance, if you want to build an RL algorithm that can beat you at chess, you first have to build a chess computer game that incorporates all the game rules. The algorithm will interface to this set of rules as part of its input.

To allow more researchers and practitioners to advance with this prerequisite, OpenAI (`https://openai.com/`), a nonprofit AI research company, has developed the open source Gym package. (You can find the code at `https://github.com/openai/gym` and the paper describing the solution at `https://arxiv.org/pdf/1606.01540.pdf`.) Gym is a complete a toolkit to help everyone develop RL algorithms applied to both basic and challenging problems by offering ready-to-use environments.

REMEMBER

OpenAI Gym lets you verify whether your algorithms are general in scope because all environments use the same command interface. You just change the environment name to test your RL solution within another situation.

The package also has a website where you can post your scores, comparing how your RL algorithm fares against other solutions. You easily install the gym package and its prerequisites on your local computer (the package h5py) from the Anaconda shell using these commands (pip will connect to the Internet to obtain the packages and install them locally):

```
pip install h5py
pip install gym
conda install -c menpo ffmpeg
```

TECHNICAL STUFF

In contrast to other book examples, the examples in this chapter can't run on Google Colab for technical reasons — the procedures are too complex. You need to run the code on your local computer.

Using Gym, you don't have to worry about the environment anymore. Different environments are available, some presenting algorithmic tasks (such as learning to copy a sequence), some text based, some robotic related (like controlling a robot's arm), and a larger number based on the old Atari arcade games, such as Space Invaders or Breakout. You can see all the environments available at https://gym.openai.com/envs/. You start with a classic environment, as described in the RL scientific literature, but you can also explore the other possibilities offered by the package.

REMEMBER

Studying how to solve games using RL also helps you devise better solutions for real-world problems. At Uber, a transportation network company, engineers study RL algorithms, contemplate how RL operates, and reverse engineer how RL makes decisions to develop trust and confidence in AI, as you can read in Uber's engineering blog at https://eng.uber.com/atari-zoo-deep-reinforcement-learning/.

Gym is structured around the core principles of RL, so you find functions and methods to describe the agent and the environment. You can also have the agent perform an action or inaction inside the environment. The environment will answer by providing feedback in two forms: a new state, which you can use to summarize the new situation within the environment; and a reward, which is a score showing success or failure. The only part you need to code is the RL, and you can start a basic example using a few lines of Python.

The environment for the RL experiment is the CartPole problem (see https://gym.openai.com/envs/CartPole-v1/ for details). A pole attaches freely to a cart that moves along a track (you don't account for friction). The pendulum starts upright, in unstable equilibrium, and the goal of the environment is to prevent it from falling over (which requires an angle greater than 15 degrees from vertical). For actions, you determine whether to increase or decrease the cart's velocity in one direction or another.

Figure 17-2 shows a representation of the environment provided by the OpenAI Gym package. You can also see an example of how to balance a CartPole in this real-world experiment by the Department of Engineering of the Technological Educational Institute of Crete at https://www.youtube.com/watch?v=XWhGjxdug0o.

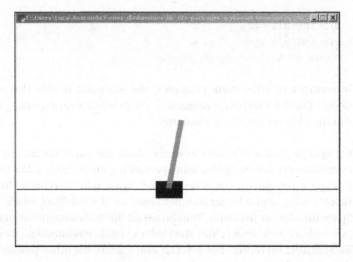

FIGURE 17-2:
The CartPole
environment in
OpenAI Gym.

The CartPole environment operates by reporting observations of these states:

>> Cart position

>> Cart velocity

>> Pole angle

>> Pole velocity at tip

You can manipulate the environment based on the these states by

>> Pushing the cart to the left

>> Pushing the cart to the right

The following code creates the environment and tests some random commands with it:

```
import numpy as np
import gym
env = gym.make('CartPole-v0')
```

```
np.random.seed(42), env.seed(42)
nb_actions = env.action_space.n
input_shape = (1, env.observation_space.shape[0])
```

You create the environment using a single make command that returns a Python class used for getting general information about the environment (for instance, about actions you can perform using the env.action_space), controlling the flow of time, or performing some specific action inside the environment.

The next few lines reset the environment just created. Everything is restarted at an initial position (some environmental aspects are randomly decided). The code uses a loop of 200 iterations to perform various random actions sampled from the range of the possible available actions (a force applied on the cart, ranging from -1 to +1). When the iterations complete, the game ends in failure (when the pole is more than 15 degrees from vertical), or the cart moves more than 2.4 units from the center, the done variable becomes true and the experiment concludes (the number of steps will vary because it's a random process of choices).

```
observation = env.reset()
for t in range(200):
  env.render()
  act = env.action_space.sample()
  obs, rwrd, done, info = env.step(act)
  if done:
      print("Episode concluded after %i timesteps" % (t+1))
      break
env.close()
```

Presenting Q-learning

Building an RL solution based on deep learning requires quite a coding effort, but you can leverage an existing package, keras-rl (https://github.com/keras-rl/keras-rl), which contains the most recent state-of-the-art RL algorithms. This package, developed by Matthias Plappert, a Research Scientist working at OpenAI, can seamlessly integrate with neural networks built with Keras and the OpenAI environments. You install the package by issuing this command on a shell:

```
pip install keras-rl
```

After you install keras-rl, you import the necessary functions from Keras (you use a neural network for your RL solution) and keras-rl specialized functions for creating an RL agent. (The details about how they work appear later in the chapter.)

```
from keras.models import Sequential
from keras.layers import Dense, Activation
from keras.layers import Flatten, Dropout
from keras.optimizers import Adam
from rl.agents.dqn import DQNAgent
from rl.policy import EpsGreedyQPolicy
from rl.memory import SequentialMemory
```

The first step is building a network capable of figuring out the outcome in terms of a reward from a certain environmental state. This is the *value-based learning* approach, and it's the idea behind Deep Q-Network and Deep Q-Learning: to approximately determine the reward after taking a certain action, given the present state. This technique doesn't directly consider past actions and the associated state, or the complete sequence of actions that an agent should take, yet it works effectively for many problems by pointing out the best single action to take among the alternatives.

```
model = Sequential()
model.add(Flatten(input_shape=input_shape))
model.add(Dense(12))
model.add(Activation('relu'))
model.add(Dense(nb_actions))
model.add(Activation('linear'))

print(model.summary())
```

The neural network that the code creates is simple, made of three layers of decreasing numbers of neurons. All the layers are activated by an ReLU function, but the final layer activates linearly to get an output value that's used as the action the bot will take.

REMEMBER

The DQN algorithm doesn't understand how the environment works. In a human sense, the algorithm simply associates state and actions to expected rewards, which is done using a mathematical function. The algorithm, therefore, can't understand whether it's playing a particular game; its understanding of the environment is limited to the knowledge of the reported state deriving from taken actions.

This neural network feeds into the DQN algorithm, together with a policy (a policy is a function that chooses a sequence of actions), and a memory of previous actions and states. The memory is necessary to allow the example to train a neural network. It records previous agent experiences with the environment, and the code can sample it to extract a series of actions given a state. The neural network uses the memory to learn how to estimate the likely reward from an action taken in a state.

For the policy, Eps Greedy Q policy does either of the following:

» Takes a random action with probability epsilon

» Takes a current best action with probability (1 – epsilon)

The two policies show the exploration/exploitation trade-off. When the Eps Greedy Q policy function chooses randomly to take a random action, the algorithm is exploring because it could decide on an unexpected action, and that action could lead to an interesting result. For instance, in the Atari Breakthrough game, digging a hole in the wall and having the ball run amok, destroying the wall from above, is clearly a strategy that emerged randomly by exploration and that the RL algorithm recorded and learned as being extremely useful.

```
policy = EpsGreedyQPolicy(eps=0.3)
memory = SequentialMemory(limit=50000,
                          window_length=1)

dqn = DQNAgent(model=model,
               nb_actions=nb_actions,
               memory=memory,
               nb_steps_warmup=50,
               target_model_update=0.01,
               policy=policy)

dqn.compile(Adam(lr=0.001))

training = dqn.fit(env, nb_steps=30000,
                   visualize=False, verbose=1)
```

The system trains itself using the same approach used by other deep learning networks. After completing its learning from 30,000 examples, it's ready to test:

```
env = gym.make('CartPole-v0')
mon = gym.wrappers.Monitor(env,
                           "./gym-results",
                           force=True)
mon.reset()
dqn.test(mon, nb_episodes=1, visualize=True)
mon.close()
env.close()
```

The test should end up in a high reward (the expected result is about 200, but it could be different because the test has a random training element). You can review the behavior of the cart using the DQN directives found in the video that recorded during the test:

```python
import io
import base64
from IPython.display import HTML

template = \
    './gym-results/openaigym.video.%s.video000001.mp4'
video = io.open(template % mon.file_infix, 'r+b').read()
encoded = base64.b64encode(video)
HTML(data='''
<video width="520" height="auto" alt="test" controls>
<source src="data:video/mp4;base64,{0}"
 type="video/mp4"/>
</video>'''.format(encoded.decode('ascii')))
```

Explaining Alpha-Go

Chess and Go are both popular board games that share characteristics, such as being played by two players who move in turns and lack a random element (no dice are thrown as in Backgammon). Apart from that, they have different game rules and complexity. In chess, each player has 16 pieces to move on the board according to type, and the game ends when the king piece is stalemated (checked) — unable to move further. Experts calculate that about 10^{123} different chess games are possible, which is a large number when you consider that scientists estimate the number of atoms in the known universe at about 10^{80}. Yet, computers can master a single game of chess by determining the future possible moves far enough ahead to have an advantage against any human opponent. In 1997, Deep Blue, an IBM supercomputer designed for playing chess, defeated Garry Kasparov, the world chess champion.

REMEMBER

A computer cannot prefigure a complete game of chess using brute force (calculating every possible move from beginning to end of the game). It uses some heuristics and its ability to look into a certain number of future moves. Deep Blue was a computer with high computational performance that could anticipate more future moves in the game than any previous computer.

In Go, you have a 19-x-19 grid of lines containing 361 spots on which each player places a stone (usually black or white color) each time a player takes a turn. The purpose of the game is to enclose in stones a larger portion of the board than one's opponent's. Considering that, on average, each player has about 250 possible moves at each turn, and that a game consists of about 150 moves, a computer would need enough memory to hold 150^{250} games, which is on the order of 10^{360} boards. From a resource perspective, Go is more complex than chess, and experts used to believe that no computer software would be able to beat a human Go master within the next decade using the same approach as Deep Blue. Yet, AlphaGo accomplished it using RL techniques.

DeepMind, a research center in London owned by Google, developed a computer system named AlphaGo in 2016 that featured Go playing skills never attained before by any hardware and software solution. After setting up the system, Deep-Mind had AlphaGo test itself against the strongest Go champion living in Europe, Fan Gui, who had been the European Go champion three times. DeepMind challenged him in a closed-door match, and AlphaGo won all the games, leaving Fan Gui amazed by the game style displayed by the computer.

Then, after Fan Gui helped refine the AlphaGo skills, the DeepMind team, led by their CEO Demis Hassabis and chief scientist David Silver, challenged Lee Sedol, a South Korean professional Go player ranked at the ninth dan, the highest level a master can attain. AlphaGo won a series of four games against Lee Sedol and lost only one. Apart from the match it lost because of an unexpected move from the champion, it actually led the other games and amazed the champion by playing unexpected, impactful moves. In fact, both players, Fan Gui and Lee Sedol, felt that playing against AlphaGo was like playing against a contestant coming from another reality: AlphaGo moves resembled nothing they had seen before.

TIP

The story behind AlphaGo is so fascinating that someone made a film out of it. It's well worth seeing: https://www.imdb.com/title/tt6700846/.

Determining if you're going to win

In chess, you can explore future moves and go far with the right computer. The number of pieces, their limited movements, and the state of the board all make determining what could happen easier. Moreover, you can get a measure of how well the game is progressing or how a move could rate because of the nature of the game itself (chess pieces have a value, for instance). In Go, you can't make these determinations because the number of possible moves explodes just a few moves ahead. In addition, you can't determine the move value because you have to see the game completed before understanding how each move contributed to the end of the game.

Because the underlying strategy of Go differs from chess, computer programs playing Go use another approach to determine which moves to make. That approach is called Monte Carlo Tree Search (MCTS). In MCTS, the computer simulates many complete games from the existing state of the board, first using random moves and then using the most successful moves that it finds during random play. This isn't too different from the exploration/exploitation approach in RL. Using this approach, a computer can determine whether a move in Go is good or not by simulating enough games to obtain a reliable answer.

AlphaGo uses MCTS but supports the algorithm's processing using neural networks. The system is made of two components:

>> **A look at a future move system:** A forecasting method similar to the one used by Deep Blue. It's a tree search system because it branches through possible games and relies on MCTS to do so.

>> **Some CNNs:** Provide the guidance to the tree search system.

The deep learning networks are of two kinds: policy networks and value networks. Both networks process the board image, looking for local and general patterns like those used in image processing used to differentiate between a dog and a cat. The roles of two policy networks (one slower but more precise, one faster but rougher) are to guide action selection. These policy networks output a probability for each possible move, so MCTS can simulate realistic games based on their suggestions, not randomly. The value network provides a likelihood of winning, given the board state.

TIP

By using both value networks, which provide an intuition of the game situation, and the policy network, which helps the computer prefigure future moves, AlphaGo can deliver the best strategy and moves during game play.

Given that such an architecture isn't really end-to-end because it involves so many different systems, engineers at Deep Mind first trained AlphaGo using games played by strong amateurs to kick-start the neural networks. (They used 160,000 amateur games collected from an online Go community.) Finally, they let AlphaGo play against itself to learn how to improve and refine its playing skills. Here, RL techniques had a key role: They taught computers to play Backgammon, chess, poker, Scrabble, and finally Go by having AlphaGo challenge itself millions of times, working in the kind of fast and intense experience-building environment that humans can't handle.

REMEMBER

David Silver, the AlphaGo project chief researcher, declared that self-learning is so effective in building smart systems because the opponent these systems face is always at the right level of skill — never too low or too high. Letting a system learn by playing itself is something seen in TD-Gammon in 1992, as well as in the WOPR computer in the 1983 *WarGames* film. (In this sense, the WOPR computer is as emblematic for AI as HAL9000 in *2001: A Space Odyssey* is.)

Applying self-learning at scale

The DeepMind team that created AlphaGo didn't stop after the success of its solution; it retired AlphaGo and created even more incredible systems. First, the team built up AlphaGo Zero, which is AlphaGo trained by playing against itself. Then it created Alpha Zero, which is a general program that can learn to play chess and shogi, the Japanese chess game, by itself.

If AlphaGo demonstrated how to solve a problem deemed impossible for computers, AlphaGo Zero demonstrated that computers can attain super-capabilities using self-learning (which is RL in its essence). In the end, its results were even better than from those starting from human experience: AlphaGo Zero has challenged AlphaGo and won 100 matches without losing one.

GRASPING THE IMPORTANCE OF ALPHA ZERO

The Alpha Zero feat is even more important than what AlphaGo achieved. This book frequently mentions the role of data in opening the way for deep learning to perform well. More data with a simple model can beat a clever algorithm using less data. Howeyer, Alpha Zero managed to reach the pinnacle of performance starting with zero data. This capability goes beyond the idea that data can achieve every AI target (as Alon Halevy, Peter Norvig, and Fernando Pereira stated just a few years ago in the whitepaper at https://static.googleusercontent.com/media/research.google.com/it//pubs/archive/35179.pdf). Alpha Zero is possible because we know the generative processes used by Go game players, and DeepMind researchers were able to recreate a perfect Go environment.

In terms of laws, many more situations than Go can be defined. For instance, scientists know the basic laws of how the physical world works because humans spent centuries investigating them, with the brightest minds endeavoring to understanding them — from Isaac Newton to Albert Einstein and Stephen Hawking. This knowledge opens the door to creating generative models that can replicate and simulate the thought processes used to create the data needed by deep learning and AI models to learn. If this process sounds really advanced, take note: It's already here. People are already discussing how a video game could help build better self-driving cars, as you can read in the article at https://www.inverse.com/article/26307-grand-theft-auto-open-ai.

A paper published in Nature (and accessible on the DeepMind website at https://deepmind.com/research/publications/mastering-game-go-without-human-knowledge/) explains that AlphaGo Zero started learning by making random moves. This activity is similar to how the reinforcement algorithm DQN learned to balance a cart in the coding example. In about 29 million self-playing games, AlphaGo Zero reached a level exceeding the previous AlphaGo system. Moreover, AlphaGo Zero is both less complex in terms of deep learning models and hardware it requires. It needs a single computer and four of Google's custom TPU chips, whereas the original AlphaGo required several machines and 48 TPUs.

AlphaGo, AlphaGo Zero, and Alpha Zero represent the new frontier of RL as well as hope for future applications. In fact, apart from playing Go, chess, and shogi, these systems aren't capable of anything else. Like Deep Blue, these systems concentrate on a single task that they can execute at a qualitatively super-human level. Researchers at DeepMind envision further possible applications that are now difficult and challenging for humans, such as protein folding, optimizing energy consumption in a network, or discovering new materials in chemistry.

4

The Part of Tens

IN THIS PART . . .

Consider real-world applications that use deep learning.

Find some of the best tools for deep learning tasks.

Discover an occupation that relies on deep learning.

Chapter **18**

Ten Applications that Require Deep Learning

This chapter is too short. It can't even begin to describe the ways in which deep learning will affect you in the future. Consider this chapter to be offering a tantalizing tidbit — an appetizer that can whet your appetite for exploring the world of deep learning further. The applications you see listed in this chapter are already common in some cases. You probably used at least one of them today, and quite likely more than just one. After reading this chapter, you might want to take the time to consider all the ways in which deep learning currently affects your life. Although the technology has begun to see widespread usage, it's really just the beginning. We're at the start of something, and AI is actually quite immature at this point.

This chapter doesn't discuss killer robots, dystopian futures, AI run amok, or any of the sensational scenarios that you might see in the movies. This chapter is about real life, discussing existing AI applications that you can interact with today.

Restoring Color to Black-and-White Videos and Pictures

You probably have some black-and-white videos or pictures of family members or special events that you'd love to see in color. Color consists of three elements: hue (the actual color), value (the darkness or lightness of the color), and saturation (the intensity of the color). You can read more about these elements at `http://learn.leighcotnoir.com/artspeak/elements-color/hue-value-saturation/`. Oddly enough, many artists are color-blind and make strong use of color value in their creations (read `https://www.nytimes.com/2017/12/23/books/a-colorblind-artist-illustrator-childrens-books.html` as one of many examples). So having hue missing (the element that black-and-white art lacks) isn't the end of the world. Quite the contrary, some artists view it as an advantage (see `https://www.artsy.net/article/artsy-editorial-the-advantages-of-being-a-colorblind-artist` for details).

When viewing something in black and white, you see value and saturation but not hue. *Colorization* is the process of adding the hue back in. Artists generally perform this process using a painstaking selection of individual colors, as described at `https://fstoppers.com/video/how-amazing-colorization-black-and-white-photos-are-done-5384` and `https://www.diyphotography.net/know-colors-add-colorizing-black-white-photos/`. However, AI has automated this process using Convolutional Neural Networks (CNNs), as described at `https://emerj.com/ai-future-outlook/ai-is-colorizing-and-beautifying-the-world/`.

REMEMBER

The easiest way to use CNN for colorization is to find a library to help you. The Algorithmia site at `https://demos.algorithmia.com/colorize-photos/` offers such a library and shows some example code. You can also try the application by pasting a URL into the supplied field. The article at `https://petapixel.com/2016/07/14/app-magically-turns-bw-photos-color-ones/` describes just how well this application works. It's absolutely amazing!

Approximating Person Poses in Real Time

Person poses don't tell you who is in a video stream, but rather what elements of a person are in the video stream. For example, using a person pose could tell you whether the person's elbow appears in the video and where it appears. The article at `https://medium.com/tensorflow/real-time-human-pose-estimation-in-the-browser-with-tensorflow-js-7dd0bc881cd5` tells you more about how this whole visualization technique works. In fact, you can see how the system works through a short animation of one person in the first case and three people in the second case.

Person poses can have all sorts of useful purposes. For example, you could use a person pose to help people improve their form for various kinds of sports — everything from golf to bowling. A person pose could also make new sorts of video games possible. Imagine being able to track a person's position for a game without the usual assortment of cumbersome gear. Theoretically, you could use person poses to perform crime-scene analysis or to determine the possibility of a person committing a crime.

Another interesting application of pose detection is for medical and rehabilitation purposes. Software powered by deep learning could tell you whether you're doing your exercises correctly and track your improvements. An application of this sort could support the work of a professional rehabilitator by taking care of you when you aren't in a medical facility (an activity called telerehabilitation; see https://matrc.org/telerehabilitation-telepractice for details).

REMEMBER

Fortunately, you can at least start working with person poses today using the tfjs-models (PoseNet) library at https://github.com/tensorflow/tfjs-models/tree/master/posenet. You can see it in action with a webcam, complete with source code, at https://ml5js.org/docs/posenet-webcam. The example takes a while to load, so you need to be patient.

Performing Real-Time Behavior Analysis

Behavior analysis goes a step beyond what the person poses analysis described in the previous section does. When you perform behavior analysis, the question still isn't a matter of whom, but how. This particular AI application affects how vendors design products and websites. Articles such as the one at https://amplitude.com/blog/2016/06/14/10-steps-behavioral-analytics go to great lengths to fully define and characterize the use of behavior analysis. In most cases, behavior analysis helps you see how the process the product designer expected you to follow doesn't match the process you actually use.

Behavior analysis has a role to play in other areas of life as well. For example, it can help people in the medical profession identify potential issues with people who have specific medical conditions, such as autism, and help the patient overcome those issues (see https://www.autismspeaks.org/applied-behavior-analysis-aba-0 for details). Behavior analysis may also help teachers of physical arts show students how to hone their skills. You might also see it used in the legal profession to help ascertain motive. (The guilt is obvious, but why a person does something is essential to fair remediation of an unwanted behavior.)

Fortunately, you can already start performing behavior analysis with Python. For example, the site at `https://rrighart.github.io/GA/` discusses the technique (and provides source code as well) with regard to web analytics.

Translating Languages

The Internet has created an environment that can keep you from knowing whom you're really talking to, where that person is, or sometimes even when the person is talking to you. One thing hasn't changed, however: the need to translate one language to another when the two parties don't speak a common language. In a few cases, mistranslation can be humorous, assuming that both parties have a sense of humor. However, mistranslation has also led to all sorts of serious consequences, including war (see `https://unbabel.com/blog/translation-errors-war-iraq-hiroshima-vietnam/`). Consequently, even though translation software is extremely accessible on the Internet, careful selection of which product to use is important. One of the most popular of these applications is Google Translate (`https://translate.google.com/`), but many other applications are available, such as, DeepL (`https://www.deepl.com/en/translator`). According to Forbes, machine translation is one area in which AI excels (see `https://www.forbes.com/sites/bernardmarr/2018/08/24/will-machine-learning-ai-make-human-translators-an-endangered-species/#114274573902`).

Translation applications generally rely on Bidirectional Recurrent Neural Networks (BRNNs) as described at `https://blog.statsbot.co/machine-learning-translation-96f0ed8f19e4`. You don't have to create your own BRNN because you have many existing APIs to choose from. For example, you can get Python access to the Google Translate API using the library found at `https://pypi.org/project/googletrans/`. The point is that translation is possibly one of the more popular deep learning applications and one that many people use without even thinking about it.

Estimating Solar Savings Potential

Trying to determine whether solar energy will actually work in your location is difficult unless a lot of other people are also using it. In addition, it's even harder to know what level of savings you might enjoy. Of course, you don't want to install solar energy if it won't satisfy your goals for using it, which may not actually include long-term cost savings (although generally it does). Some deep reinforcement learning projects now help you take the guesswork out of solar energy, including Project Sunroof found at https://www.google.com/get/sunroof. Fortunately, you can also get support for this kind of prediction in your Python application at https://github.com/ColasGael/Machine-Learning-for-Solar-Energy-Prediction.

Beating People at Computer Games

The AI-versus-people competition continues to attract interest. From winning at chess to winning at Go, AI seems to have become unbeatable — at least, unbeatable at one game. Unlike humans, AI specializes, and an AI that can win at Go is unlikely to do well at chess. Even so, 2017 is often hailed as the beginning of the end for humans over AI in games, as described at https://newatlas.com/ai-2017-beating-humans-games/52741/. Of course, the competition has been going on for some time, And you can likely find competitions that the AI won far earlier than 2017. Indeed, some sources (https://en.wikipedia.org/wiki/AlphaGo) place the date for a Go win as early as October 2015. The article at https://interestingengineering.com/11-times-ai-beat-humans-at-games-art-law-and-everything-in-between describes 11 other times that the AI won.

The problem is to custom create an AI that can win a particular game and realize that in specializing at that game, the AI may not do well at other games. The process of building an AI for just one game can look difficult. The article at https://medium.freecodecamp.org/simple-chess-ai-step-by-step-d55a9266977 describes how to build a simple chess AI, which actually won't defeat a chess master but could do well with an intermediate player.

TIP

However, it's actually a bit soon to say that people are out of the game. In the future, people may compete against the AI with more than one game. Examples of this sort of competition already abound, such as people who perform in a triathlon of games, which consists of three sporting events, rather than one. The competition would then become one of flexibility: the AI couldn't simply hunker down and learn only one game, so the human would have a flexibility edge. This sort of AI use demonstrates that humans and AI may have to cooperate in the future, with the AI specializing in specific tasks and the human providing the flexibility needed to perform all required tasks.

Generating Voices

Your car may already speak to you; many cars speak regularly to people now. Oddly, the voice generation is often so good that it's hard to tell the generated voice from a real one. Articles such as the one at https://qz.com/1165775/googles-voice-generating-ai-is-now-indistinguishable-from-humans/ talk about how the experience of finding computer voices that sound quite real are becoming more common. The issue attracts enough attention now that many call centers tell you that you're speaking to a computer rather than a person.

TIP

Although call output relies on scripted responses, making it possible to generate responses with an extremely high level of confidence, voice recognition is a little harder to perform (but it has greatly improved). To work with voice recognition successfully, you often need to limit your input to specific key terms. By using keywords that the voice recognition is designed to understand, you avoid the need for a user to repeat a request. This need for specific terms gives it away that you're talking to a computer — simply ask for something unexpected and the computer won't know what to do with it.

The easy way to implement your own voice system is to rely on an existing API, such as Cloud Speech to Text (https://cloud.google.com/speech-to-text/). Of course, you might need something that you can customize. In this case, using an API will prove helpful. The article at https://medium.com/@sundarstyles89/create-your-own-google-assistant-voice-based-assistant-using-python-94b577d724f9 tells how to build your own voice-based application using Python.

Predicting Demographics

Demographics, those vital or social statistics that group people by certain characteristics, have always been part art and part science. You can find any number of articles about getting your computer to generate demographics for clients (or potential clients). The use of demographics is wide ranging, but you see them used for things like predicting which product a particular group will buy (versus that of the competition). Demographics are an important means of categorizing people and then predicting some action on their part based on their group associations. Here are the methods that you often see cited for AIs when gathering demographics:

>> **Historical:** Based on previous actions, an AI generalizes which actions you might perform in the future.

>> **Current activity:** Based on the action you perform now and perhaps other characteristics, such as gender, a computer predicts your next action.

» **Characteristics:** Based on the properties that define you, such as gender, age, and area where you live, a computer predicts the choices you are likely to make.

WARNING

You can find articles about AI's predictive capabilities that seem almost too good to be true. For example, the article at `https://medium.com/@demografy/artificial-intelligence-can-now-predict-demographic-characteristics-knowing-only-your-name-6749436a6bd3` says that AI can now predict your demographics based solely on your name. The company in that article, Demografy (`https://demografy.com/`), claims to provide gender, age, and cultural affinity based solely on name. Even though the site claims that it's 100 percent accurate, this statistic is highly unlikely because some names are gender ambiguous, such as Renee, and others are assigned to one gender in some countries and another gender in others. Yes, demographic prediction can work, but exercise care before believing everything that these sites tell you.

If you want to experiment with demographic prediction, you can find a number of APIs online. For example, the DeepAI API at `https://deepai.org/machine-learning-model/demographic-recognition` promises to help you predict age, gender, and cultural background based on a person's appearance in a video. Each of the online APIs do specialize, so you need to choose the API with an eye toward the kind of input data you can provide.

Creating Art from Real-World Pictures

Chapter 15 provides you with some good ideas on how deep learning can use the content of a real-world picture and an existing master for style to create a combination of the two. In fact, some pieces of art generated using this approach are commanding high prices on the auction block. You can find all sorts of articles on this particular kind of art generation, such as the *Wired* article at `https://www.wired.com/story/we-made-artificial-intelligence-art-so-can-you/`.

However, even though pictures are nice for hanging on the wall, you might want to produce other kinds of art. For example, you can create a 3-D version of your picture using products like Smoothie 3-D. The articles at `https://styly.cc/tips/smoothie-3d/` and `https://3dprint.com/38467/smoothie-3d-software/` describe how this software works. It's not the same as creating a sculpture; rather, you use a 3-D printer to build a 3-D version of your picture. The article at `https://thenextweb.com/artificial-intelligence/2018/03/08/try-this-ai-experiment-that-converts-2d-images-to-3d/` offers an experiment that you can perform to see how the process works.

REMEMBER

The output of an AI doesn't need to consist of something visual, either. For example, deep learning enables you to create music based on the content of a picture, as described at https://www.cnet.com/news/baidu-ai-creates-original-music-by-looking-at-pictures-china-google/. This form of art makes the method used by AI clearer. The AI transforms content that it doesn't understand from one form to another. As humans, we see and understand the transformation, but all the computer sees are numbers to process using clever algorithms created by other humans.

Forecasting Natural Catastrophes

People have been trying to predict natural disasters for as long as there have been people and natural disasters. No one wants to be part of an earthquake, tornado, volcanic eruption, or any other natural disaster. Being able to get away quickly is the prime consideration in this case given that humans can't control their environment well enough yet to prevent any natural disaster.

Deep learning provides the means to look for extremely subtle patterns that boggle the minds of humans. These patterns can help predict a natural catastrophe, according to the article on Google's solution at http://www.digitaljournal.com/tech-and-science/technology/google-to-use-ai-to-predict-natural-disasters/article/533026. The fact that the software can predict any disaster at all is simply amazing. However, the article at http://theconversation.com/ai-could-help-us-manage-natural-disasters-but-only-to-an-extent-90777 warns that relying on such software exclusively would be a mistake. Overreliance on technology is a constant theme throughout this book, so don't be surprised that deep learning is less than perfect in predicting natural catastrophes as well.

Chapter **19**

Ten Must-Have Deep Learning Tools

D eep learning is a complex task, and if you try to write every last bit of code you need, you won't ever have time to perform any analysis, which takes considerable time by itself. Consequently, you need tools that will help you get the job done with less effort. Throughout the book, you have seen a number of tools described and used. However, except for TensorFlow and Keras, the tools described previously are generally a good starting point, or something to consider to ease the learning curve. The tools in this chapter are special. They help you accomplish a variety of tasks with professional results.

Compiling Math Expressions Using Theano

Theano (http://deeplearning.net/software/theano/) is a Python library that makes it easier for you to work with various math expressions quickly. You can replace the copy of TensorFlow you installed in the "Getting your copy of Tensor-Flow and Keras" section of Chapter 4 with Theano when desired. The choice of which to use can be quite complicated, as shown by the discussions at https://www. analyticsindiamag.com/tensorflow-vs-theano-researchers-prefer-artificial-intelligence-framework/ and https://www.reddit.com/r/MachineLearning/comments/4ekywt/tensorflow_vs_theano_which_to_learn/. However, Theano's fast speed doesn't seem to be in question.

After training a few models in this book, you already know that speed is important — even essential. For example, the Chapter 12 code really could use some speeding up, and libraries like this one could help you make that happen (see the "Considering the cost of realistic output" sidebar in Chapter 12 for a discussion of speed issues). Here are the underlying features that make Theano so incredibly fast:

>> Transparent GPU use

>> Dynamic C-code generation

>> Specialized optimizations

WARNING

Theano is currently the fourth most-used framework (as shown at `https://towardsdatascience.com/deep-learning-framework-power-scores-2018-23607ddf297a`), which is why it appears in this chapter. However, as stated at `https://groups.google.com/forum/m/#!msg/theano-users/7Poq8BZutbY/rNCIfvAEAwAJ`, the Theano developers aren't doing anything more with it. You can see the final update notes at `http://www.deeplearning.net/software/theano/NEWS.html` and read developer reactions to the loss at `https://www.quora.com/Is-Theano-deep-learning-library-dying`. Many developers still make a strong case for using it, as discussed at `https://www.reddit.com/r/MachineLearning/comments/47qh90/is_there_a_case_for_still_using_torch_theano/`.

Augmenting TensorFlow Using Keras

Chapter 4 and various other chapters in this book describe using Keras (`https://keras.io/`) with TensorFlow. The "Getting your copy of TensorFlow and Keras" section of Chapter 4 tells you how to obtain a copy of these products and install them. Many of the book examples won't run without Keras, so you may have already seen a smidgen of what Keras can do for you.

Fortunately, if you choose to go the Theano route instead of working with TensorFlow, you still have the option of using Keras alongside it. You can also use the built-in version of Keras with TensorFlow (see `https://www.tensorflow.org/api_docs/python/tf/keras` for details). The connection between Keras and TensorFlow will only get stronger when TensorFlow 2.0 is finally released (see `https://medium.com/tensorflow/standardizing-on-keras-guidance-on-high-level-apis-in-tensorflow-2-0-bad2b04c819a` for details).

TIP

Oddly enough, you can also use Keras with your Microsoft Cognitive Toolkit (CNTK) installation. Keras supports all three through a backend, as described at `https://keras.io/backend/`. You simply need to use a different underlying toolkit to make a change to a configuration file. As a result, you can experiment to see which toolkit serves your needs best, and your Keras code will remain the same. One caveat, however: You must write your code using the abstract Keras backend API for it to be compatible with multiple underlying toolkits. This book doesn't show you how to use the abstract Keras backend API, so this technique would require additional learning time on your part.

Dynamically Computing Graphs with Chainer

At one time, you might have used a library such as Pylearn2 (which is built on TensorFlow; (see http://deeplearning.net/software/pylearn2/ for details) to bridge the gap between algorithms and deep learning. However, new products, such as Chainer (https://chainer.org/) have taken the stage for reasons such as those discussed at https://www.quora.com/Which-is-better-for-deep-learning-TensorFlow-or-Chainer. The emphasis is on making it easier to access the functionality that most systems can provide today or access through online hosts. Consequently, you can look to Chainer to provide these features:

>> CUDA support for GPU access

>> Multiple GPU support with little effort

>> Support for a variety of networks including feed-forward nets, CNNs, recurrent nets, and recursive nets

>> Per-batch architecture support

>> Control of flow statements in forward computation without losing backpropagation

>> Significant debugging functionality to make finding errors easier

Creating a MATLAB-Like Environment with Torch

To get optimal performance from deep learning solutions, you need GPU support, which is where Torch (http://torch.ch/) comes into play. It puts the GPU first when you develop solutions, which allows you to get the additional cores and optimized processing features that GPUs can provide. To offer maximum speed, Torch relies on the LuaJIT compiler (http://luajit.org/) to compile your application instead of interpreting it. (Interpreters can make applications run slower.) It also has an underlying C language and CUDA (https://www.geforce.com/hardware/technology/cuda) implementation that turns your high-level code into a low-level language to run as quickly as possible.

Torch comes with some features that are similar to those found in NumPy, but with an emphasis on deep learning. (You can find the package documentation at http://torch.ch/docs/package-docs.html.) For example, you'll find:

» N-dimensional arrays

» Matrix manipulation features

» Linear algebra routines

In addition to these features, you find some that are specifically devoted to AI needs, including deep learning:

» Neural network models

» Energy-based models

» Numeric optimization routines

» Fast and reliable GPU support

Performing Tasks Dynamically with PyTorch

PyTorch (https://pytorch.org/) is a serious competitor for TensorFlow. One item on the main page that will likely pique your attention is that you can click various options to be shown the required installation instructions for your platform using the technique you really want to use. In fact, of all of the products you find online, this one might be the easiest to install. The ease of installation extends to other aspects of this product as well, such as debugging, as described at https://medium.com/@NirantK/the-silent-rise-of-pytorch-ecosystem-693e74b33f1e. Note that this article also describes a few missing elements and how to fix them.

You use PyTorch much as you would TensorFlow and Keras, but there are differences that you need to know about, as described at https://hub.packtpub.com/what-is-pytorch-and-how-does-it-work/. These differences aren't bad, and you could easily argue that they have contributed to PyTorch's fast growth (see `https://venturebeat.com/2018/10/16/github-facebooks-pytorch-and-microsofts-azure-have-the-fastest-growing-open-source-projects/` for details). Many developers pair PyTorch with other products such as Fastai, whichisdescribedat`https://twimlai.com/twiml-talk-186-the-fastai-v1-deep-learning-framework-with-jeremy-howard/`.

Accelerating Deep Learning Research Using CUDA

You can find CUDA (`https://developer.nvidia.com/how-to-cuda-python`) in various forms for various languages and a range of needs. For example, the C/C++ version appears at `https://developer.nvidia.com/cuda-math-library`. This section looks at the Python offering, but other versions exist as well, and their features differ from the version discussed in this section. No matter what form it takes, CUDA is about using GPUs, specially the GPUs on NVIDIA devices, such as the Titan V (`https://www.nvidia.com/en-us/titan/titan-v/`).

You don't actually need a GPU in your system to use CUDA. Instead, you can access the GPUs on any of a number of hosted sites, including Amazon AWS, Microsoft Azure, and IBM SoftLayer. In fact, your installation comes with the NVIDIA-maintained CUDA Amazon Machine Image (AMI) on AWS, so you don't even have to work very hard to access this support.

WARNING

CUDA gives you a great deal of flexibility in using a variety of GPU sources. Flexibility comes with the price of a higher learning curve and additional coding in most cases because you can't make as many assumptions about package use. Consequently, before you even install this package, make sure to read the blog post at `https://devblogs.nvidia.com/numba-python-cuda-acceleration/` that tells you more about how to use CUDA to perform real-world tasks. However, after you get past the learning curve, you find that you can perform an incredible array of tasks that you might not be able to do otherwise.

When working with CUDA, many developers couple it with the CUDA Deep Neural Network (cuDNN) library (`https://developer.nvidia.com/cudnn`). This is a special library of optimized routines that support using CUDA for deep learning needs.

CONSIDERING THE ETHICS OF AI

It would be easy to write an entire book on ethics and AI because the technology has such an incredible potential for misuse. For example, the recent article at https://medium. com/futuresin/facebooks-suicide-algorithms-is-invasive-25e4ef33beb5 discusses the use of suicide prevention algorithms by Facebook to monitor its users. In fact, Facebook regularly uses algorithms to monitor people using the service and it feels that doing so without permission is perfectly acceptable. CEO Mark Zuckerberg feels that privacy is dead and everyone should get used to it (see the article at http://www. nbcnews.com/id/34825225/ns/technology_and_science-tech_and_gadgets/t/ privacy-dead-facebook-get-over-it/#.XFh14FVKhpg for details).

Books like 1984 by George Orwell have seen a surge in sales (see https://www.nytimes. com/2017/01/25/books/1984-george-orwell-donald-trump.html) partly because of people's feelings of insecurity over their personal information. The tendency of Facebook to keep your information in public view forever is one of the reasons that it's losing users, according to the article at https://www.recode.net/2018/2/12/16998750/ facebooks-teen-users-decline-instagram-snap-emarketer. All these articles share the realization that people know that a company is misusing a technology in a big way and aren't happy about it.

The problem comes when people aren't aware of what a company is doing. Keeping up with all the technology changes today isn't possible because technology moves so quickly. In this case, employees of the organization need to bring their concerns before the organization, as happened when Amazon employees took Jeff Bezos to task over the sale of Rekognition (https://aws.amazon.com/rekognition/) to law enforcement, who would be using it to perform mass surveillance through facial recognition (https://www.pcmag.com/commentary/366229/ the-ai-industrys-year-of-ethical-reckoning).

After WWII, society became progressively more complex but also more frail. To protect people from dangers appearing inside and outside the state, military and law enforcement have sometimes leveraged these new technologies for surveillance, control, and influence. If scientists don't complain and regulate the use of the new technologies for such purposes, their extensive and indiscriminate use may erode people's rights and even create a totalitarian state akin to the one in 1984. Only the ethical behavior of scientists who are aware of how their technology is used will help mitigate this decidedly unethical behavior.

Supporting Business Needs with Deeplearning4j

Businesses could be viewed as boring because they perform the same repetitive tasks with different parameters when it comes to data. Using a neural network to deal with a business's data needs is tricky, though, because the various tasks differ too much for a single neural network model to fit all situations. The Deeplearning4J (https://deeplearning4j.org/) lets you combine various shallow nets (layers) to create a deep neural net. This approach greatly reduces the time required to train a deep neural net, and time is something that businesses usually have in extremely short supply.

REMEMBER

This particular solution is written in Java and will work with any JVM-compatible language, including Scala, Clojure, or Kotlin. The underlying computations are written in C and CUDA, so you can also use this solution with those languages if all you want to do is access the underlying computations. To use this solution with Python, you need to run it on Keras. The example at https://www.javacodegeeks.com/2018/11/deep-learning-apache-kafka-keras.html demonstrates what is involved in creating a solution in this environment. Make sure to spend some time reviewing it before you take the plunge.

Mining Data Using Neural Designer

Many of the products listed in this chapter don't feel quite finished; they have that rough feel that researchers and experimenters love. However, some people just need a solution that works. Neural Designer (https://www.neuraldesigner.com/) is that solution, and it performs a variety of tasks, including:

» Discovering complex relationships

» Recognizing unknown patterns

» Predicting trends

» Recognizing associations from data

Unlike many of the other solutions you find, Neural Designer also places specific emphasis on particular industries. You can find specific information for the following:

» Banking and insurance (https://www.neuraldesigner.com/solutions/solutions-banking-insurance)

- » Engineering and manufacturing (https://www.neuraldesigner.com/solutions/solutions-engineering-manufacturing)

- » Retail and consumer (https://www.neuraldesigner.com/solutions/solutions-retail)

- » Healthcare (https://www.neuraldesigner.com/solutions/solutions-health)

Training Algorithms Using Microsoft Cognitive Toolkit (CNTK)

Microsoft Cognitive Toolkit (CNTK) (https://www.microsoft.com/en-us/cognitive-toolkit/) is another back-end framework used for deep learning, much like TensorFlow and Theano. You can run Keras on any of the three. Consequently, people constantly compare the three to see which performs best, such as this comparison between CNTK and TensorFlow at https://minimaxir.com/2017/06/keras-cntk/. You can get a quick overview of all three back ends at http://kaggler.com/keras-backend-benchmark-theano-vs-tensorflow-vs-cntk/.

Besides comparing the three frameworks' speed and other performance issues, you also need to look at features. Obviously, all three will run Keras — usually with some modifications (see the "Augmenting TensorFlow Using Keras" section of this chapter for details). However, each of the three back ends also sport some special functionality. For example, if you want to use Azure, CNTK is probably your best solution because the Microsoft scientists are the most familiar with current and upcoming Azure features. Of course, you'd expect this sort of functionality from CNTK.

TIP

One of the nicer features of CNTK is the extensive model gallery at https://www.microsoft.com/en-us/cognitive-toolkit/features/model-gallery/. You find examples in multiple languages, with some of the examples specific to one language and other examples supporting multiple languages. Look carefully at this page and you see that it includes models for C++, C#, and .NET in general, which you might be hard pressed to find with other back ends.

Exploiting Full GPU Capability Using MXNet

MXNet (https://mxnet.apache.org/) has some interesting features that are good for experimenting with at this point, but the product probably isn't ready for a production because the site tells you that it's still incubating. This product provides some amazing models that will significantly reduce the time required to create many deep learning applications.

REMEMBER

To work with MXNet, you rely on Gluon (you can theoretically also use the module API, but it looks a little painful at this point). Gluon is the imperative interface described at https://beta.mxnet.io/guide/crash-course/index.html (note again that this is a beta site, not a finished site). When going through the crash course, the first thing you notice is that Gluon really does look easy. To use Gluon with Python, you want to read about the Python package at https://mxnet.incubator.apache.org/api/python/gluon/gluon.html. The information at https://beta.mxnet.io/ will help you get a reasonably good install, albeit with some fuss.

Fortunately, the MXNet documentation for Gluon is great (https://mxnet.apache.org/api/python/gluon/model_zoo.html), and you can find additional resources on Medium (https://medium.com/apache-mxnet). Most impressive is the huge number of models that this product already supports. In addition, you can find a considerable number of examples to ease your learning curve (https://github.com/apache/incubator-mxnet/tree/master/example) and tutorials as well (https://mxnet.apache.org/versions/master/tutorials/index.html). Overall, this is a product to watch because of its significant potential for reducing your workload.

Chapter **20**

Ten Types of Occupations that Use Deep Learning

This books covers a lot of different uses for deep learning — everything from the voice-activated features of your digital assistant to self-driving cars. Using deep learning to improve your daily life is nice, of course, but most people need other reasons to embrace a technology, such as getting a job. Fortunately, deep learning doesn't just affect your ability to locate information faster but also offers some really interesting job opportunities, and with the "wow" factor that only deep learning can provide. This chapter gives you an overview of ten interesting occupations that rely on deep learning to some extent today. This material represents only the tip of the iceberg, though; more occupations than can fit in this book are already using deep learning, and more are added every day.

Managing People

A terrifying movie called *The Circle* (https://www.amazon.com/exec/obidos/ASIN/B071GB3P5N/datacservip0f-20/) would have you believe that modern technology will be even more invasive than Big Brother in the book *1984*, by George

Orwell. Part of the movie's story involves installing cameras everywhere — even in bedrooms. The main character wakes up every morning to greet everyone who is watching her. Yes, it can give you the willies if you let it.

However, real deep learning isn't about monitoring and judging people, for the most part. It's more like Oracle's Global Human Resources Cloud (https://cloud.oracle.com/en_US/global-human-resources-cloud). Far from being scary, this particular technology can make you look smart and on top of all the activities of your day, as shown in the video at https://www.youtube.com/watch?v=NMm_cIHeEZ0&list=PL2Gxt-CBX-Ep2n5ytNGkl3bRUnUKAMI1Z. The video is a little over the top, but it gives you a good idea of how deep learning can currently make your job easier.

REMEMBER

The idea behind this technology is to make success easier for people. If you look at Oracle's video and associated materials, you find that the technology helps management suggest potential paths to employees' goals within the organization. In some cases, employees like their current situation, but the software can still suggest ways to make their work more engaging and fun. The software keeps employees from getting lost in the system and helps to manage the employee at a custom level so that each employee receives individualized input.

Improving Medicine

Deep learning is affecting the practice of medicine in many ways, as you can see when you go to the doctor or spend time at a hospital. Deep learning assists with diagnosing illnesses (https://www.cio.com/article/3305951/health-care-industry/the-promise-of-artificial-intelligence-in-diagnosing-illness.html) and finding their correct cure (https://emerj.com/ai-sector-overviews/machine-learning-medical-diagnostics-4-current-applications/). Deep learning is even used to improve the diagnostic process for hard-to-detect issues, including those of the eye (https://www.theverge.com/2018/8/13/17670156/deepmind-ai-eye-disease-doctor-moorfields). However, one of the most important uses for deep learning in medicine is in research.

The seemingly simple act of finding the correct patients to use for research purposes isn't really that simple. The patients must meet strict criteria or any testing results may prove invalid. Researchers now rely on deep learning to perform tasks like finding the right patient (https://emerj.com/ai-sector-overviews/ai-machine-learning-clinical-trials-examining-x-current-applications/), designing the trial criteria, and optimizing the results. Obviously, medicine will need a lot of people who are trained both in medicine and in the use of deep learning techniques for medicine (https://healthitanalytics.com/features/what-is-deep-learning-and-how-will-it-change-healthcare) to continue achieving advances at their current pace.

Developing New Devices

Innovation in some areas of computer technology, such as the basic system, which is now a commodity, has slowed down over the years. However, innovation in areas that only recently became viable has greatly increased. An inventor today has more possible outlets for new devices than ever before. One of these new areas is the means to perform deep learning tasks (https://www.oreilly.com/ideas/specialized-hardware-for-deep-learning-will-unleash-innovation). To create the potential for performing deep learning tasks of greater complexity, many organizations now use specialized hardware that exceeds the capabilities of GPUs — the currently preferred processing technology for deep learning.

This book talks a lot about various deep learning technologies, but the technology is in its infancy, so a smart inventor could come up with something interesting without really working all that hard. The article at https://blog.adext.com/en/artificial-intelligence-technologies-2019 tells about new AI technologies, but even these technologies don't begin to plumb the depths of what could happen.

TIP

Deep learning is attracting the attention of both inventors and investors because of its potential to upend current patent law and the manner in which people create new things (https://marketbrief.edweek.org/marketplace-k-12/artificial-intelligence-attracting-investors-inventors-academic-researchers-worldwide/). An interesting part of most of the articles of this sort is that they predict a significant increase in jobs that revolve around various kinds of deep learning, most of which involve creating something new. Essentially, if you can make use of deep learning in some way and couple it with a current vibrant occupation, you can find a job or develop a business of your own.

Providing Customer Support

Many of the discussions in this book refer to chatbots (see Chapters 1, 2, 11, and 14) and other forms of customer support, including translation services. In case you're curious, you can have an interactive experience with a chatbot at https://pandorabots.com/mitsuku/. The use of chatbots and other customer support technologies have stirred up concern, however.

Some consumer groups that say human customer support is doomed, as in the article at https://www.forbes.com/sites/christopherelliott/2018/08/27/chatbots-are-killing-customer-service-heres-why/. However, if you have ever had to deal with a chatbot to perform anything complex, you know the experience is less than appealing. So the new paradigm is the human and chatbot combination, as described at https://chatbotsmagazine.com/bot-human-hybrid-the-new-era-of-customer-support-346e1633e910.

REMEMBER

Much of the technology you see used today supposedly replaces a human, but in most cases, it can't. For the time being, you should expect to see many situations that have humans and bots working together as a team. The bot reduces the strain of performing physically intense tasks as well as the mundane, boring chores. The human will do the more interesting things and provide creative solutions to unexpected situations. Consequently, people need to obtain training required to work in these areas and feel secure that they'll continue to have gainful employment.

Seeing Data in New Ways

Look at a series of websites and other data sources and you notice one thing: They all present data differently. A computer doesn't understand differences in presentation and isn't swayed by one look or another. It doesn't actually understand data; it looks for patterns. Deep learning is enabling applications to collect more data on their own by ensuring that the application can see appropriate patterns, even when those patterns differ from what the application has seen before (see https://www.kdnuggets.com/2018/09/data-capture-deep-learning-way.html for details). Even though deep learning will enhance and speed up data collection, however, a human will still need to interpret the data. In fact, humans still need to ensure that the application collects good data because the application truly understands nothing about data.

Another way to see data in new ways is to perform data augmentation (https://medium.com/nanonets/how-to-use-deep-learning-when-you-have-limited-data-part-2-data-augmentation-c26971dc8ced). Again, the application does the grunt work, but it takes a human to determine what sort of augmentation to provide. In other words, the human does the creative, interesting part, and the application just trudges along, ensuring that things work.

REMEMBER

These first two deep learning uses are interesting and they'll continue to generate jobs, but the most interesting using of deep learning is for activities that don't exist yet. A creative human can look at ways that others are using deep learning and come up with something new. This article describe some interesting uses of

AI, machine learning, and deep learning that are just now becoming practical: `https://www.wordstream.com/blog/ws/2017/07/28/machine-learning-applications`.

Performing Analysis Faster

When most people speak of analysis, they think about a researcher, some sort of scientist, or a specialist. However, deep learning is becoming entrenched in some interesting places that will require human participation to see full use, such as predicting traffic accidents: `https://www.hindawi.com/journals/jat/2018/3869106/`.

Imagine a police department allocating resources based on traffic flow patterns so that an officer is already waiting at the site of an expected accident. The police lieutenant would need to know how to use an application of this sort. Of course, this particular use hasn't happened yet, but it very likely could because it's already feasible using existing technology. So performing analysis will no longer be a job for those with "Dr." in front of their names; it will be for everyone.

Analysis, by itself, isn't all that useful. It's the act of combining the analysis with a specific need in a particular environment that becomes useful. What you do with analysis defines the effect of that analysis on you and those around you. A human can understand the concept of analysis with a purpose; a deep learning solution can only perform the analysis and provide an output.

Creating a Better Work Environment

This book discusses how deep learning works, but what it all really means is that deep learning will make your life better and your employment more enjoyable if you happen to have skills that allow you to interact successfully with an AI. The article at `https://www.siliconrepublic.com/careers/future-ai-workplace-office` describes how AI could change the workplace in the future. An important element of this discussion is to make work more inviting.

At one point in human history, work was actually enjoyable for most people. It's not that they ran around singing and laughing all the time, but many people did look forward to starting each day. Later, during the industrial revolution, other people put the drudge into work, making every day away from work the only pleasure that some people enjoyed. The problem has become so severe that you can find popular songs about it, like "Working for the Weekend" (https://www.youtube.com/watch?v=ahvSgFHzJIc). By removing the drudge from the workplace, deep learning has the potential to make work enjoyable again.

TIP
Deep learning will strongly affect the work environment in a number of ways, and not just the actual performance of work. For example, technologies based on deep learning have the potential to improve your health (https://www.entrepreneur.com/article/317047) and therefore your productivity. It's a win for everyone because you'll enjoy life and work more, while your boss gets more of that hidden potential from your efforts.

One of the things that you don't see mentioned often is the effect on productivity of a falling birth rate in developed countries. The article at https://www.mckinsey.com/featured-insights/future-of-work/ai-automation-and-the-future-of-work-ten-things-to-solve-for takes this issue on to some extent and provides a chart showing the potential impact of deep learning on various industries. If the current trend continues, having fewer available workers will mean a need for augmentation in the workplace.

However, you might wonder about your future if you worry that you might not be able to adapt to the new reality. The problem is that you might not actually know whether you're safe. In *Artificial Intelligence For Dummies*, by John Paul Mueller and Luca Massaron [Wiley], you see discussions of AI-safe occupations and new occupations that AI will create. You can even discover how you might end up working in space at some point. Unfortunately, not everyone wants to make that sort of move, much as the Luddites didn't during the industrial revolution (see https://www.history.com/news/industrial-revolution-luddites-workers for details). Certainly, what AI promises is going to have consequences even greater than the industrial revolution did (read about the effects of the industrial revolution at https://www.britishmuseum.org/research/publications/online_research_catalogues/paper_money/paper_money_of_england__wales/the_industrial_revolution.aspx) and will be even more disruptive. Some politicians, such as Andrew Wang (https://www.yang2020.com/policies/), are already looking at short-term fixes like basic universal income. These policies, if enacted, would help reduce the impact of AI, but they won't provide a long-term solution. At some point, society will become significantly different from what it is today as a result of AI — much as the industrial revolution has already changed society.

Researching Obscure or Detailed Information

Computers can do one thing — pattern matching — exceptionally well (and much better than humans. If you've ever had the feeling that you're floating in information and none of it relates to your current need, you're not alone. Information overload has been a problem for many years and worsens every year. You can find a lot of advice on dealing with information overload, such as the site at https://www.interaction-design.org/literature/article/information-overload-why-it-matters-and-how-to-combat-it. The problem is that you're still drowning in information. Deep learning enable you to find the needle in a haystack, and in a reasonable amount of time. Instead of months, a good deep learning solution could find the information you need in a matter of hours in most cases.

However, knowing that the information exists is usually not sufficient. You need information that's detailed enough to fully answer your question, which often means locating more than one source and consolidating the information. Again, a deep learning solution could find patterns and mash the data together for you so that you don't have to combine the input from multiple sources manually.

REMEMBER

After AI finds the data and combines the multiple sources into a single cohesive report (you hope), it has done everything it can for you. It's still up to the human to make sense of the information and determine a way to use it successfully. The computer won't remove the creative part of the task; it removes the drudgery of finding the resources required to perform the creative part of the task. As information continues to increase, expect to see an increase in the number of people who specialize in locating detailed or obscure information.

The information broker is becoming an essential part of society and represents an interesting career path that many people haven't even heard about. The article at https://www1.cfnc.org/Plan/For_A_Career/Career_Profile/Career_Profile.aspx?id=edMrqnSJebpXYIKXsDcurwXAP3DPAXXAP3DPAX offers a good summary of what information brokers do.

Designing Buildings

Most people view architecture as a creative trade. Imagine designing the next Empire State Building or some other edifice that will that will stand the test of time. In the past, designing such a building took years. Oddly enough, the contractor actually built the Empire State Building in just a little over a year (see http://www.designbookmag.com/empirestatebuilding.htm for details), but this isn't usually the case. Deep learning and computer technology can help reduce the time to design and build buildings considerably by allowing things like virtual walkthroughs (https://pdf.wondershare.com/real-estate/virtual-tour-software-for-real-estate.html). In fact, the use of deep learning is improving the lives of architects in significant ways, as stated at https://www.autodesk.com/redshift/machine-learning-in-architecture/.

However, turning a design into a virtual tour isn't even the most impressive feat of deep learning in this field. Using deep learning enables designers to locate potential engineering problems, perform stress testing, and ensure safety in other ways before the design ever leaves the drawing board. These capabilities minimize the number of issues that occur after a building becomes operational, and the architect can enjoy the laurels of a success rather than the scorn and potential tragedy of a failure.

Enhancing Safety

Accidents happen! However, deep learning can help prevent accidents from happening — at least for the most part. By analyzing complex patterns in real time, deep learning can assist people who are involved in various aspects of safety assurance. For example, by tracking various traffic patterns and predicting the potential for an accident well in advance, a deep learning solution could provide safety experts with suggestions for preventing the accident from happening at all. A human couldn't perform the analysis because of too many variables. However, a deep learning solution can perform the analysis and then provide output to a human for potential implementation.

REMEMBER

As with every other occupation that involves deep learning, the human acts as the understanding part of the solution. Various kinds of accidents will defy the capability of any deep learning solution to provide precise solutions every time. Humans aren't predictable, but other humans can reduce the odds of something terrible happening given the right information. The deep learning solution provides that correct information, but it requires human foresight and intuition to interpret the information correctly.

Index

A

abscissa, 113

access control, 16

accuracy, neural network, 154, 157–158, 193, 230, 266–267

activation functions
  backpropagation problems, 174–175
  choosing correct, 149, 158–160
  coding, 153
  defined, 152
  in feed-forward process, 141, 142
  in LSTMs, 210–211
  neurons, 137–138
  vanishing gradients, 173, 174

adversarial examples, 245–249

adversarial training, 246. *See also* Generative Adversarial Networks

agent, in RL, 294–295

AI. *See* artificial intelligence; *specific types of AI*

albumentations package, 223

AlexNet, 197

Algorithmia, 310

algorithms. *See also specific algorithms*
  analogizers, 36
  association-rule, 37
  Bayesian, 35–36, 37
  bias, 44
  categorized by similarity, 36–40
  classifier, 31
  clustering, 37
  decision-tree, 37–38
  deep learning, 38
  defined, 26
  dimensionality reduction, 38
  ensemble, 38
  evolutionary, 35
  instance-based, 39
  as insufficient for deep learning, 168–169
  introducing bias, 33

learning process, 26–28
learning styles used to create, 28–30
main approaches to, 34
neural networks, 35, 36–37
optimization, 105–109
optimizers, 160–161
regression, 39
regularization, 39
reinforcement, 30
reinforcement learning, 296
role in computer generated art, 272–273
self-supervised, 29–30
supervised, 28–29
Support Vector Machines, 39
symbolic reasoning, 34
training process, 30, 31
unsupervised, 29

allclose function, 102

Alpha Zero, 305

AlphaGo, 293, 294, 302–304

AlphaGo Zero, 305–306

Amazon
  Mechanical Turk crowdsourcing platform, 196, 237
  recommender systems, 41
  Rekognition, 322

Amazon Web Services (AWS), 20

Anaconda 3 environment
  add-on products, 47
  installing, 47–53
  literate programming, 55
  obtaining, 46–47
  screenshots in book, 53
  TensorFlow and Keras installation, 86–88

Anaconda Navigator, 89–90

analogizers, 36

analysis
  of convolutions, 195
  deep learning in, 331

Anderson, Chris, 168

animal protection, 16

annotation, for multiple-object detection, 237

ANNs (artificial neural networks). *See* neural networks

Application Programming Interfaces (APIs), 76. *See also Keras; specific APIs*

applications. *See also specific applications*

   adversarial examples, 245–249

   comments, 66–69

   creating, 62–64

   employing deep learning in, 19

   framework, choosing for, 78

   indentation, 65–66

   requiring deep learning, 309

Arcade Learning Environment, 169

architecture, deep learning in, 333–334

art, generating

   artistic style transfer, 271, 276

   artists, mimicking, 274–278

   versus creation, 274

   examples, 272

   overview, 270, 315–316

   statistics in, 272–273

artificial intelligence (AI). *See also specific types of AI*

   AI winters, 133, 163, 189, 218

   deep learning, relation to, 10–15

   deep learning versus other forms, 163–164, 171–178

   ethics, 322

   failures, 23

artificial neural networks. *See* neural networks

artistic style transfer, 195–196, 271, 276

asarray function, 98

asmatrix function, 98

association-rule algorithms, 37

AT&T, 188, 189

attention mechanism, LSTM, 212–213

augmentation

   data, 330

   image, 221–223, 230

automatic indention, Jupyter Notebook, 65

automation, AI in, 14

automobile voice interface, 18

autonomous supervised learning, 29–30

autonomous vehicles, 22, 239–245

AWS (Amazon Web Services), 20

B

backend API, Keras, 318–319

Backgammon, 295

backpropagation

   adjusting learning with, 143–145

   exploding gradients problem, 174

   overview, 35, 107

   performing, 154–155

   ReLU activation function, 174–175

   in RNNs, 208

   vanishing gradients, 173

bag-of-words approach, 254–256, 259

batch learning, 176

batch updates, 109, 145

batches, defined, 193

Bayesian algorithms, 35–36, 37

behavior analysis, 311–312

beta coefficients, 113, 114, 115, 127–130

bias

   in linear regression, 112–113

   in machine learning, 32–33, 44

   in neural networks, 35

   in word embeddings, 259

Bidirectional Encoder Representations from Transformers (BERT), Google, 258

bidirectional LSTM, 265–266

Bidirectional Recurrent Neural Networks (BRNNs), 312

big data, 164

bi-grams, 254

binary encoding, 118, 254–255

binary response, in linear regression, 121–122

binary step (linear) activation function, 137–138, 159

black-and-white photos/video, colorization of, 310

Boston house prices dataset, 61–62, 116–117, 120–121, 122–124

bounding boxes, 220, 235, 245

brain imaging, 13

breaking changes, Python, 46

build tools, C++, 88–89

buildings, designing, 333–334

business needs, supporting, 323

C

C++ build tools, 88–89

Caffe framework, 79

Caffe2 framework, 79–80

canonical poses, 247

caption generation, 206–207

CartPole environment, OpenAI Gym, 297–299

cat neuron, 172

categorizing objects, 111–112

CBOW (continuous bag-of-words), 259

celebrities, GAN creation of, 289–290

cells

Jupyter Notebook, 62–64

RNN, 203

CGANs (conditional GANs), 290

CGI (Computer Generated Imagery), 272

Chainer framework, 80, 319

channels, image, 183

character encoding, 252

character recognition, 180

chatbots, 205, 329–330

cheat sheet, explained, 4

chess, 302

classification problems, 28–29, 121–124. *See also* image recognition

classifier algorithms, 31

cleaning text, 253, 254

cloud hosting, framework compatibility with, 78

cloud resources, 70–72. *See also specific cloud resources*

cloud solutions, deep learning, 20. *See also specific cloud solutions*

clustering algorithms, 37

CNNs. *See* Convolutional Neural Networks; image recognition

co-adaptation, 175

code repository, defining, 56–61. *See also* Jupyter Notebook; Python

coefficient of determination (R²), 116, 124–125

coefficient vector (w vector), perceptron, 133, 134

cognitive modeling approach, 13

Cognitive Toolkit (CNTK), Microsoft, 81, 82, 324

Colaboratory (Colab), Google

GAN, building, 286

overview, 45

realistic output, cost of, 229

screenshots, in book, 53

TensorFlow support, 83

traffic signs, distinguishing, 225

use of, 70–72

color images, 180–181, 183

Color shift image augmentation, 222

colorization, 310

commenting out, 69

comments, in Python code, 66–69

community support, programming languages, 21

competition between networks, in GANs, 280–282

complex analysis, AI in, 14

complex relations, in linear regression, 119–121

complexity, in machine learning, 33

composition, music, 277–278

computational graphs, TensorFlow support for, 83

computer generated art, 270–274

Computer Generated Imagery (CGI), 272

concatenation, 65, 66

conda environment product, 86–87

conditional GANs (CGANs), 290

confidence threshold, RetinaNet object detection, 243–244

connectionism, 133

connections, in neural networks, 140, 142

content images, 275

content loss, neural style transfer, 275

continuous bag-of-words (CBOW), 259

continuous skip-gram, 259

Continuum Analytics Anaconda. *See* Anaconda 3 environment

contraction, in U-NETs, 238

Contrast change image augmentation, 222

Conv2D layer, Keras, 186

Convolutional Neural Networks (CNNs or ConvNets). *See also* image recognition
  adversarial examples, 245–249
  architecture update process, 196–197
  art, generating, 273, 274–276
  colorization, 310
  convolutions, understanding, 183–186
  convolutions, visualizing, 194–196
  detecting edges and shapes from images, 193–199
  language processing, 252
  LeNet5 architecture, 188–193
  overview, 170, 179–180
  pooling layers, 187–188
  transfer learning, 197–199
Convolutional Neural Networks for Visual Recognition, 169
cost, of programming languages, 21
cost functions (loss functions), 105–107, 144, 147
creativity, in deep learning, 269–270, 274, 282
criterion variable, in linear regression, 111
cross entropy, 106
CUDA, 321
customer service, 15, 43, 329–330
Cycle GAN, 290

D

data. *See also* math; matrixes
  augmentation, 330
  benefits of additional, 167–169
  big, 164
  complex, in neural networks, 131–132, 136–145
  from deep learning perspective, 163, 164–169
  defined, 94
  entry errors, reducing, 42
  forms of, 96
  introducing bias, 32–33
  Moore's Law, 165–167
  nonlinearly separable, 135–136
  seeing in new ways, 330–331
  structured versus unstructured, 164–165
  timeliness and quality of, 168–169
  working with, 94–95

data points, in linear regression, 111–112
data shuffling, SGD, 128
datasets. *See also specific datasets*
  for caption generation, 206–207
  defined, 96
  getting and using, 54, 61–62
  Kaggle, 70
DCGAN, 289–290
dead neurons, 175
debugging, 80
decision-tree algorithms, 37–38
decoder, segmentation, 238
deduction, in symbolic reasoning, 34
Deep Blue, 302
deep convolutional layers, 193–195
deep learning. *See also* neural networks; *specific applications of deep learning*; *specific deep learning tools*
  adversarial examples, 245–249
  algorithms for, 38
  artificial intelligence, 10–15
  breakthroughs in, 40
  creativity, 269–270, 274, 282
  data from perspective of, 163, 164–169
  defined, 95
  end-to-end learning, 177–178
  ethics of, 322
  hype associated with, avoiding, 22–23
  issues with, 17–18
  layers, 172–173
  machine learning, 15–18
  math needed for, 94–96
  online learning, 176–177
  versus other forms of AI, 163–164, 171–178
  overview, 1–5, 9–10, 163–164
  processing speed, improving, 163, 169–171
  programming environment for, 19–21
  in real world, 18–19
  regularization by dropout, 175–176
  ReLU activation function, 174–175
  start-up ecosystem, 22
  transfer learning, 177
  when not to use, 22–23

Deep Learning Studio, 19–20
Deep Q-Learning, 296, 300–302
Deep Q-Network (DQN), 294, 300–302
DeepAI API, 315
deepdream images, 195
Deeplearning4j, 323
DeepMind, Google, 169, 296, 303–306
define and run approach, 80
define-by-run approach, 80
degenerate (singular) matrixes, 102
deleting notebooks, 59–60
Demografy, 315
demographics, predicting, 314–315
dense convolutional layers, 193–195
dense prediction, 237–238
derivative handling, optimizers, 160–161
detection, multiple-object, 233, 234–237, 239–245
device development, 329
differentiable activation functions, 153
digits dataset, Keras, 190
dimensionality reduction algorithms, 38
dimensions
  matrix, 97–98
  tensor, 102–103
discriminator, GAN, 277, 281, 284–285, 287–289
distillation, 249
distributional hypothesis, Word2vec, 259
DL4Denv environment
  accessing, 89–90
  creating, 86–87
DNN Frameworks support, programming
  languages, 21
doAdd function, 104
documentation cells, Jupyter Notebook, 63–64
Dollár, Piotr, 240
dot products, 99–100
downsampling, 240
DQN (Deep Q-Network), 294, 300–302
Drive, Google, 71, 72
dropout, 175–176
dying ReLU, 159
dynamic execution, 83
dynamic graphs, 83

E

eager execution, 83
early stopping, 107, 147
edges, detecting from images, 193–199
ElasticNet, 221
element-by-element matrix multiplication, 99, 100
ELU (Exponential Linear Unit) activation function, 160
Embedding layer, 265
embeddings, word, 251, 257–261, 265
employee downtime, forecasting, 42
encoder, segmentation, 238
encoding, character, 252
end-to-end learning, 177–178
ensemble algorithms, 38
enterprise frameworks, 77
environment
  DL4Denv, accessing, 89–90
  DL4Denv, creating, 86–87
  in RL, 294–295, 296–299
epochs, 156, 193, 229, 230
Eps Greedy Q policy, 301
error correction, 106–107. *See also* backpropagation
ethics, 322
evolutionary algorithms, 35
exclusive or (XOR), 136–137
expansion, in U-NETs, 238
expert systems, 19, 22, 218, 252–253
exploding gradients problem, 152, 174
exporting notebooks, 58
extensibility, TensorFlow, 82

F

Face Aging, 291
face recognition, 178, 249
Facebook, ethics of AI used by, 322
Facebook AI Research (FAIR), 258
fake images, GAN generation of, 282, 287
FastAnnotationTool, 237
fastText, 259
FCNs (Fully Convolutional Networks), 238
feature creation, 17, 182–183
feature space, creating new, 136

feature visualization, 195

features
  complex relations, dealing with, 119–121
  incompatible, defining outcome of, 124–125
  modeling with linear regression, 118–119
  multiple linear regression, 114
  selecting correct, 112, 124–126

feedback loop, in RL, 30. *See also* reinforcement learning

feed-forward process, neural networks, 138–140, 141–142, 153–154

film reviews, sentiment analysis of, 261–267

filter depth, 184

filters, convolution, 183, 184, 185

financial rule and modeling precision, improving, 42

fine-tuning, 198

first-order optimization, 161

fitting process, 26, 31–32. *See also* training data

Flickr 30K dataset, 206–207

Flip image augmentation, 221, 222

focal loss solution, 240–241

Fold extension, TensorFlow, 83

folder, creating new, 56, 57

forget gate, in LSTMs, 210

forward procedure, 153–154

fractals, 272

frameworks. *See also specific frameworks*
  choosing, 78
  downsides of, 77
  focus on specific issues, 77–78
  Keras use with, 85–86
  low-end, 79–82
  open source, 171
  overview, 73–74
  popularity of, 75–76
  programming language support, 21
  types of, 74–75

fraud detection, 14

frequency encoding of text, 254–255

frozen spots, in frameworks, 75, 77–78

Fully Convolutional Networks (FCNs), 238

functions. *See also specific functions*
  for importing datasets, 61
  vector and matrix array-creation, 98

G

games, deep learning in, 295–299, 313

Gated Recurrent Units (GRUs), 211–212

gates
  in GRUs, 211
  in LSTMs, 209–210

General Data Protection Regulation (GDPR), 18, 44

generalization, 31–32, 41, 107

generated art, 270–274

Generative Adversarial Networks (GANs)
  art, generating, 273, 276
  building, 282–289
  competition between networks in, 280–282
  fake images, 282, 287
  overview, 246, 279–280
  variants of, 289–291

generator, GAN, 277, 281, 284, 285, 287–289

geometrical meaning of regression, 112–114

German Traffic Sign Recognition Benchmark (GTSRB), 218, 224, 225

Girshick, Ross, 240

GitHub, 71

Global Human Resources Cloud, Oracle, 328

global minimum, 108, 145

GloVe (Global Vectors), 259

Gluon, 325

Go game, 302–305

Goodfellow, Ian, 280, 295

Google. *See also* Colaboratory, Google
  attention mechanism, 213
  BERT, 258
  Deep Q-Network, 294, 300–302
  natural disasters, predicting, 316
  Neural Image Caption, 207
  transfer learning, 177, 197

Google Brain team, 172, 219–220

Google Cloud, 78

Google DeepMind, 169, 296, 303–306

Google Drive, 71, 72

Google Neural Machine Translation (GNMT), 206

Google Translate, 312

GoogleLeNet, 169, 195

Goyal, Priya, 240

gradient descent, 107–109, 115, 127, 144–145
Graphics Processing Units (GPUs)
  Colab support, 83
  CUDA, working with, 321
  GAN, building, 286
  improving processing speed with, 170
  realistic output, cost of, 229
  TensorFlow support for, 84
graphs, dynamic, 83
grayscale images, 181
GRUs (Gated Recurrent Units), 211–212
GUI. *See* Jupyter Notebook
Gui, Fan, 303
Gym package, OpenAI, 293–294, 296–299

H

hackers, 245–249
hardware, improving processing speed with, 170
He, Kaiming, 240
headings, 64, 66
Heaviside step function, 153
help resources, Python, 69
hidden functionality, 43–44
hidden layers, 140
Hinton, Geoffrey, 170–171, 173–175
Histograms of Oriented Gradients (HOG), 182
Hochreiter, Sepp, 208
hot spots, in frameworks, 75, 77–78
Hubel, David Hunter, 183
human processes
  AI as simulating, 11–13
  versus deep learning, 18–19
  introducing bias, 33
  versus rational processes, 14
hyperbolic tangent (tanh) activation function, 137–138, 159, 192, 210–211
hyperparameters, 17
hyperplane, 113–114

I

icons, explained, 3–4
ICs (integrated circuits), 165–166

identity function, 102
identity matrix, 102
IDEs (Integrated Development Environments), 55, 75. *See also* Anaconda 3 environment
image augmentation, 221–223, 230
image generator, 228
image pyramids technique, 236
image recognition. *See also* Convolutional Neural Networks
  advanced, overview, 233–234
  adversarial examples, 245–249
  ambiguous and confusing images, 247
  annotation process, 237
  architecture update process, 196–197
  basics of, 180–183
  classification tasks, distinguishing, 234–235
  competitions, role of, 217, 218–223
  convolutions, understanding, 183–186
  convolutions, visualizing, 194–196
  detecting edges and shapes from images, 193–199
  GoogleLeNet, 169
  image augmentation, 221–223
  LeNet5 architecture, 188–193
  localization, 235
  multiple-object detection, 234–237
  overview, 172, 217–218
  pooling convolutional layers, 187–188
  segmentation, 237–238
  testing RetinaNet object detection, 239–245
  traffic signs, distinguishing, 218, 223–231
  transfer learning, 197–199
ImageDataGenerator function, 222–223
ImageNet, 169, 196–197, 218–220, 237
images. *See also* image recognition
  caption generation for, 206–207
  combining in single piece of art, 274–276
  repairing, 291
imaging, brain, 13
IMDb dataset, 261–262
imdb function, 262
indentation, in Python code, 65–66
induction (inverse deduction), 34
industrial revolution, 332

information brokers, 333
Information loss image augmentation, 222
information overload, 333
innovation, data as supporting, 168
input gate, in LSTMs, 210
input images, neural style transfer, 275
input layer, neural networks, 139
input padding, 264
instance segmentation, 235
instance spotting, 235
instance-based algorithms, 39
integrated circuits (ICs), 165–166
Integrated Development Environments (IDEs), 55, 75.
    See also Anaconda 3 environment
intelligence. *See also* artificial intelligence
  defining, 11–12
  versus learning, 15–16
introspection, in cognitive modeling, 13
inverse deduction (induction), 34
inversion, matrix, 101–102
Iris dataset, 139
iterations, 127, 128

J

Jupyter Notebook
  accessing new environment in, 89–90
  application, creating, 62–64
  C++ build tools, 88
  cells, 62–64
  closing notebook, 59
  code repository, defining, 56–61
  comments, 66–69
  creating notebook, 56–58
  exporting notebook, 58
  folder creation, 56, 57
  Google Colaboratory use, 70–72
  importing notebook, 60–61
  indentation, 65–66
  literate programming, 55
  overview, 54
  removing notebook, 59–60
  saving notebook, 59
  screenshots in book, 53

starting, 54–55
stopping, 56

K

Kaggle datasets and kernels, 70
Kasparov, Garry, 302
Keras
  augmenting TensorFlow with, 318–319
  building LeNet5 architecture with, 189–193
  Conv2D layer, 186
  GAN, building, 282–289
  image augmentation, 222–223
  language processing, 252
  LSTM, 211
  obtaining, 86–88
  overview, 85–86
  sentiment analysis, 261–267
  traffic signs, distinguishing, 223–231
  transfer learning, 199
  transformations to manipulate text, 254–255
Keras-RetinaNet, 239, 241–245
keras-rl, 294, 299–302
kernels
  convolution, 184, 185–186
  Kaggle, 70
Kornblith, Simon, 219–220

L

L1 regularization (Lasso), 126, 221
L2 regularization (Ridge), 126, 221
LabelImg tool, 237
labeling
  in image classification, 237
  in machine learning, 43
LabelMe tool, 237
language processing
  bag-of-words approach, 254–256
  overview, 251–253
  sentiment analysis, 261–267
  transformations to manipulate text, 253–254
  word embeddings, 251, 257–261

language translation, 204–206, 258, 312

languages, programming, 20–21. *See also specific languages*

Lasso (L1 regularization), 126, 221

layers
  attention, 213
  convolutional, 186–188, 193–195
  in deep learning, 17, 172–173
  neural networks, 138, 139, 140
  pooling, 187–188
  skip, 197
  tensors, 103–104

Le, Quoc V., 219–220

LeakyReLU activation function, 160

learning. *See also* deep learning; machine learning; reinforcement learning
  approaches to, 33–40
  human versus computer, 18
  versus intelligence, 15–16
  one-example-at-a-time approach, 127–130
  as optimization, 93–94, 105
  programming languages, 21
  styles used to create algorithms, 28–30
  unsupervised, 293

learning rates
  backpropagation, 145
  for neural network, setting, 150–151, 161
  update strategy of perceptron, 134

LeCun, Yann, 170, 171, 179, 188–189, 194, 279

lemmatization, 253

LeNet5 architecture, 188–193, 218

Li, Fei-Fei, 196, 218

Lin, Tsung-Yi, 240

linalg.inv function, 102

linear (binary step) activation function, 137–138, 159

linear algebra manipulation functions, 99

linear models, 132. *See also* perceptron

linear regression
  combining variables, 112–117
  complex relations, dealing with, 119–121
  example of, 116–117
  features, modeling, 118–119
  features, selecting correct, 112, 124–126
  gradient descent, 115, 127

mixing variable types, 117–121
  multiple, 111, 113–114, 115
  one-example-at-a-time approach, 127–130
  overview, 111–112
  probabilities, 121–124
  responses, modeling, 117–118
  simple, 111, 112–113, 115
  stochastic gradient descent, 127–130

link function, 122

Linux, installing Anaconda on, 47–48

literate programming, 55. *See also* Jupyter Notebook

Local Interpretable Model-Agnostic Explanations (LIME), 44

local minima, 108, 145

localization, 233–234, 234–235

log loss, 106

logistic (sigmoid) activation function, 137–138, 153, 159, 210–211

logistic regression, 122–124

long short-term memory (LSTM)
  architecture, 209–211
  attention mechanism, 212–213
  overview, 207–209
  sentiment analysis, 265–266
  variants, 211–212

loss functions (cost functions), 105–107, 144, 147

loss measures, neural style transfer, 275

low-end frameworks, 79–82

M

machine efficiency, 15

machine learning. *See also* deep learning; *specific machine learning applications*
  benefits of, 41–43
  bias, 32–33
  breakthroughs in, 40
  complexity, 33
  deep learning, relation to, 15–18
  deep learning versus, 163–164, 171–176
  defined, 26
  generalization, 31–32, 41
  learning approaches, 33–40
  learning styles used to create algorithms, 28–30
  limitations of, 43–44

machine learning *(continued)*
  math in, 27–28
  overview, 25–26
  process of, 26–27
  reinforcement learning algorithms, 30
  self-supervised learning algorithms, 29–30
  simplicity in, 33
  supervised learning algorithms, 28–29
  training, validating, and testing data, 30–31
  true uses of, 40–44
  unsupervised learning algorithms, 29
machine translation, 205–206, 312
MacOS, installing Anaconda on, 48–49
maintenance needs, predicting, 42
make_moons function, 155–156
management, deep learning in, 327–328
many to many RNN configuration, 205–206
many to one RNN configuration, 205
marketing, machine learning in, 41
mat function, 98
math. *See also* neural networks
  data, working with, 94–95
  data forms, 96
  defined, 94
  in machine learning, 27–28
  matrix operations, 95–102
  needed for deep learning, 94
  optimization, 105–109
  overview, 93–94
  tensors, 102–104
  vectorization, 104
MATLAB language, 20–21
MATLAB product, 20
matrix class, 98, 100
matrix computations, 95
matrix factorization, 259
matrixes
  advanced operations, 100–102
  bag-of-words approach, 254–256
  creating, 97–98
  defined, 96
  identity, 102
  inversion, 101–102
  linear regression, 115

multiplication, 99–100
neural network architecture, defining, 151–152
operations, 97–102
overview, 95–96
reshaping vector into, 100–101
singular, 102
tensors, 102–104
transposition, 101
word embeddings, 258
MCTS (Monte Carlo Tree Search), 303–304
mean squared error, 106
Mechanical Turk, Amazon, 196, 237
medicine, deep learning in, 328–329
memory. *See also* long short-term memory
  modeling sequences using, 202–204
  in RL, 300
  short-term, in RNNs, 204, 207–209, 210
Microsoft Cognitive Toolkit (CNTK), 81, 82, 324
Microsoft Common Objects in the Context (MS COCO) dataset, 207, 220
Microsoft ResNet, 197
Microsoft Windows
  C++ build tools, 88–89
  installing Anaconda on, 49–53
Midi Net, 291
mini-batch (stochastic) updates, 109, 145
misclassified examples, perceptron handling of, 134
missing data, in linear regression, 118–119
mnist command, 190
MNIST dataset, 282–283
model zoos, 79, 238
Monte Carlo Tree Search (MCTS), 303–304
Moore's Law, 165–167
Mordvintsev, Alexander, 195
movie reviews, sentiment analysis of, 261–267
multiclass classification problems, 224–231
multiline comments, 67–68, 69
multilingual applications, 258
multiple linear regression, 111, 113–114, 115
multiple RNNs, 204–205
multiple-object detection
  overview, 233, 234–237
  RetinaNet, testing, 239–245

multiplication, matrix, 99–100
multiply function, 99, 100
music, generating from picture, 316
music composition, 277–278
MXNet framework, 81, 325

N

NATO Innovation Challenge, 241
natural disasters, predicting, 316
Natural Language Processing (NLP), 251, 252–253. *See also* language processing
Neural Designer, 323–324
Neural Image Caption (NIC), Google, 207
Neural Information Processing Systems (NeurIPS) conference, 279
neural networks. *See also* Convolutional Neural Networks; deep learning; Recurrent Neural Networks; *specific neural network applications*; weights, neural network
  activation function, choosing, 149, 158–160
  architecture of, 138–139, 151–152
  backpropagation, 143–145
  competition between, in GANs, 280–282
  connections, 140, 142
  core functionalities, coding, 153–155
  feed-forward process, 138–140, 141–142, 153–154
  versus human learning, 18
  image feature creation, 182–183
  images, connecting directly to, 181
  layers, 140, 172–173
  learning rate, setting, 150–151, 161
  LeNet5 architecture, 190–193
  neurons, 35, 136–138
  optimizers, 150–151, 160–161
  overfitting, 146–147
  overview, 17, 35, 36–37, 131–132, 149
  perceptron, 132–136
  tensors, 103–104
  testing, 155–158
  understanding, 150–151
  updating, 109
neural style transfer, 195–196, 275–276, 290
neurons
  activation functions, 137–138, 158
  dead, 175

  in deep learning, 17
  defined, 151
  human visual perception, 183
  in neural networks, 35, 136–138
  regularization by dropout, 175–176
  saturation of, 152
n-grams, 254, 259
Noise addition image augmentation, 222
nonlinearly separable data, 135–136
nonprogramming solutions, for deep learning, 19–20
normalization, 253, 254, 257, 283
Notebook. *See* Jupyter Notebook
numeric estimates, transforming into probabilities, 122–124
numeric values, in neural networks, 139
NumPy library
  advanced matrix operations, 100–102
  matrix creation, 97–98
  matrix multiplication, 99–100
  overview, 97
  tensors, 102–104
  vectorization, 104
NVIDIA, 239

O

object categorization, 111–112
object recognition. *See* image recognition
Occam's Razor, 33
occupations using deep learning
  analysis, 331
  architecture, 333–334
  customer support, 329–330
  data, seeing in new ways, 330–331
  device development, 329
  information broker, 333
  management, 327–328
  medicine, 328–329
  overview, 327
  safety, enhancing, 334
  work environment, improving, 331–332
Octave language, 20–21
Olah, Chris, 195
one to many RNN configuration, 205
one to one RNN configuration, 205

1-D pooling, 188
one-hot encoding, 118, 255, 256
ones function, 98
one-stage detection, 236, 239–245
online learning, 176–177
online mode, weight updates, 145
OpenAI Gym, 293–294, 296–299
operations, math, 97–102
optimization
  versus backpropagation, 143
  cost functions, 105–106
  error correction, 106–107
  gradient descent, 107–109, 115
  learning as, 93–94, 105
  updating, 109
optimizers, neural network, 150–151,
    160–161
Oracle Global Human Resources Cloud, 328
ordinate, 113
out of core learning, 145
outliers, 119
output gate, in LSTMs, 210
output layer, neural networks, 139
overfitting
  generalization, 31–32, 107
  image augmentation for, 221–223
  ImageNet dataset, 219
  overview, 132
  regularization, 125–126
  solving, 146–147

P

packages, Python, 46
pad_sequences function, 264
padding
  convoluted images, 184, 185
  input, 264
paradigms, 17
parallelism, 170
Pascal Sentence Dataset, 206–207
PASCAL VOC (Visual Object Classes) dataset, 220
pastiches, 276
PATH environment variable, 51–52
pattern recognition, 36

peephole connections, in LSTM variants, 211
perceptron
  functionality, 132–134
  neurons as evolution of, 136–137
  nonlinearly separable data, 135–136
  overview, 131, 132, 171
  update strategy of, 134–136
person poses, 310–311
perturbations, 248
Pix2Pix, 291
platform-specific issues, 3
policy, in RL, 300, 301
policy networks, AlphaGo, 304
polynomial expansion, 120–121
pooling convolutional layers, 187–188
Pose Guided Person Image Generation, 290
PoseNet library, 311
pos-tagging text, 253
post-processing, 238
precision, RetinaNet object detection, 244
predict function, 155
predictors, in linear regression, 111, 113
PReLU (Parametric Rectified Linear Unit) activation
    function, 160
pretrained networks
  for language processing, 258
  neural style transfer, 275–276
  segmentation, 238
  transfer learning, 197–199
privacy, AI and, 322
probabilities
  in linear regression, 121–124
  softmax in neural networks, 139–140
problem domains, 74–75
processing speed, improving, 163, 169–171
product marketing, 41
programming, literate, 55. See also Jupyter Notebook
programming environment, 19–21
programming languages, 20–21. See also specific
    languages
psychological testing, 13
Python. See also Anaconda 3 environment
  application, creating, 62–64
  breaking changes, 46
  C++ build tools, 88–89

cloud-related activities, 70–72
code repository, defining, 56–61
comments, 66–69
datasets, getting and using, 61–62
help resources, 69
hype associated with deep learning, avoiding, 22
indentation, 65–66
Jupyter Notebook, 54–61
knowledge needed to work with book, 3
linear regression example, 116–117
literate programming, 55
matrix operations, 97–102
neural network architecture in, 151–152
neural network core functionalities in, 153–155
neural network, testing, 155–158
versus other languages for deep learning, 20–21
overview, 45–46
packages, 46
working with, 46
PyTorch framework, 80–81, 320–321

Q

Q-learning, 169, 296, 299–302
qualitative variables, 117–118, 139

R

R language, 20–21
R^2 (coefficient of determination), 116, 124–125
Random crop image augmentation, 222
random sampling, SGD, 128
rational processes, in AI, 13, 14
realistic output, cost of, 229
recognition, image. See image recognition
recommender systems, 36, 41
Recurrent Neural Networks (RNNs)
  caption generation, 206–207
  language processing, 252, 256
  long short-term memory, 207–213
  modeling sequences using memory, 202–204
  multiple, 204–205
  overview, 201–204
  recognizing and translating speech, 204–206
  sentiment analysis, 261–267

recursion, 35, 203
region of interest, 236
regression, linear. See linear regression
regression algorithms, 39
regression beta, 113
regression line, 115
regression problems, 28–29
regression result, 122
regressor model, 235
regularization, 39, 125–126, 146–147, 175–176
reinforcement learning (RL)
  algorithms for, 30
  AlphaGo, 293, 294, 302–306
  basics of, 294–296
  keras-rl, 299–302
  overview, 293–294
  simulating game environments, 296–299
Rekognition, Amazon, 322
ReLU (Rectified Linear Units) activation function, 137, 159–160, 174–175, 179, 192
Remember icon, explained, 4
reminders, using comments to leave, 68
reordering image dimensions, 223
repository, defining code, 56–61
representation capability, 143
rescaling images, 223
reset gate, GRUs, 211
reshape function, 100–101
residuals, 119
ResNet, Microsoft, 197
resource scheduling, 14
responses, modeling with linear regression, 117–118
RetinaNet object detection, 239–245
rewards, in RL, 295
RGB images, 181, 183
Ridge (L2 regularization), 126, 221
Rosenblatt, Frank, 132–133, 136
Rotation image augmentation, 222

S

saddle points, 108
safety systems, 15, 334
sales predictions, 42
same padding, 184

sampling, to solve unbalanced classification, 240

saturation of neurons, 152

saving notebooks, 59

scalars, 95, 96

Schmidhuber, Jürgen, 208

Schubert, Ludwig, 195

scientific innovation, data as supporting, 168

Scikit-learn library, 61–62, 116–117, 118

screenshots, in book, 53

second-order optimization, 161

Sedol, Lee, 303

segmentation, 233–235, 237–238, 240

segmentation models package, 238

self-driving cars, 22, 239–245

self-learning, 304–306. *See also* reinforcement learning

self-supervised learning algorithms, 29–30

semantic segmentation, 233–235, 237–238, 240

semantic similarity, 258

semantics, understanding by word embeddings, 257–261

semi-supervised learning, 30

sentiment analysis, 203, 261–267

sequence labeling, 205

sequences, processing, 202–204. *See also* Recurrent Neural Networks

SGD (stochastic gradient descent), 127–130

shapes, detecting from images, 193–199

sharing notebooks, 58

Shlens, Jonathon, 219–220

short-term memory, in RNNs, 204, 207–209, 210

Show and Tell network, Google, 207

sigmoid (logistic) activation function, 137–138, 153, 159, 210–211

Silver, David, 304

simple linear regression, 111, 112–113, 115

simplicity, in machine learning, 33

simulating game environments, 296–299

single-line comments, 67, 69

single-object classification. *See* image recognition

singular (degenerate) matrixes, 102

skip layers, 197

skip-gram version, Word2vec, 259

sliding window technique, 236

Smoothie 3-D, 315

softmax, neural networks, 139–140

solar savings potential, estimating, 312–313

solutions, deep learning, 19–20, 22

solving by closed form, 115

sparse data problems, 257–258

speech recognition, 204–206

standard normal distribution, 152

standardization, image, 223

start-up ecosystem, deep learning, 22

state
  in RL, 295
  RNNs, 204, 209

static graphs, 83

statistics, role in computer generated art, 272–273. *See also* linear regression

stemming, text, 253

stickers, adversarial examples in form of, 249

stochastic (mini-batch) updates, 109, 145

stochastic gradient descent (SGD), 127–130

stop word removal, text, 253

stride, convolution, 184, 185

structured data, 164–165

style images, 275

style loss, neural style transfer, 275

style transfer, artistic, 195–196, 271, 276

SUN dataset, 220

Super Resolution GAN (SRGAN), 290

supervised learning algorithms, 28–30

Support Vector Machines (SVM), 39

symbolic reasoning, 34

T

tangent hyperbolic (tanh) activation function, 137–138, 159, 192, 210–211

TD-Gammon, 295

Technical Stuff icon, explained, 4

Tensor Processing Units (TPUs), 78

TensorBoard extension, TensorFlow, 84

TensorFlow framework
  accessing new environment in Notebook, 89–90
  augmenting with Keras, 318–319
  benefits of using, 82–84
  C++ build tools, 88–89
  cloud options, 78

Colab support, 83
define and run approach, 80
define-by-run approach, 80
Fold extension, 83
GAN, building, 282–289
Keras, 85–86
LSTM, 211
obtaining, 86–88
overview, 74, 82
sentiment analysis, 261–267
TensorBoard extension, 84
TFLearn, 84–85
traffic signs, distinguishing, 223–231
tensors, 102–104
Term Frequency-Inverse Document Frequency
  (TF-IDF) score, 255–256
Tesauro, Gerald, 295
testing
  data, in machine learning, 30–31
  neural networks, 155–158
  RetinaNet object detection, 239–245
tetrachromats, 181
text. *See also* language processing
  sentiment analysis of, 261–267
  transformations to manipulate, 253–254
texts_to_matrix method, 256
TFLearn package, 84–85
Theano, 80, 317–318
thinking
  human, in AI, 12–13
  rational, in AI, 13
3-D art, generating, 315
3-D pooling, 188
three-dimensional matrixes, 97–98
Tip icon, explained, 3
tokenization, 253, 254
Tokenizer function, 254–255, 256, 263
Torch, 319–320
Total Turing Test, 12
TPUs (Tensor Processing Units), 78
traffic accidents, predicting, 331
traffic signs, distinguishing
  classification task, running, 228–231
  overview, 218, 223–224
  preparing image data, 224–227

training data
  generalization, 31–32
  image recognition, 228–231
  introducing bias, 33
  in machine learning, 26, 28, 30–31, 43
  optimization, 107
transfer learning, 177, 197–199, 219–220
transformations to manipulate text, 253–254
Transformer attention mechanism, Google, 213
translation, language, 204–206, 258, 312
translation invariance, 182, 193
transpose function, 101
transposition, matrix, 101
tri-grams, 254
triple-quoted strings, 67
Turing Test, 12
tutorial kernels, Kaggle, 70
2-D pooling, 188
two-dimensional matrixes, 97
two-stage detection, 236

U

Uber, 297
unbalanced learning, 240
underfitted models, 31
U-NETs, 238
universal approximators, neural networks as,
  143, 172
University of Toronto, 173–175
unstructured data, 164–165
unsupervised learning, 29, 30, 293
update gate, GRUs, 211
updates
  book, 4
  CNN architecture, 196–197
  perceptron strategy for, 134–136
  weight, in neural networks, 109,
    145, 155
upsampling, 240

V

valid padding, 184
validating data, 30–31, 228–231
value networks, AlphaGo, 304

value-based learning, 300
vanishing gradients, 159, 173, 174, 208
variables, in linear regression
  combining, 112–117
  mixing types of, 117–121
vectAdd function, 104
vectorization, 104
vectors
  defined, 96
  overview, 95
  reshaping into matrix, 100–101
  word, 260–261
version numbers, Python packages, 46
VGG-19 pretrained network, 275–276
VGGNet architecture, 197
virtualenv environment product, 86
visual art. *See* art, generating
visual perception, 183
visual recognition. *See* image recognition
visual relationship detection, 245
Visual Studio C++ build tools, 88–89
visualizing convolutions, 194–196
vocabulary size, for language processing, 254–255
voice generation, 314
voice interface, in automobiles, 18
voice recognition, 314

W

w vector (coefficient vector), perceptron, 133, 134
wait time prediction, 16
Warning icon, explained, 3
weighted summation meaning of regression, 114

weighting tensors, 103–104
weights, neural network
  basic architecture, 151–152
  connections between neurons, 140
  constraining, 221
  defined, 35
  feed-forward process, 142
  image recognition, 227
  updates, 109, 145, 155
Wiesel, Torsten, 183
Windows, Microsoft
  C++ build tools, 88–89
  installing Anaconda on, 49–53
winters, AI, 133, 163, 189, 218
Wissner-Gross, Alexander, 168–169
word embeddings, 251, 257–261, 265
word vectors, 260–261
Word2vec, 259, 260–261
work environment, improving, 331–332

X

XOR (exclusive or), 136–137

Y

Yao, Mariya, 247

Z

ZCA whitening, 223
Zubarev, Vasily, 206
Zuckerberg, Mark, 322

About the Authors

John Mueller is a freelance author and technical editor. He has writing in his blood, having produced 112 books and more than 600 articles to date. The topics range from networking to artificial intelligence and from database management to heads-down programming. Some of his current books include discussions of data science, machine learning, and algorithms. His technical editing skills have helped more than 70 authors refine the content of their manuscripts. John has provided technical editing services to various magazines, performed various kinds of consulting, and writes certification exams. Be sure to read John's blog at http://blog.johnmuellerbooks.com/. You can reach John on the Internet at John@JohnMuellerBooks.com. John also has a website at http://www.johnmuellerbooks.com/. Be sure to follow John on Amazon at https://www.amazon.com/John-Mueller/.

Luca Massaron is a data scientist and marketing research director who specializes in multivariate statistical analysis, machine learning, and customer insight, with more than a decade of experience in solving real-world problems and generating value for stakeholders by applying reasoning, statistics, data mining, and algorithms. Starting from being a pioneer of web audience analysis in Italy to achieving the rank of top-ten Kaggler on kaggle.com, he has always been passionate about everything regarding data and analysis and about demonstrating the potentiality of data-driven knowledge discovery to both experts and non experts. Favoring simplicity over unnecessary sophistication, he believes that a lot can be achieved in data science by understanding and practicing the essentials of it. Luca is also a Google Developer Expert (GDE) in machine learning.

John's Dedication

This book is dedicated to my exceptionally kind neighbors, Donnie and Shannon Thompson. They redefined the term neighbor for me in so many ways that I've lost count.

Luca's Dedication

I would like to dedicate this book to my family, Yukiko and Amelia, to my parents, Renzo and Licia, and to Yukiko's family, Yoshiki, Takayo, and Makiko.

John's Acknowledgments

Thanks to my wife, Rebecca. Even though she is gone now, her spirit is in every book I write, in every word that appears on the page. She believed in me when no one else would.

Russ Mullen deserves thanks for his technical edit of this book. He greatly added to the accuracy and depth of the material you see here. Russ worked exceptionally hard helping with the research for this book by locating hard-to-find URLs and also offering a lot of suggestions.

Matt Wagner, my agent, deserves credit for helping me get the contract in the first place and taking care of all the details that most authors don't really consider. I always appreciate his assistance. It's good to know that someone wants to help.

A number of people read all or part of this book to help me refine the approach, test scripts, and generally provide input that all readers wish they could have. These unpaid volunteers helped in ways too numerous to mention here. I especially appreciate the efforts of Eva Beattie, Glenn A. Russell, Mr. Osvaldo Téllez Almirall, and Simone Scardapane, who provided general input, read the entire book, and selflessly devoted themselves to this project.

Finally, I would like to thank Katie Mohr, Susan Christophersen, and the rest of the editorial and production staff.

Luca's Acknowledgments

My greatest thanks go to my family, Yukiko and Amelia, for their support and loving patience. I also want to thank Simone Scardapane, an assistant professor at Sapienza University (Rome) and a fellow Google Developer Expert, who provided invaluable feedback during the writing of this book.

Publisher's Acknowledgments

Associate Publisher: Katie Mohr
Project Manager and Copy Editor:
  Susan Christophersen
Technical Editor: Russ Mullen

Sr. Editorial Assistant: Cherie Case
Production Editor: Mohammed Zafar Ali
Cover Image: © agsandrew/Shutterstock

PERSONAL ENRICHMENT

Staying Sharp
9781119187790
USA $26.00
CAN $31.99
UK £19.99

Facebook
9781119179030
USA $21.99
CAN $25.99
UK £16.99

Guitar
9781119293354
USA $24.99
CAN $29.99
UK £17.99

Investing
9781119293347
USA $22.99
CAN $27.99
UK £16.99

Beekeeping
9781119310068
USA $22.99
CAN $27.99
UK £16.99

Digital Photography
9781119235606
USA $24.99
CAN $29.99
UK £17.99

Meditation
9781119251163
USA $24.99
CAN $29.99
UK £17.99

Pregnancy
9781119235491
USA $26.99
CAN $31.99
UK £19.99

Samsung Galaxy S7
9781119279952
USA $24.99
CAN $29.99
UK £17.99

iPhone
9781119283133
USA $24.99
CAN $29.99
UK £17.99

Crocheting
9781119287117
USA $24.99
CAN $29.99
UK £16.99

Nutrition
9781119130246
USA $22.99
CAN $27.99
UK £16.99

PROFESSIONAL DEVELOPMENT

Windows 10
9781119311041
USA $24.99
CAN $29.99
UK £17.99

AutoCAD
9781119255796
USA $39.99
CAN $47.99
UK £27.99

Excel 2016
9781119293439
USA $26.99
CAN $31.99
UK £19.99

QuickBooks 2017
9781119281467
USA $26.99
CAN $31.99
UK £19.99

macOS Sierra
9781119280651
USA $29.99
CAN $35.99
UK £21.99

LinkedIn
9781119251132
USA $24.99
CAN $29.99
UK £17.99

Windows 10
9781119310563
USA $34.00
CAN $41.99
UK £24.99

SharePoint 2016
9781119181705
USA $29.99
CAN $35.99
UK £21.99

Fundamental Analysis
9781119263593
USA $26.99
CAN $31.99
UK £19.99

Networking
9781119257769
USA $29.99
CAN $35.99
UK £21.99

Office 2016
9781119293477
USA $26.99
CAN $31.99
UK £19.99

Office 365
9781119265313
USA $24.99
CAN $29.99
UK £17.99

Salesforce.com
9781119239314
USA $29.99
CAN $35.99
UK £21.99

Coding
9781119293323
USA $29.99
CAN $35.99
UK £21.99

dummies.com

dummies®
A Wiley Brand